HEMPSTEAD PLAINS

FROM ABOVE

RICHARD PANCHYK

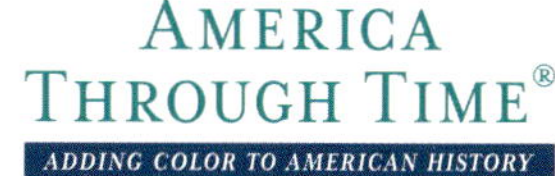

America Through Time is an imprint of Fonthill Media LLC
www.through-time.com
office@through-time.com

Published by Arcadia Publishing by arrangement with Fonthill Media LLC
For all general information, please contact Arcadia Publishing:
Telephone: 843-853-2070
Fax: 843-853-0044
E-mail: sales@arcadiapublishing.com
For customer service and orders:
Toll-Free 1-888-313-2665

www.arcadiapublishing.com

First published 2020

ISBN 978-1-63499-201-5

Typeset in Mrs Eaves XL Serif Narrow
Printed and bound in England

CONTENTS

ACKNOWLEDGMENTS

Thanks to Alan Sutton for developing this series, and thanks to Kena Longabaugh for getting the manuscript ready for publication. Also, thanks to Matthew and Elizabeth for their help and their company on many Hempstead Plains adventures.

PHOTO CREDITS

Library of Congress	p12, p29 bottom, p30 top, p31 top, p32 bottom, p37 top, p48, p49 bottom, p50 top, p73 top
National Archives	p21 top, p29 top, p32 top, p35 top, p45 top, p49 top, p52 top, p53, p54 top, p62, p63, p64, p67 bottom, p69, p70 bottom, p71, p72, p101, p108 top
United States Geologic Survey	p73 bottom, p74, p75, p76
Historical Society of the Westburys	p15

All other images courtesy of the author

FOREWORD

by Ed Mangano

President Theodore Roosevelt said: "No one cares how much you know, until they know how much you care." It is my honor to read the works of Richard Panchyk, a citizen who cares so much about Nassau County's natural beauty and rich history that he spent countless hours researching and preserving Nassau's wonders in several books he has authored. Having served as County Executive, I know just how wonderful Nassau County is and just how tirelessly Richard worked to recount its historic events in this wonderful book.

Nassau has birthed citizens that put men on the moon and brought them safely home, led the defense industry in engineering and reinvented its economy several times over. Moreover, I believe it is important to acknowledge citizens and authors who sought to preserve our history through literary works and museums like the Old Bethpage Village Restoration, Cradle of Aviation Museum, Museum of American Armor, Holocaust Memorial and Tolerance Center, the Nassau Museum of Fine Arts, the African American Museum, and President Roosevelt's home, just to name a few important repositories of our history. Richard's latest book, *Hempstead Plains From Above*, captures this spirit and much more, in preserving our history. Richard's unique approach will provide you with a visual perspective seldom utilized in recounting how the Hempstead Plains' changing landscape shaped Nassau County and in many instances that of our Nation.

Hempstead Plains From Above will take you on a trip back in time to when the Hempstead Plains was the largest prairie east of the Mississippi River and stretched across present-day Elmont, Franklin Square, New Hyde Park, Garden City Park, Stewart Manor, Garden City, East Garden City, Hempstead, Uniondale, Mineola, Carle Place, Westbury, East Meadow, Hicksville, and Levittown. You will learn of historic events in aviation, transportation, military operations, and sports, and discover what physical traces remain of this history today. I am certain you will appreciate this wonderful historic journey.

Enjoy Richard's book and then share it with your friends and family.

Edward P. Mangano served as Nassau County Executive from 2010-2017. Prior to that he was a Nassau County Legislator from 1996-2009.

Introduction

Hempstead Plains From Above is part of a new book series that strives to capture history from a different angle, one that is seldom seen in the thousands of local history books currently on the market. This is the second book in the *From Above* series; *Westbury From Above* was the first. It was appropriate that it was the first book in this series, given that Westbury contains the spot where Charles Lindbergh's plane became airborne on its famous transatlantic voyage. Westbury is a subset of the larger area that has long been of interest to me—so it was natural that Hempstead Plains follow as a second topic. *Hempstead Plains From Above*, like the Westbury title before it, was born simply out of a natural curiosity to see my environs from a new perspective. After studying local history in the area for several years, it was exciting to have a look at the places I thought I knew so well, from above. These "from above" adventures wound up turning into the idea to create something new to share with other history enthusiasts.

The concept of the bird's-eye view itself is nothing new. It actually dates back several centuries, but was most popular in the nineteenth century and was a great way to depict the growth of the many villages, towns, and cities across the United States. No mere street-level view can capture the essence of a neighborhood the way a bird's-eye view can—literally called that because only birds could see such sights in those days, as people had not yet gained the ability to fly. Context and perspective reveal things that simply cannot be seen or understood at ground level. This is true everywhere but especially for the Hempstead Plains, which holds many hidden secrets and remnants of a storied past.

With the advent of airplanes in the early twentieth century, aerial photographic views were now possible, but most of these were taken from heights well over 1,000 feet. New technology has made possible the capturing of views from lesser altitudes, where more detail can be captured and a greater sense of place can be established—perfect for historians and more broadly, those with curious minds. The photos in this book offer a twofold benefit: seeing the Hempstead Plains from above for the first time, but more importantly, providing a better understanding of how today's landscape was shaped by yesterday's history. With historic aerial photos and other vintage images mixed in, as well as present-day ground views, this book offers a wealth of visual information on one of the most geographically interesting and history-packed areas in the eastern United States.

Once upon a time, a vast swath of flat, grassy land across what is now central Nassau County was the largest prairie east of the Mississippi River. At 40,000 acres, the Hempstead Plains was a natural wonder that stretched across present-day Elmont, Franklin Square, New Hyde Park, Garden City Park, Stewart Manor, Garden City, East Garden City, Hempstead, Uniondale, Mineola, Carle Place, Westbury, East Meadow, Hicksville, and Levittown.

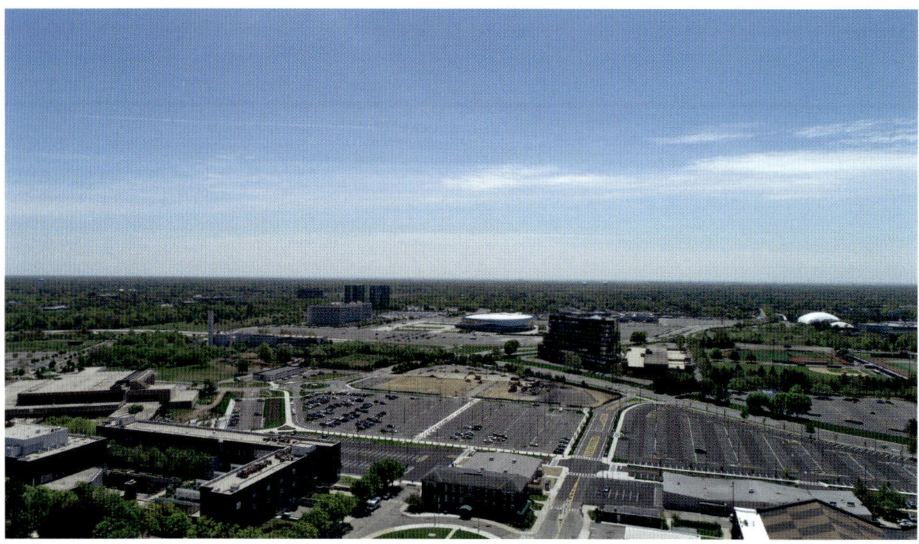

The heart of the Hempstead Plains, a location filled with history. This image offers a little bit of several important Hempstead Plains features—from left to right: the NCC parking lot, a Mitchel Field runway remnant, Eisenhower Park, the Hempstead Plains preserve, and the Meadowbrook Parkway.

However, it was not just a giant field of grass; there were numerous species of plants and shrubs that were native to the Plains, as well as birds and other animals that visited or lived in the area. Left unchecked, some of the plant life could grow several feet tall, with pretty flowers in spring and summer.

By the mid-seventeenth century, American colonists began to settle on the Hempstead Plains. The village of Hempstead was the biggest settlement and for years an outpost of sorts on an otherwise empty prairie. Early on, the Hempstead Plains was recognized as an ideal place for sports. Horse racing was the first major Hempstead Plains attraction, starting when Governor Richard Nicholls established a race course called New Market in 1665, and decreed that a sterling silver plate would be the prize for an annual race to be run there.

An early American colonist named Daniel Denton, who published a book about New York in 1670, wrote of the Hempstead Plains:

Toward the middle of Long Island lyeth a plain, sixteen miles long and four broad, upon which plain grows very fine grass, that makes excellent good hay, and is very good pasture for sheep and other cattle; where you shall find neither stick nor stone to hinder the horses' heels or endanger them in their races.

The horse races grew in popularity (and frequency) over the years and large crowds came from far and wide to watch the races and other special events. Bull baiting was a popular attraction held after the horse races; though one time a bull broke loose and rampaged through the stands. The New Market course later became the Washington Race Course, which was also the site of the annual Huckleberry Frolic, a carnival-like festival that took place in August during huckleberry season. The *Queens County Sentinel* of August 6, 1861, described the commotion following the horse races that day: "This is commonly a furious stampede through the village at the peril of horse and vehicle, life and limb. The clouds of dust exceed the clouds of a thunder storm, but generally 'nobody is hurt.'" An article in the same paper a few years later explained, "drinking bad rum, swearing and lighting are some of the necessary accompaniments" on Frolic Day. Other activities during the Huckleberry Frolic included sack races, acrobatic tumblers, and fire eaters.

What did the Plains look like in the mid-nineteenth century? Winslow C. Watson wrote in his 1860 book titled *The Plains of Long Island*:

Unoccupied, uncultivated, without enclosures, [the plains] present to the eye a wide expanse, clothed in rich and beautiful verdure. This vast surface is almost perfectly level, interrupted by slight undulations, and stretching from the ridge towards the ocean, by a declination so gradual as to be imperceptible. Scarcely a bush or tree interrupts the view. Nature formed it a broad, upland meadow. Its appearance recalls at once the memory of a Western prairie, and the herds of cattle ranging over it, which fancy may readily conceive to be the Buffalo, do not lessen the similitude.

Still, over the centuries, more and more of the Hempstead Plains had been developed. At the time of Watson's book, he claimed the Hempstead Plains had decreased in size by 30% from their original expanse. The size of the virgin prairie was soon to be reduced even more, for less than ten years later in 1869, the wealthy Alexander T. Stewart purchased 7,170 acres of prairie from the Town of Hempstead for $55 an acre, and turned much of that land into Garden City over the next few years. The coming of the railroad to this part of Long Island was also critical in its development. Garden City was served both by the Hempstead branch and the now defunct Central branch of the Long Island Rail Road.

Most of the remaining plains that were unaffected by Stewart's development were owned by his heirs, and would within a few decades be developed, too, as golf courses and flying fields were built. By 1914, what was left of the Plains lay east of Garden City and was owned by The Hempstead Plains Company. By 1917 and America's entry into World War I, more land was needed for Camp Mills and army flying fields, including Aviation Field #2, which would be renamed Mitchel Field.

Though the flying fields in their early iterations did preserve sizeable open patches of grass (which was almost certainly not allowed to grow to its full height), 1917 was really the end of the old Hempstead Plains—the last large pieces of it were no longer intact as undeveloped parcels. With the closing and subsequent development of Roosevelt Field in the 1950s, that left mainly the bits and pieces of Plains that lay within Mitchel Field, which itself closed in 1961. Subsequent development of the Mitchel Field property left only fragments of the Hempstead Plains. Construction of the Nassau Coliseum turned what was once part of the Mitchel Field runway complex into a world-class concert and sports venue. The roads that cross the former prairie are some of Nassau County's busiest, and the heart of the former Hempstead Plains is also known as the Nassau Hub because of its critical importance as a shopping and recreation center. Though the runways are largely gone, there are many Mitchel Field buildings remaining, with a number of them reused by Nassau Community College and others left vacant and abandoned.

One exciting development on the Hempstead Plains was the opening of the Cradle of Aviation Museum in 2002, which preserves and celebrates the area's aviation heritage and its role in the aircraft industry. The museum itself is partly in an old Mitchel Field hangar, preserving a piece of history.

There are three main pieces of Hempstead Plains prairie that are left today. One is adjacent to Nassau Community College, another is between the Meadowbrook Parkway and the Marriott Hotel, and the third is located on the northern edge of the Red Course at Eisenhower Park. A study of the soils and vegetation in these three areas shows that the least disturbed spot—the best-preserved piece of the Hempstead Plains—is around the periphery of the Red Course at Eisenhower. This bit of prairie was still intact when it became part of a golf course in 1914, and had no real disturbances since then, whereas the other two locations were adjacent to an air base.

Some of the hundreds of grasses and plants that grow on the Hempstead Plains remnants include big bluestem, little bluestem, Indian grass, switchgrass rush, wild indigo, Canada cinquefoil, gray goldenrod, early goldenrod, butterfly-weed, stargrass, fringed violet, and stiff-leaf aster. The Plains also attract birds of all kinds. Thanks to groups such as The Friends of the Hempstead Plains (run through Nassau Community College), the important grassland fragments are being maintained and preserved for future generations to study and enjoy. Invasive species are nearly impossible to eliminate, but keeping them at bay can preserve the authentic feel of the remaining plains.

The Hempstead Plains is a special place to see from above. Many of its secrets are revealed only through aerial views, so fasten your seatbelts and enjoy your tour through one of Long Island's most fascinating areas.

Note: I have arranged the images in this book by theme, which works well to tell the story of the Hempstead Plains.

HEMPSTEAD PLAINS

The Hempstead Plains in its natural state began to shrink by the mid-seventeenth century with the settlement of Hempstead, and continued to decrease in size over time. Even by 1860, the author of a book called *The Plains of Long Island* wrote that, "The territory known as the Hempstead plains formerly included a much more extended area than it now embraces." Ironically, the very land uses that suited development of the largest prairie on the East Coast and led to the ultimate destruction of the vast majority of its acreage also wound up saving a few small segments of the prairie from permanent destruction. The once vast Hempstead Plains have now been reduced to a tenuous few acres that were salvaged and preserved from the remnants of an air base's runway infrastructure and two nearby golf courses, one active and one inactive. As it turned out, the land between strips of Mitchel Field runway and the land on the periphery of manicured golf courses were the only true survivors of what was once tens of thousands of acres of grasslands. From above, the Plains remnants and the surrounding areas are seen in context, making it easy to imagine what the entire area once used to look like.

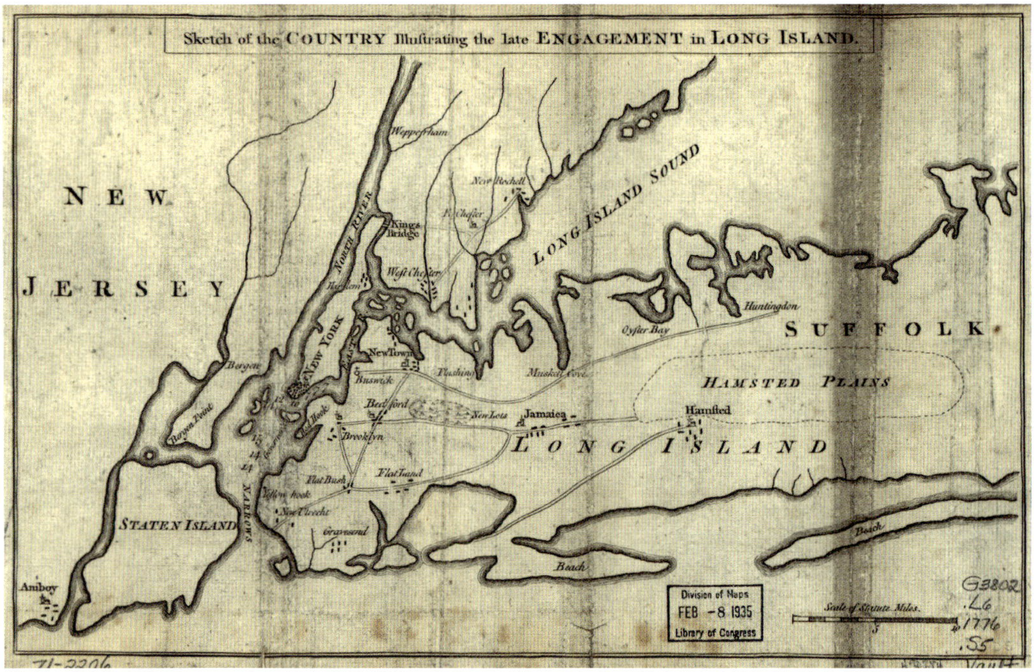

Sketch of the COUNTRY Illustrating the late ENGAGEMENT in LONG ISLAND.

NEW JERSEY

NEW YORK

Weppertham

New Rochell

E. Chester

Kings Bridge

West Chester

Harlem

LONG ISLAND SOUND

Huntingdon

Oyster Bay

SUFFOLK

Bergen

NewTown

Buswick

Flushing

Muskat Cove

HAMSTED PLAINS

Hamsted

Bergen Point

Red Hook

Bedford

New Lots

Jamaica

LONG ISLAND

Brooklyn

Flat Bush

Flat Iand

Yellow hook

New Utrecht

Gravsand

STATEN ISLAND

Beach

Amboy

Scale of Statute Miles

NEW MAP OF KINGS AND QUEENS COUNTIES NEW YORK.
FROM ACTUAL SURVEYS
PUBLISHED BY J. B. BEERS & CO, 36 Vesey St. NEW YORK.

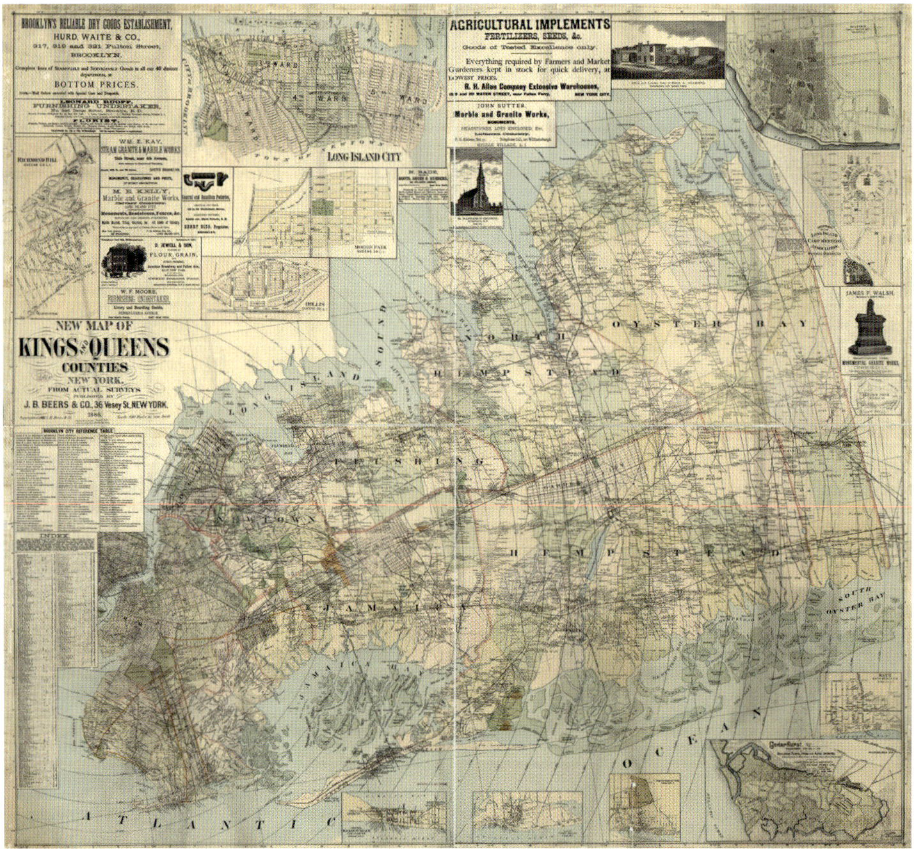

BROOKLYN'S RELIABLE DRY GOODS ESTABLISHMENT,
HURD, WAITE & CO.,
317, 319 and 321 Fulton Street,
BROOKLYN.
BOTTOM PRICES.

AGRICULTURAL IMPLEMENTS
FERTILIZERS, SEEDS, &c.
Goods of Tested Excellence only.
Everything required by Farmers and Market
Gardeners kept in stock for quick delivery, at
LOWEST PRICES.
R. H. Allen Company Extensive Warehouses,
NEW YORK CITY.

JOHN SUTTER,
Marble and Granite Works,
MONUMENTS.

WM. E. RAY,
STEAM GRANITE & MARBLE WORKS.

M. M. SCHLY,
Marble and Granite Works.

HENRY RUSS, Engraver.

D. JEWELL & SON,
FLOUR, GRAIN.

W. F. MOORE,
FURNISHING UNDERTAKER.

LONG ISLAND CITY

LONG ISLAND SOUND

NORTH OYSTER BAY

HEMPSTEAD

FLUSHING

JAMAICA

SOUTH OYSTER BAY

ATLANTIC

OCEAN

JAMES F. WALSH.

BROOKLYN CITY REFERENCE TABLE

INDEX

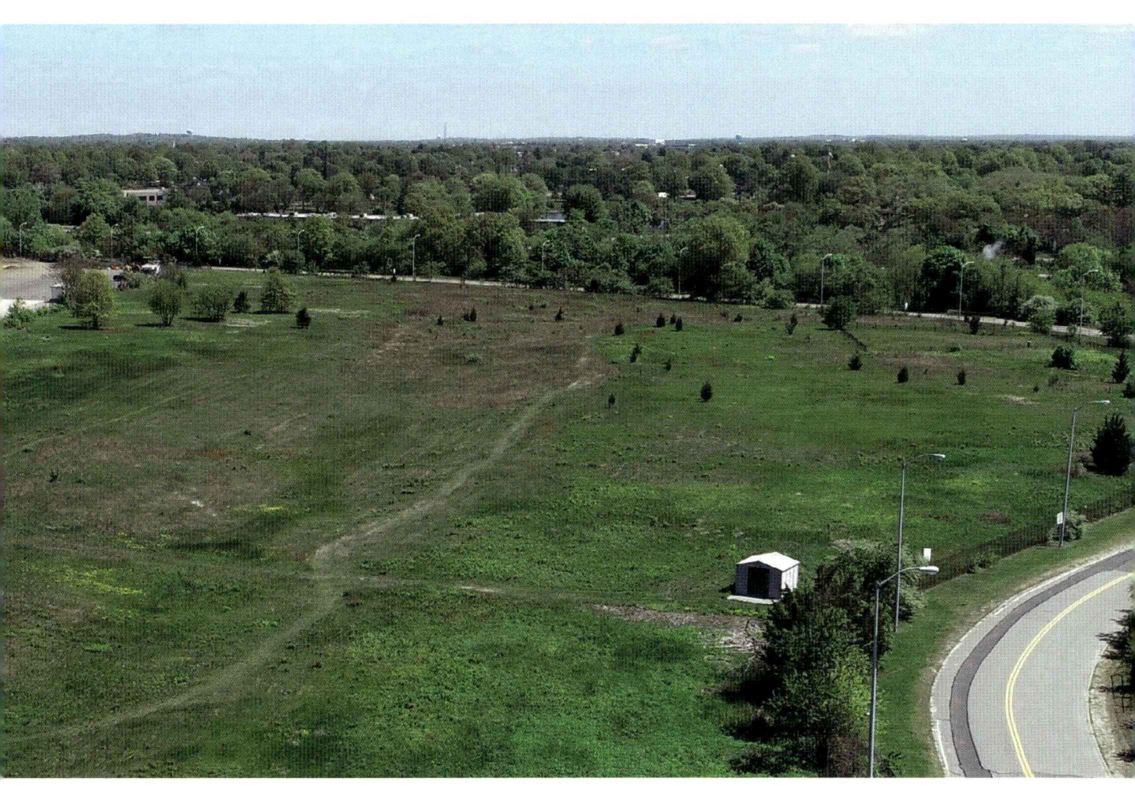

Until the mid-nineteenth century, much of the Hempstead Plains looked like this, a preserved section of the plains adjacent to the Nassau Community College campus.

Above: This map of Long Island dates to 1776 and shows the "Hamsted Plains," but it exaggerates the extent of the plains, depicting this area extending far into Suffolk County.

Below: An 1886 map shows the recently created Garden City as a laid-out grid with very little yet constructed. The entire expanse of what it shows as "Garden City" was part of the Hempstead Plains that was purchased by A. T. Stewart in the 1860s. Note the Meadowbrook Hunt property marked to the east of Garden City.

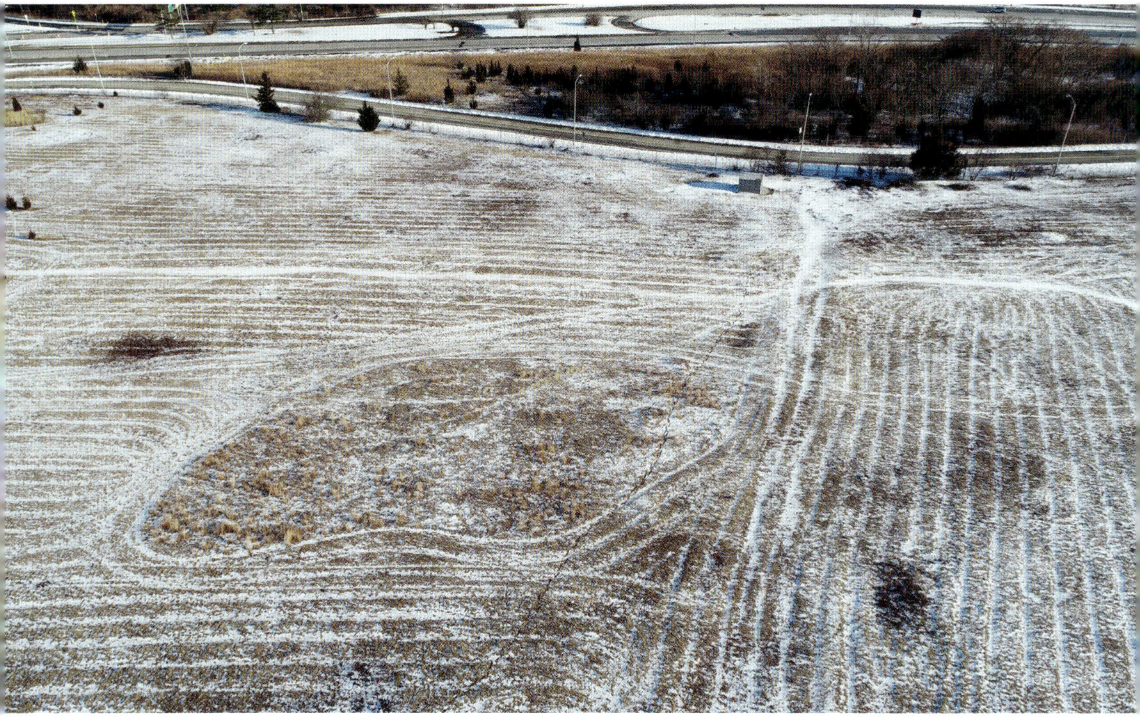

Seen under a dusting of snow, it's easy to imagine miles and miles of grasslands coated in white during winters past in the areas north and east of the village of Hempstead and south of the village of Westbury.

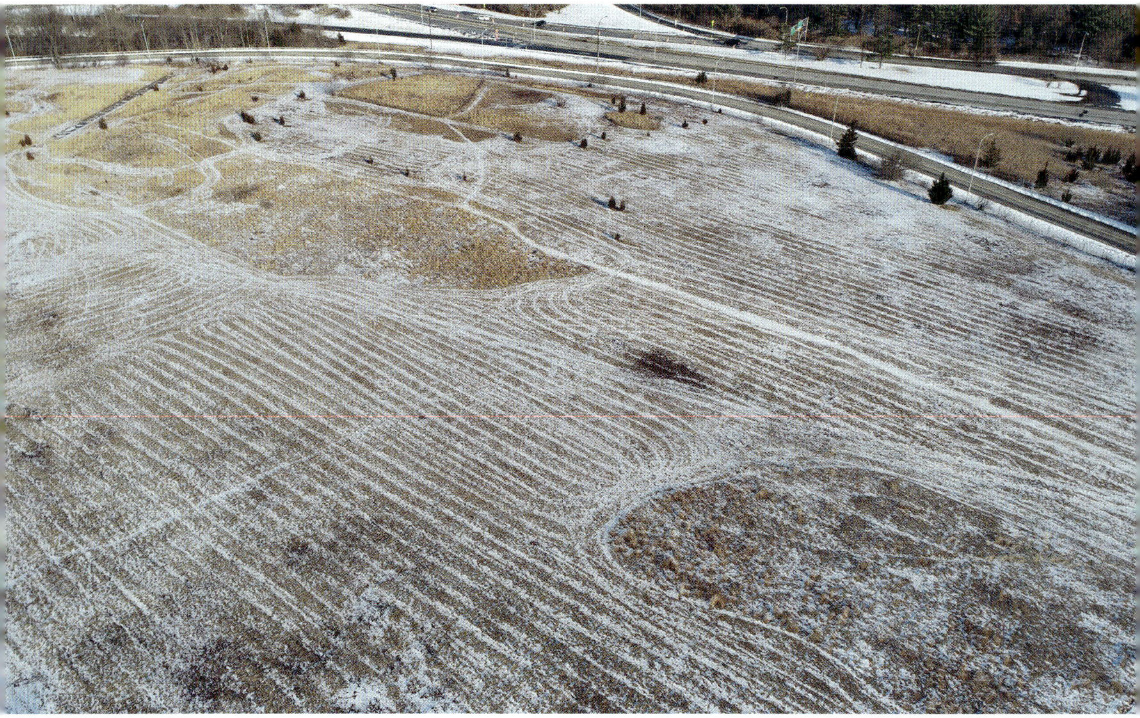

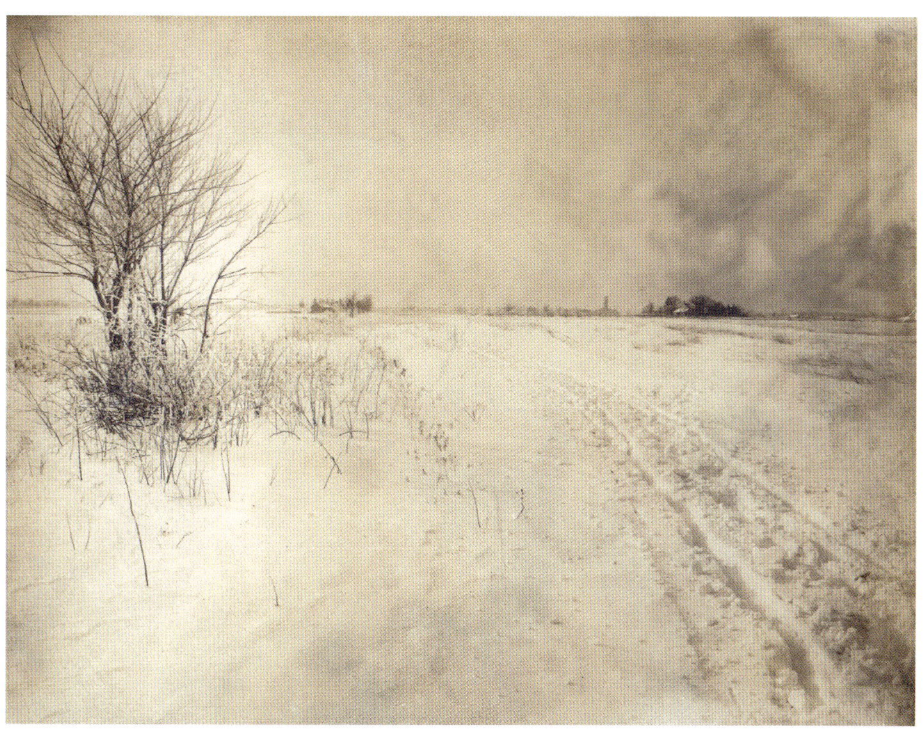

A vintage image *circa* early twentieth century shows how rural part of the Hempstead Plains still looked back then, before it was developed.

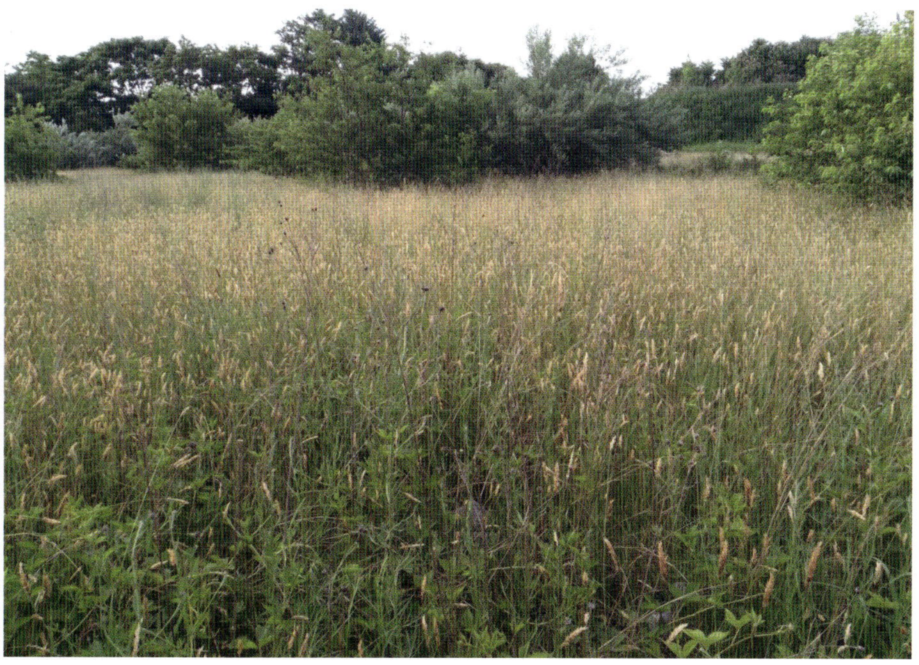

There are a few spots in the area that are still reminiscent of the old days of the great plains, even if the greenery is not fully native and untouched by outside influence—this is in Eisenhower Park just north of the Merrick Avenue/Stewart Avenue entrance.

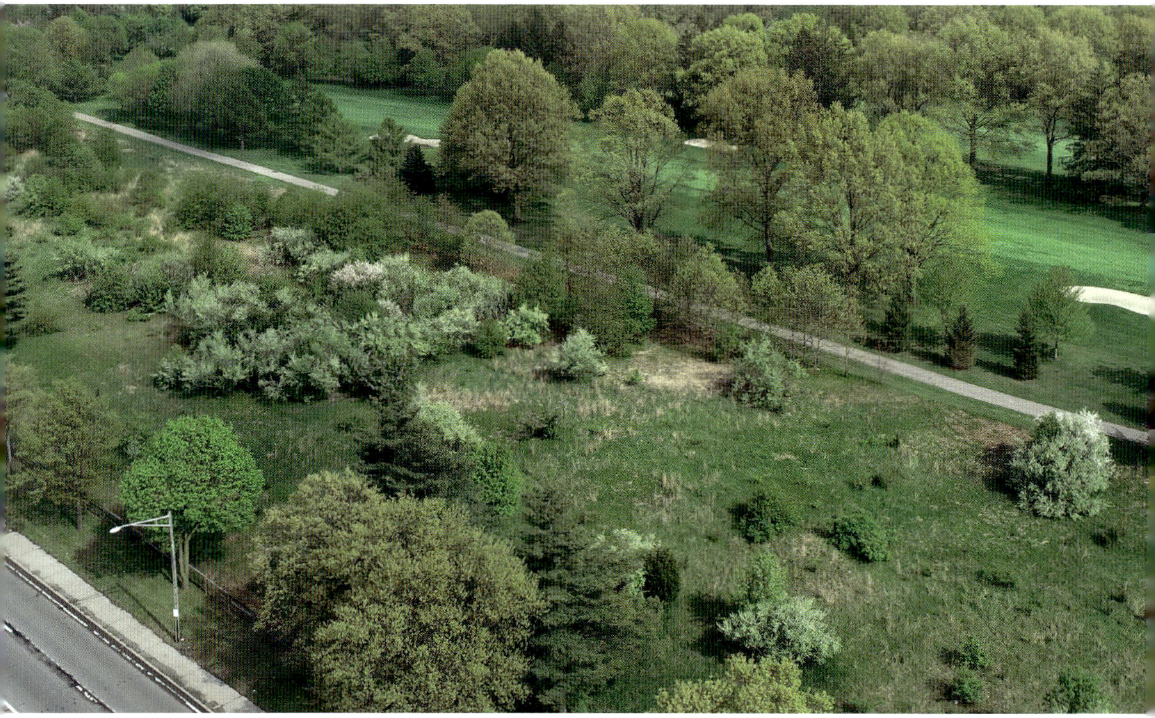

A closeup of the northern edge of the Red Course at Eisenhower Park shows some of the native grasses still left from the Hempstead Plains, mixed in with shrubs and trees.

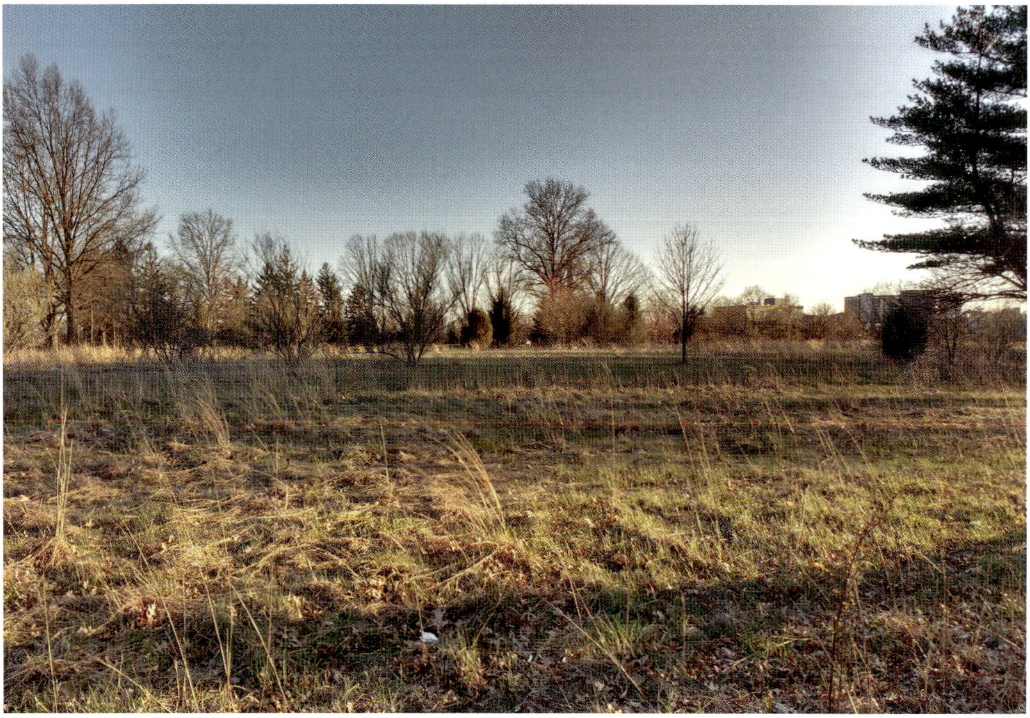

A ground-level view of northern edge of the Red Course.

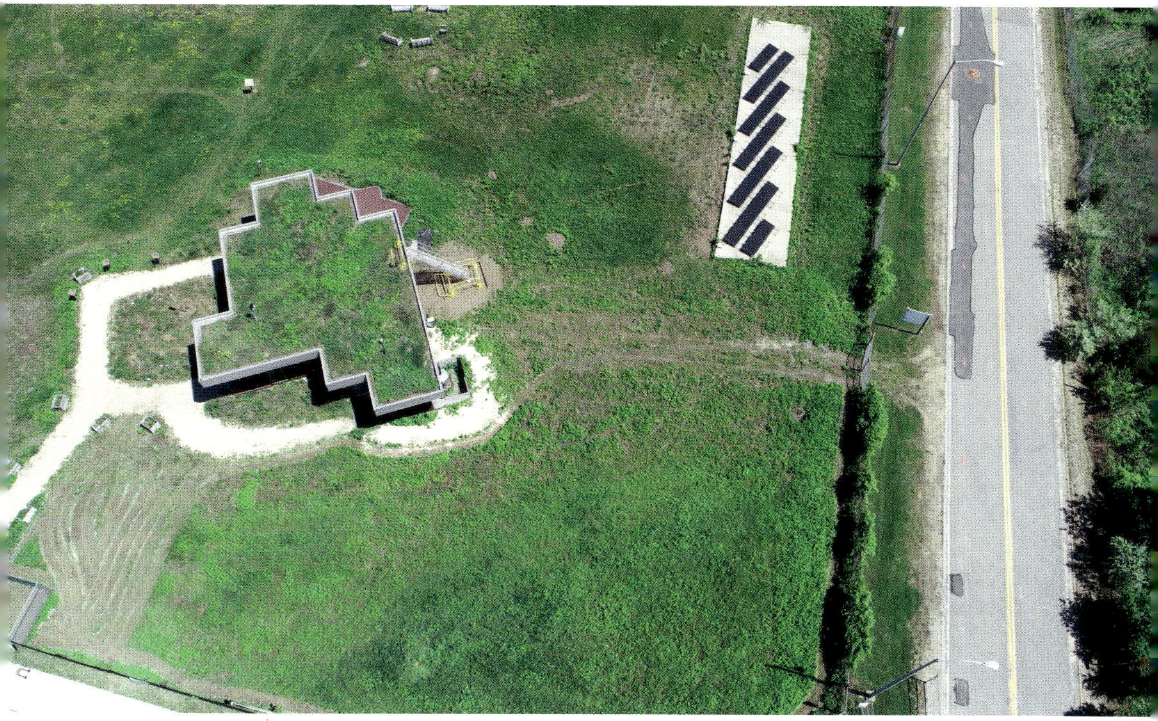

Two views of the interpretive center at the Hempstead Plains Preserve. It's a continuing challenge for volunteers to ensure that this small piece of the plains is not overrun with weeds and invasive species.

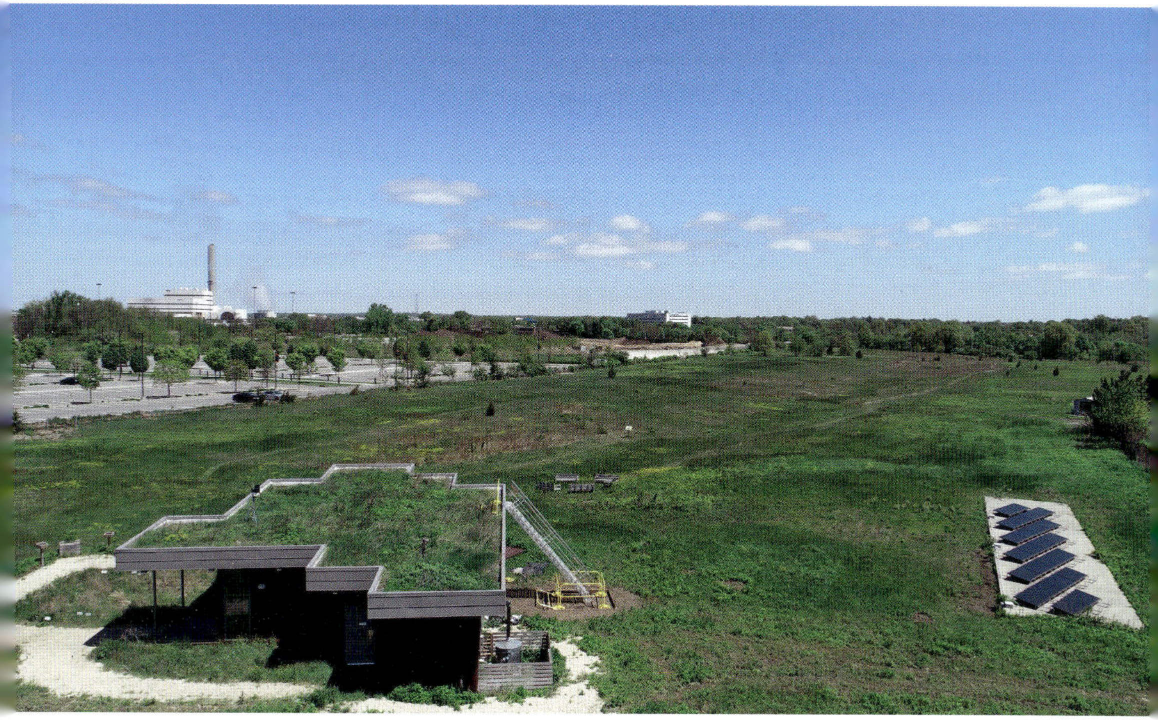

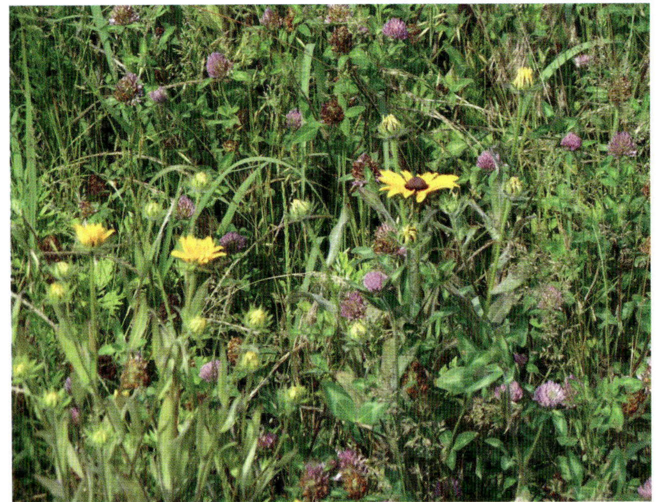

Wildflowers in late spring at the Hempstead Plains Preserve. Black-eyed Susans may not be native, but they sure are pretty.

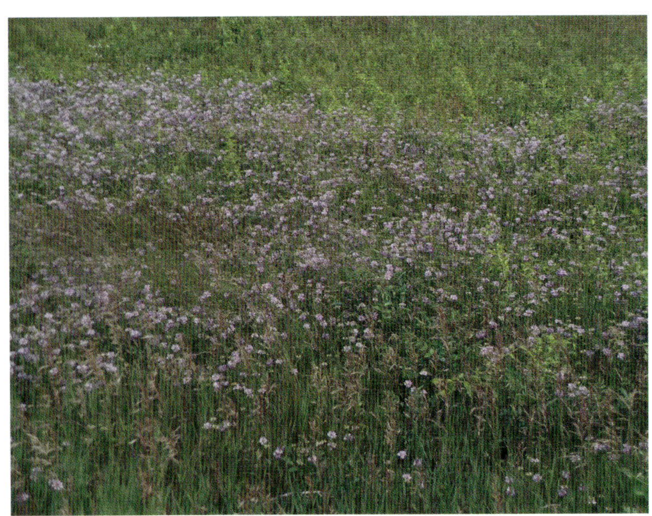

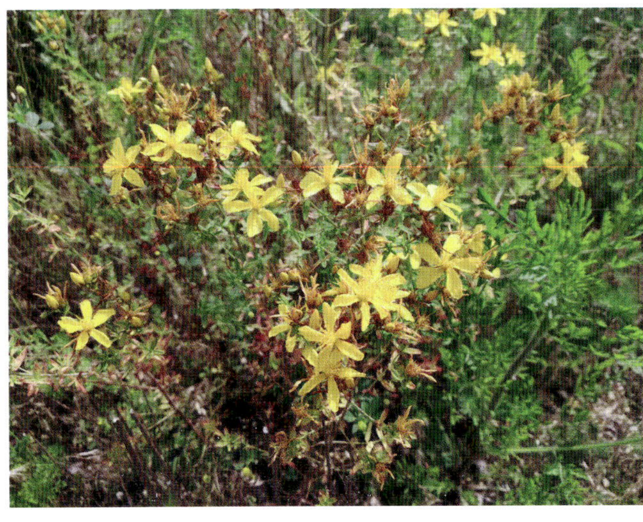

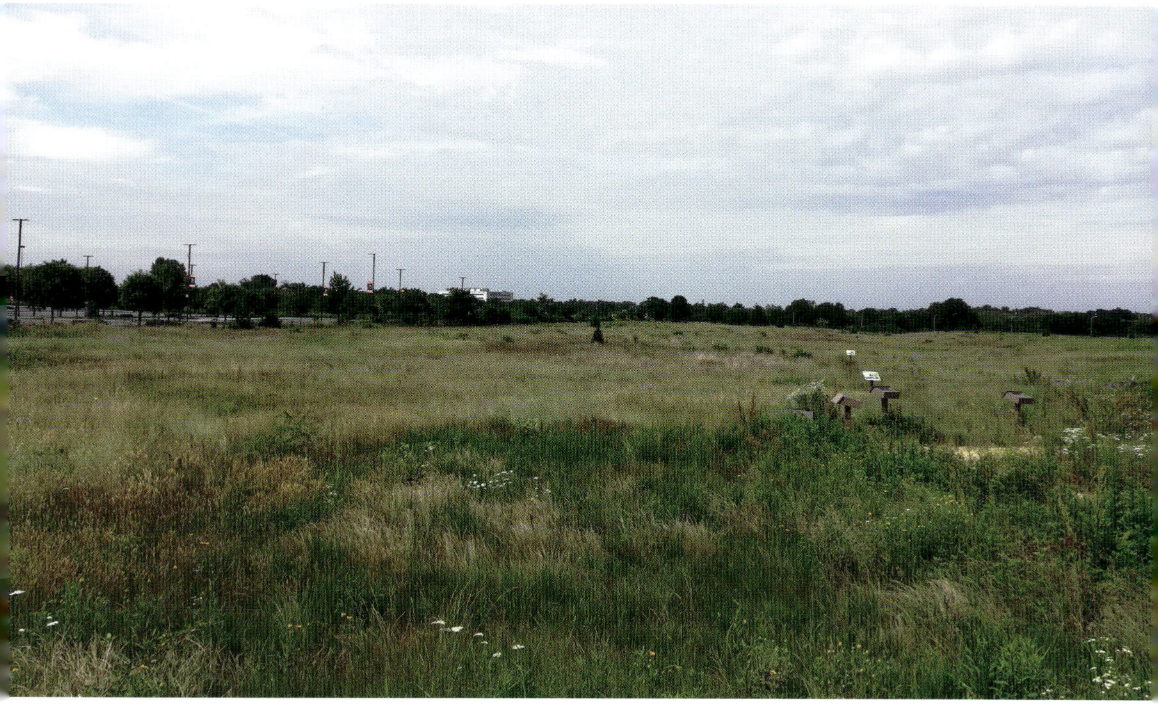

The Hempstead Plains Preserve in spring from a low-flying bird's-eye view.

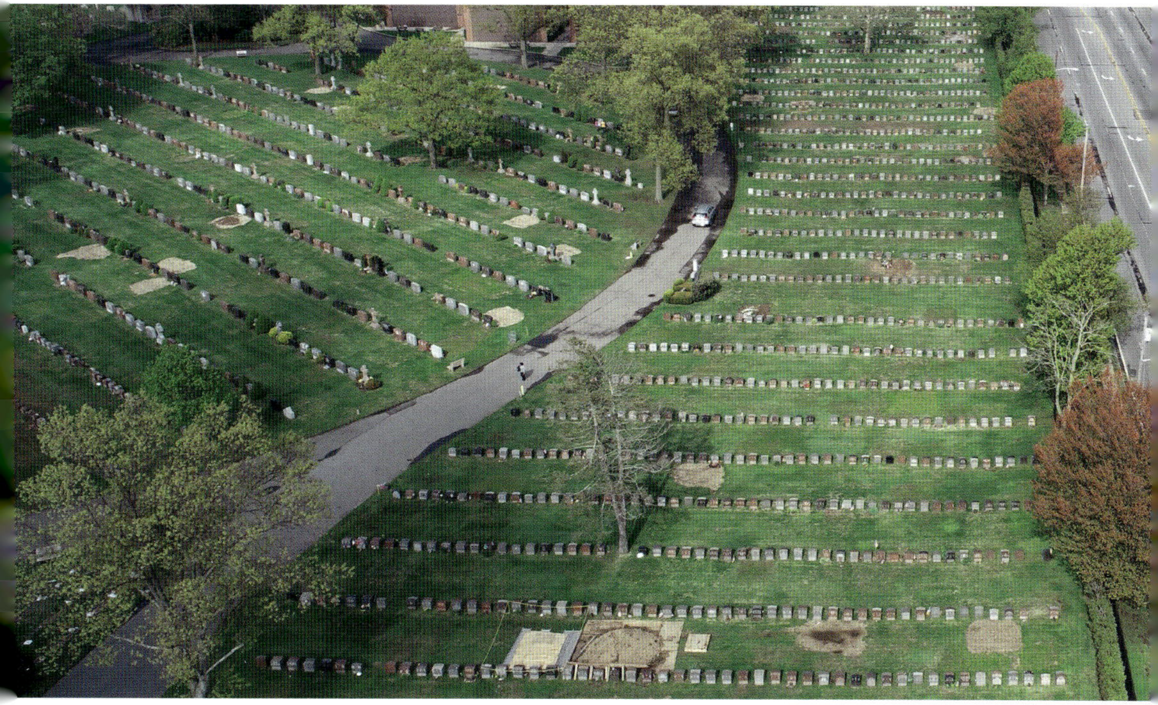

Though the more traditional understanding of the Hempstead Plains limits take it only as far north as Old Country Road, a study of soil characteristics shows that the plains really extended as far north as Jericho Turnpike in spots. What is now the Holy Rood Cemetery, on the north side of Old Country Road, was certainly part of the plains.

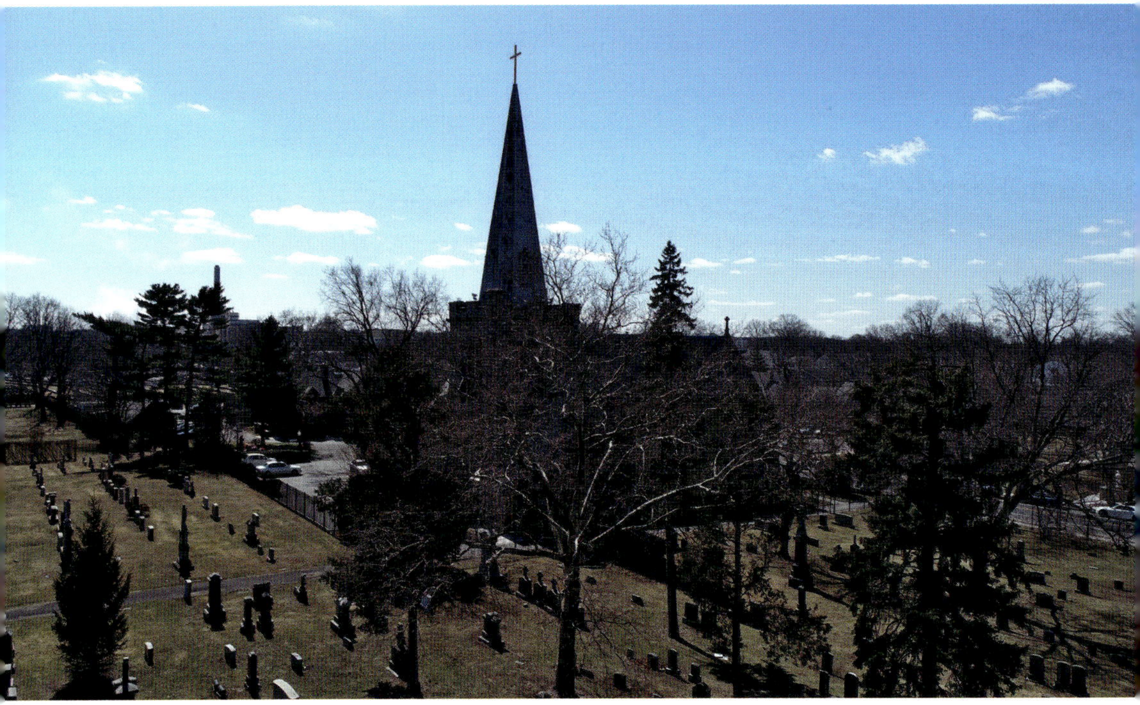

Holy Rood Cemetery originated with the church cemetery of St. Brigid's Church, which was first built in 1854. The church was likely built to be close to the railroad station that was just to the north.

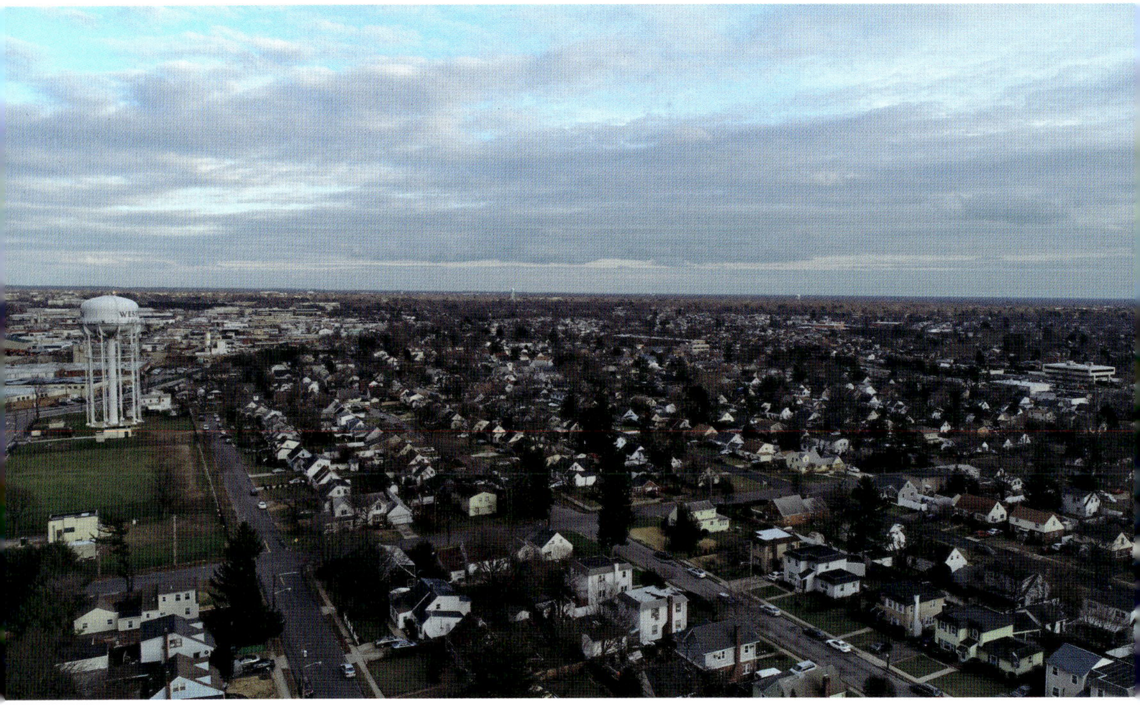

Looking toward Hicksville and the eastern end of the Hempstead Plains.

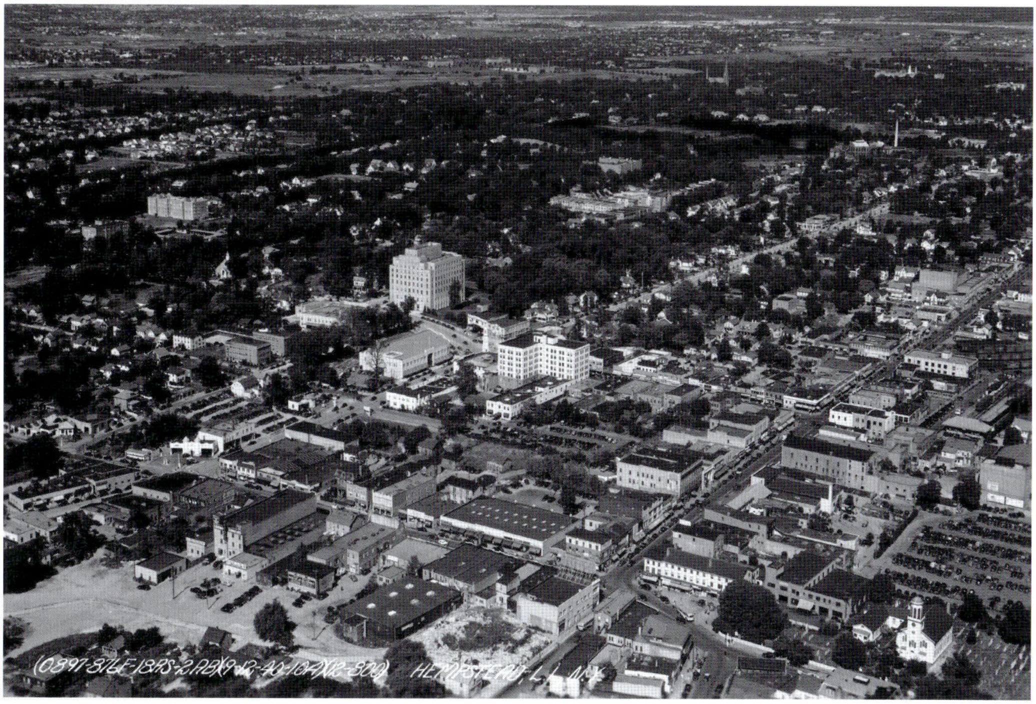

A 1940 aerial view looking northeast at the Hempstead Plains from downtown Hempstead at 800 feet. The early buildings of Adelphi University and the Garden City cathedral are visible in the distance.

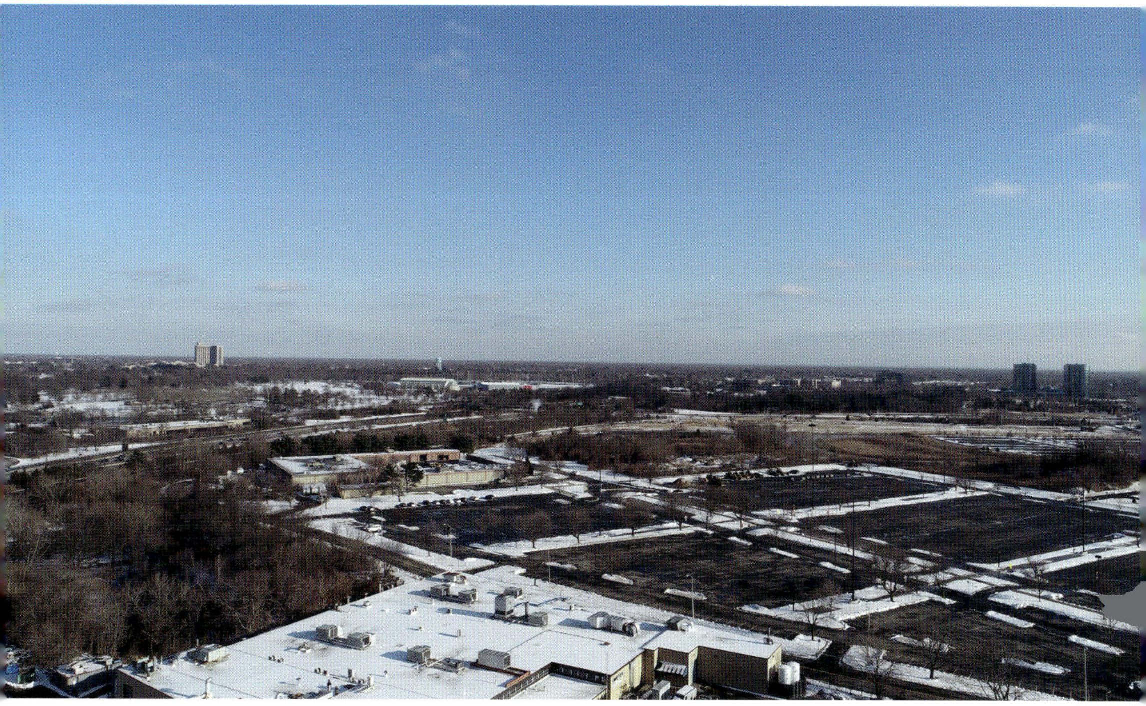

Looking southeast from the heart of the Hempstead Plains, the vista is entirely flat—even beyond the plains. We have the retreating glaciers of the last ice age to thank for that.

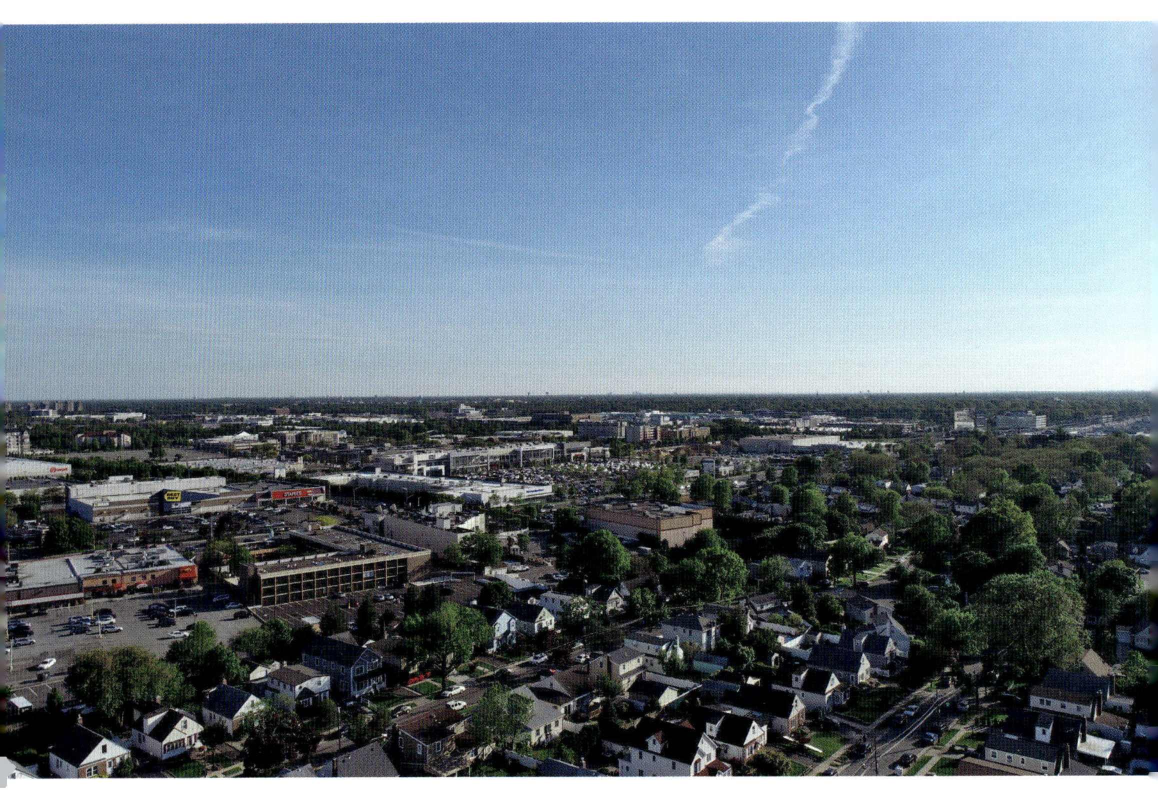

Looking southwest from Carle Place toward Garden City at the expanse of what was once a great prairie.

OPPOSITE PAGE:

A pair of ground-level views of the Francis T. Purcell Preserve adjacent to the Long Island Marriott property. This parcel was dedicated in 2004, and is comprised of what used to be Mitchel Field on the west side and the Meadowbrook Golf Course on the east side.

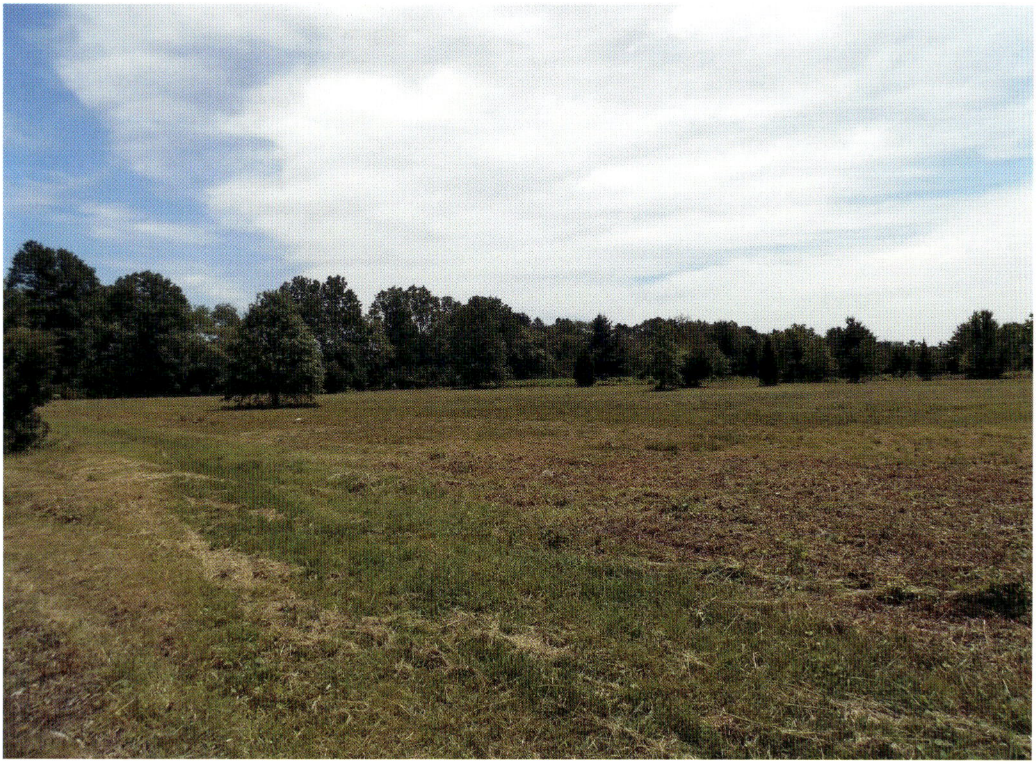

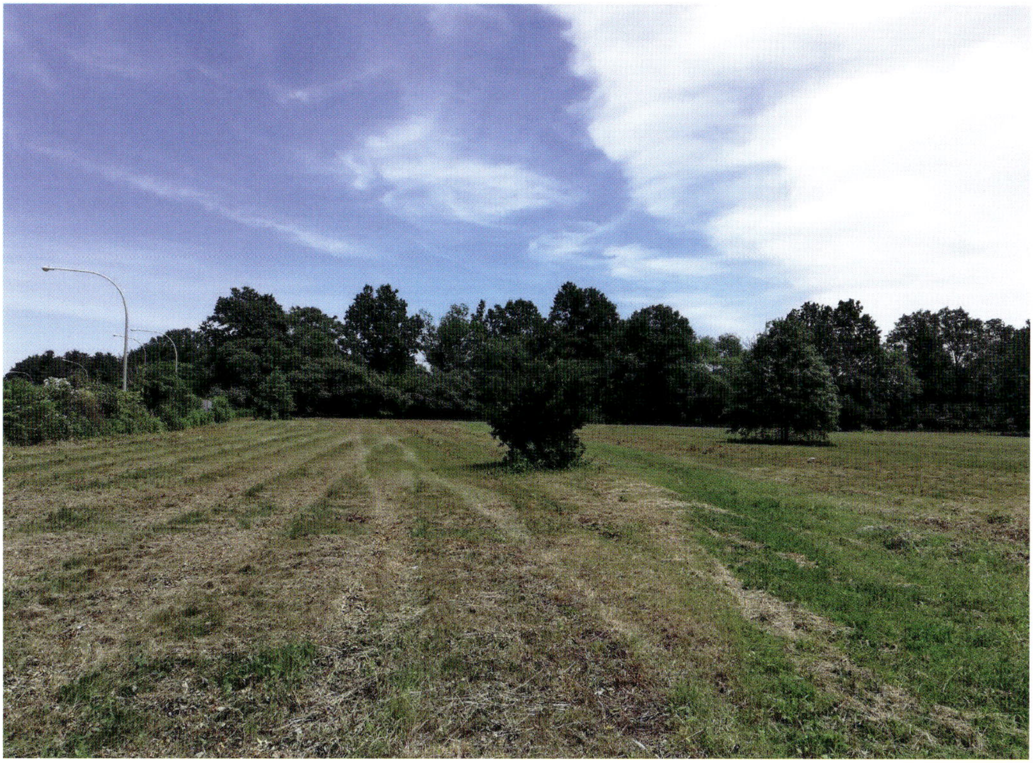

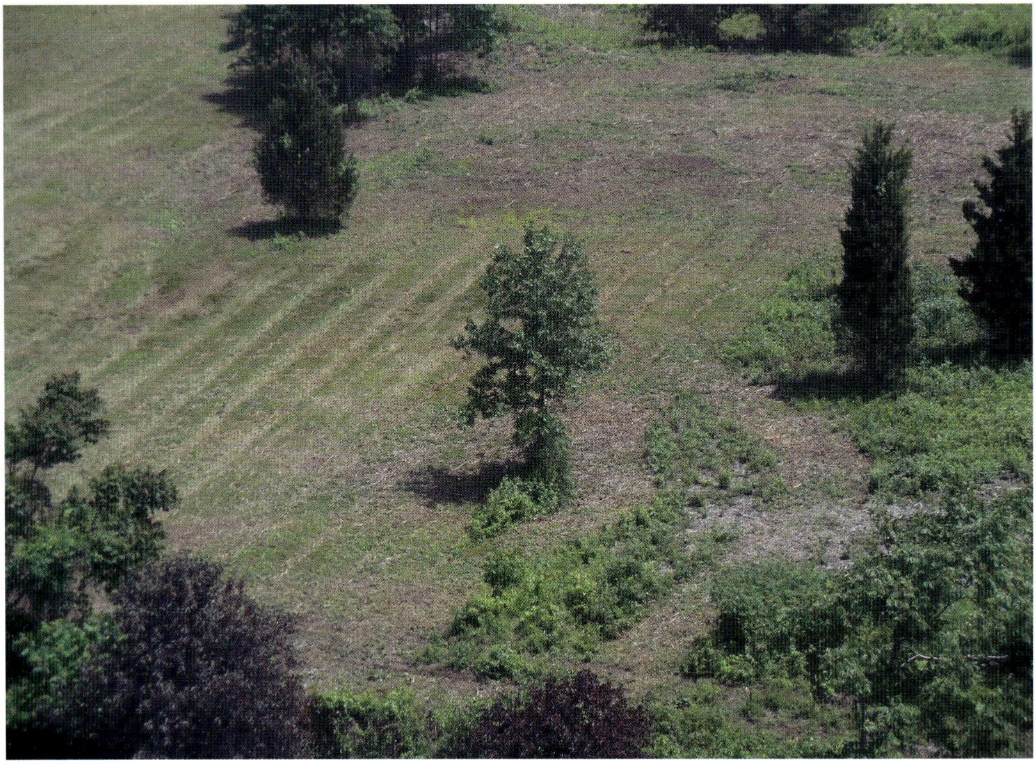

Views of the Francis T. Purcell Preserve from above.

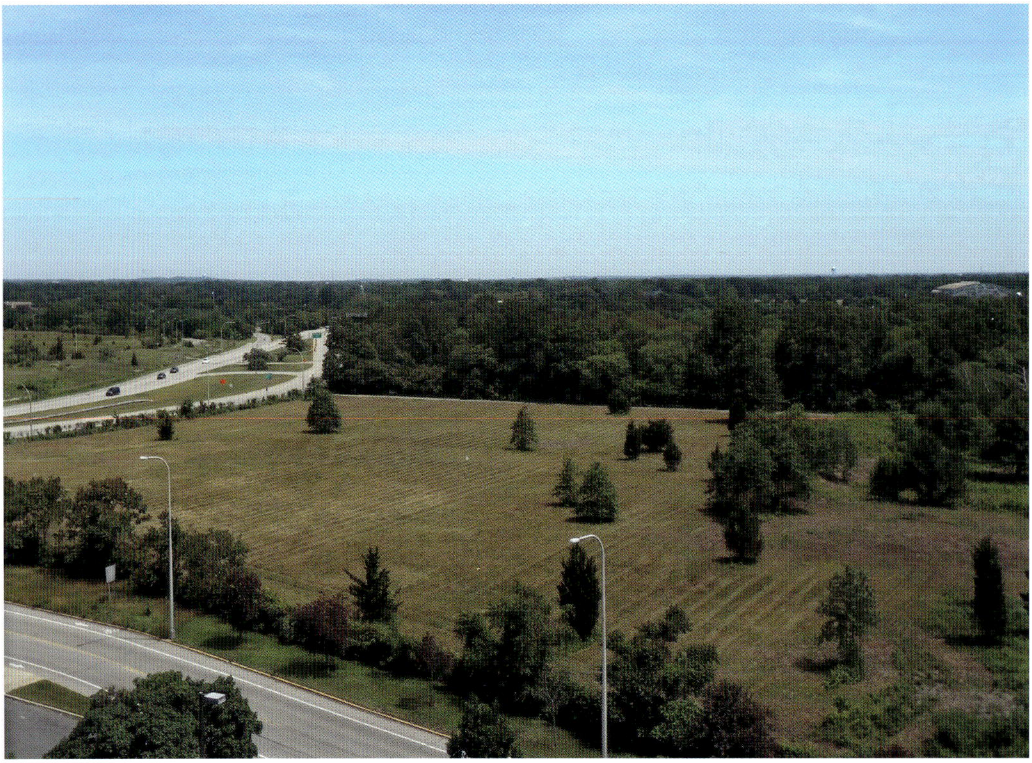

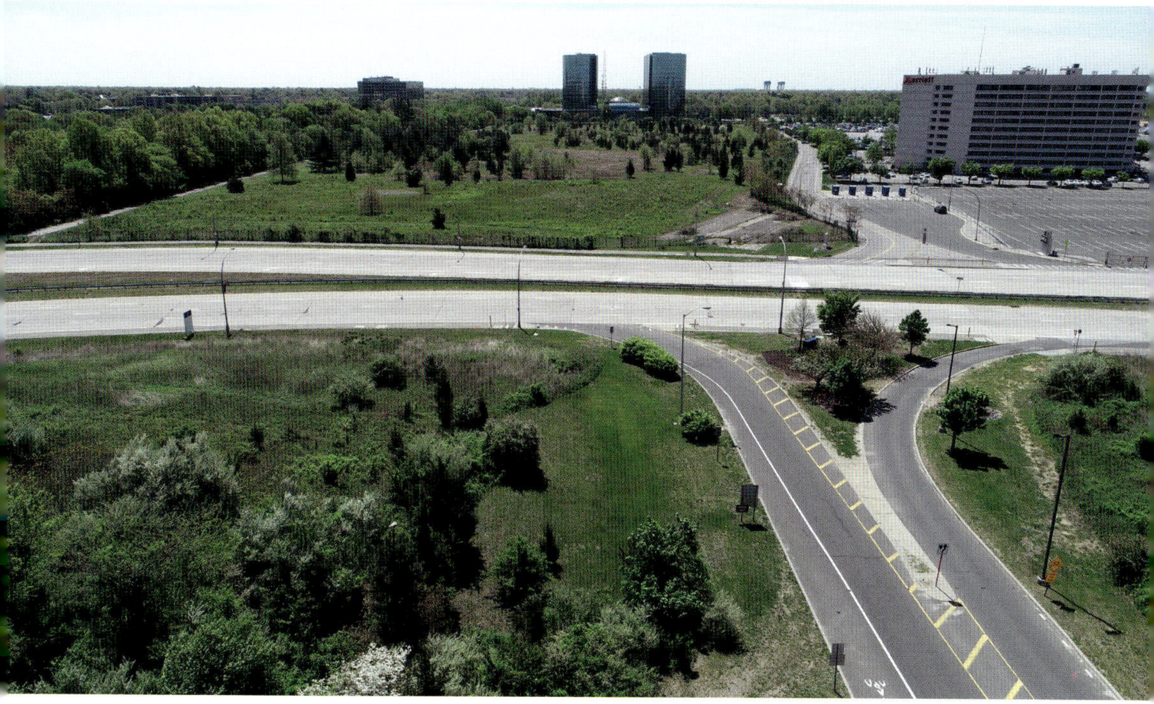

Looking south at the Francis T. Purcell Preserve. Note the bit of Mitchel Field runway/roadway in the right corner of the preserve. More on that later.

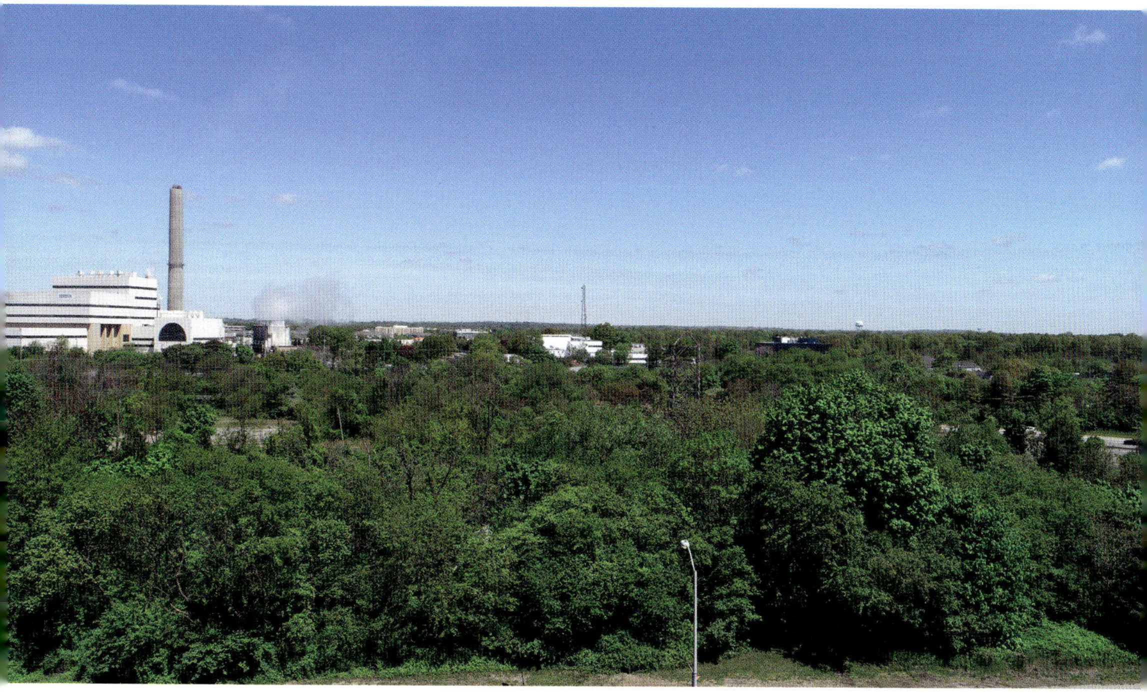

Looking east toward the Meadowbrook Parkway from a Nassau Community College parking lot, there is a lot of green, but in this view of what was once the Hempstead Plains it's all trees and no prairie.

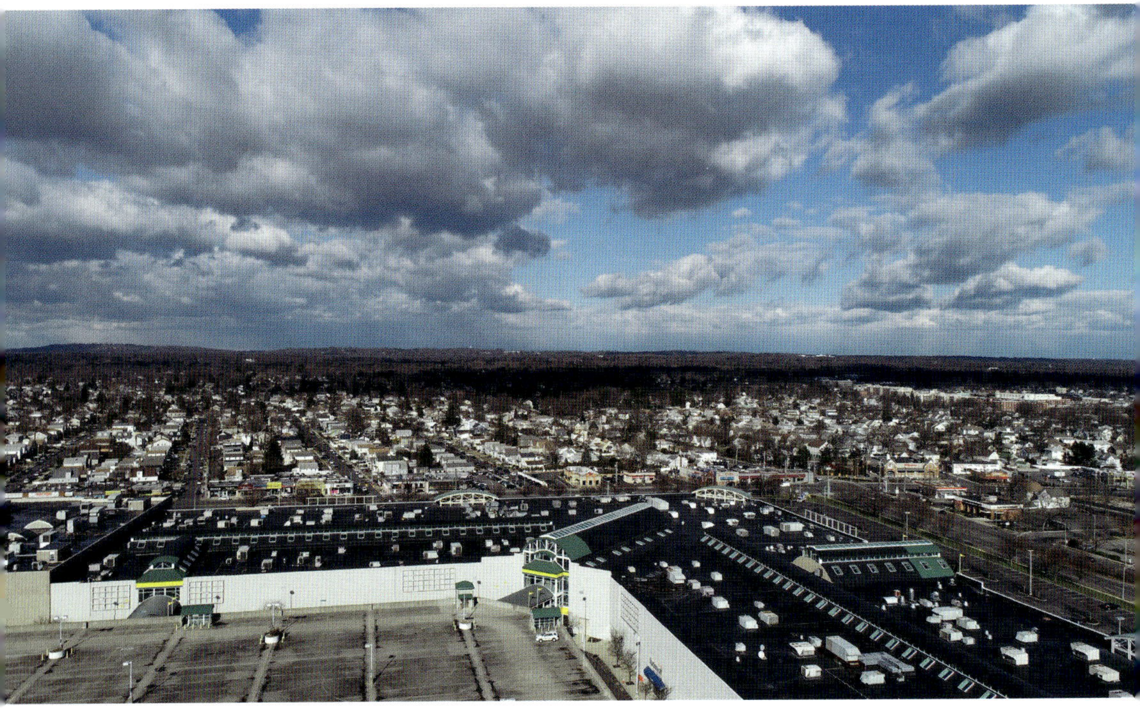

Looking north from Westbury just south of Old Country Road, it's easy to see how the flatness of the Hempstead Plains gives way to the hills of the north shore.

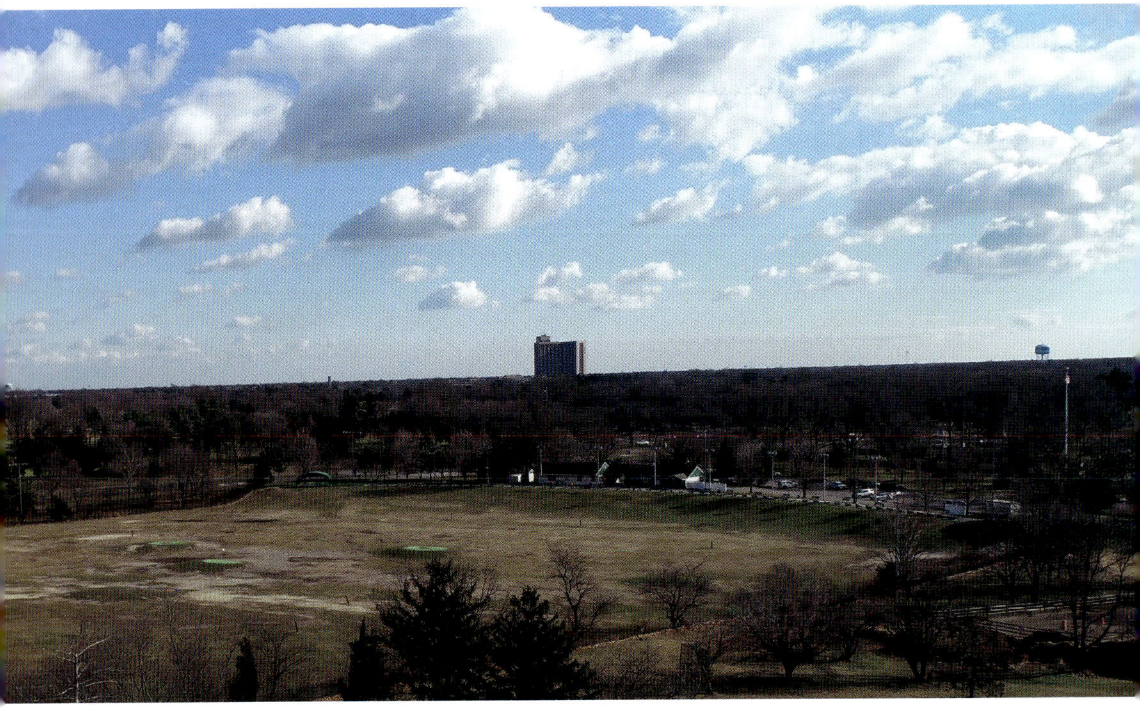

The nineteen-story Nassau University Medical Center (NUMC) is the tallest building in Nassau County, at 299 feet, and seems even taller springing up from the flatness of the Hempstead Plains.

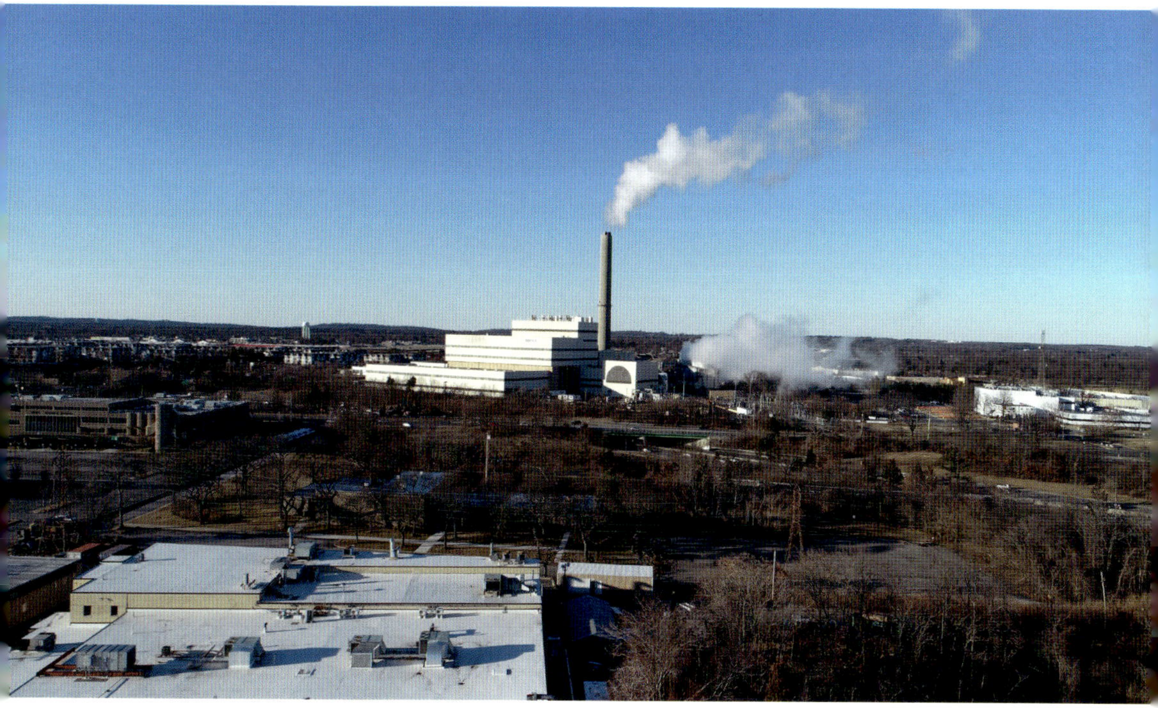

The Covanta waste-to-energy plant (opened 1989) smokestack at 600 Merchants Concourse is one of the tallest structures on all of Long Island, and can be seen from miles away.

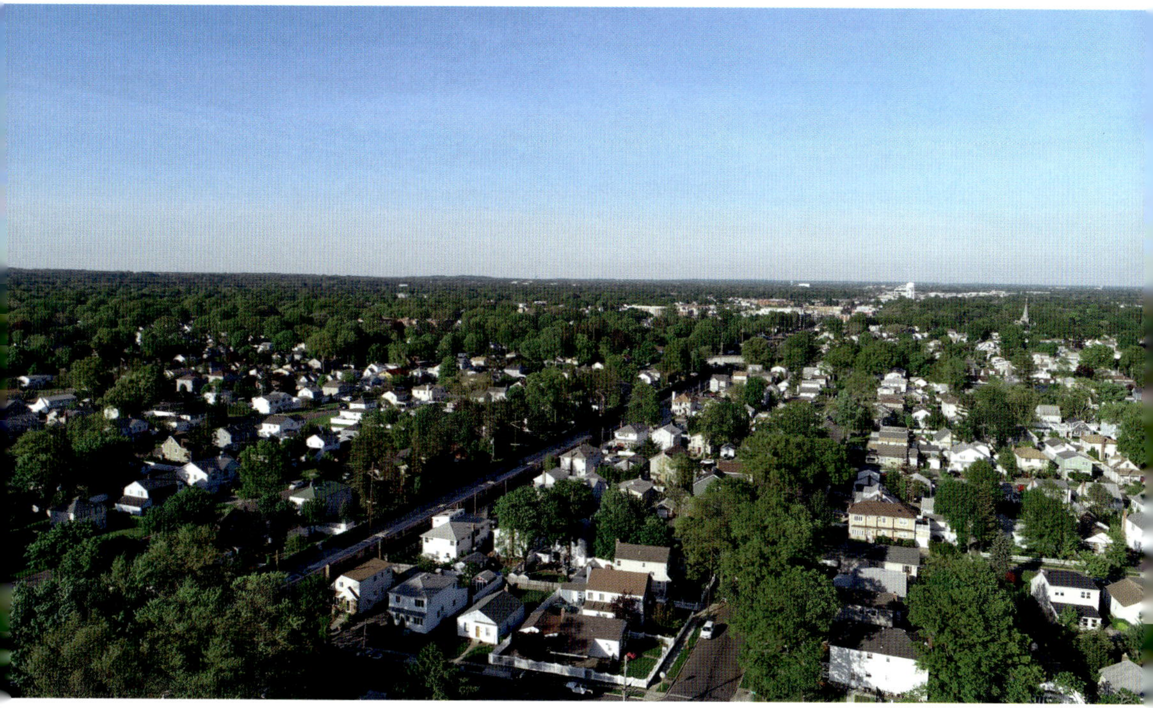

A view looking southeast at the Hempstead Plains from southern Carle Place.

2

SPORTS

From the early days of colonial settlement, the Hempstead Plains have been recognized as a great place to hold sporting events. The flat expanse of land was perfect for horse racing, and later, for another horse-powered sport—polo. By the turn of the twentieth century, the Hempstead Plains became the epicenter of this sport, with its biggest stars, Tommy Hitchcock, and then his son, Tommy Hitchcock, Jr. (known as "the Babe Ruth of polo"), living nearby. With the advent of golf, the area was also attractive, because its easily landscaped open space was well suited to a game that requires 100-150 acres of land per course. The golf courses on the Hempstead Plains as of 1927 included the Garden City Golf Club, Salisbury Golf Links, Meadowbrook Club, the Intercollegiate Golf Club, and the Cold Stream Golf Club. In fact, the 1926 PGA Championship was held at what was then the Salisbury Golf Club and is now Eisenhower Park. Car racing was also popular here, from the very earliest days of the automobile when William K. Vanderbilt ran his famous Vanderbilt Cup Races on Long Island starting in 1904 (a later Vanderbilt Cup Race in 1936 was held on a course that would be reconfigured to become the popular Roosevelt Raceway). Horse racing continued to be a steady presence through the twentieth century at the Roosevelt Raceway on the eastern end of Roosevelt Field (closed 1988), and at Belmont Park (still active as of 2019).

Above: The site of the first horse racing course in America, the Newmarket Course (named after a famous English racecourse), is believed to have been near the site of the Garden City Hotel, seen here in a 1936 aerial view. The first races were held in 1665, the year after the British took over New York from the Dutch. An article in the *New York Postboy* in 1750 explained that for one race, "upwards of seventy chairs and chaises were carried over Brooklyn Ferry the day before, besides a great number of horses."

Below: Belmont Park in Elmont is located on the western end of the Hempstead Plains. Seen here, a horse named Golden Chimes wins a race at Belmont in June 1913.

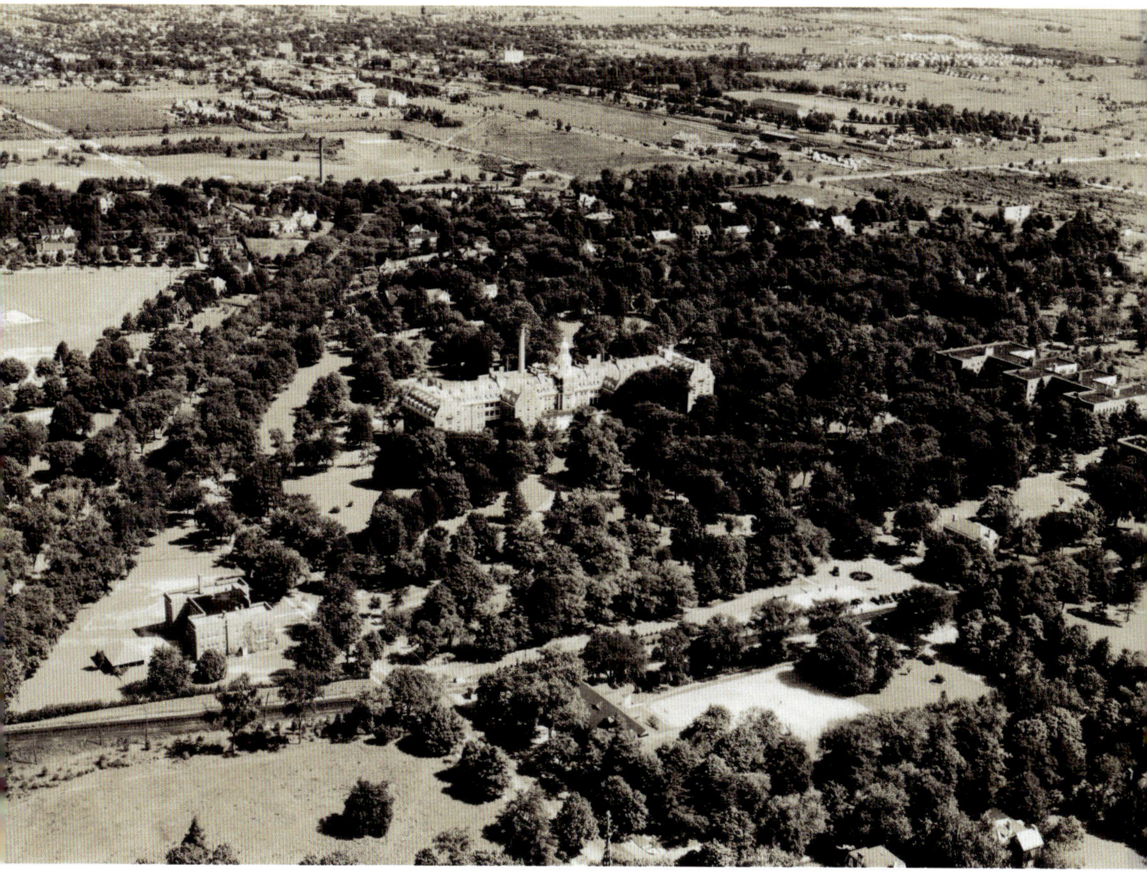

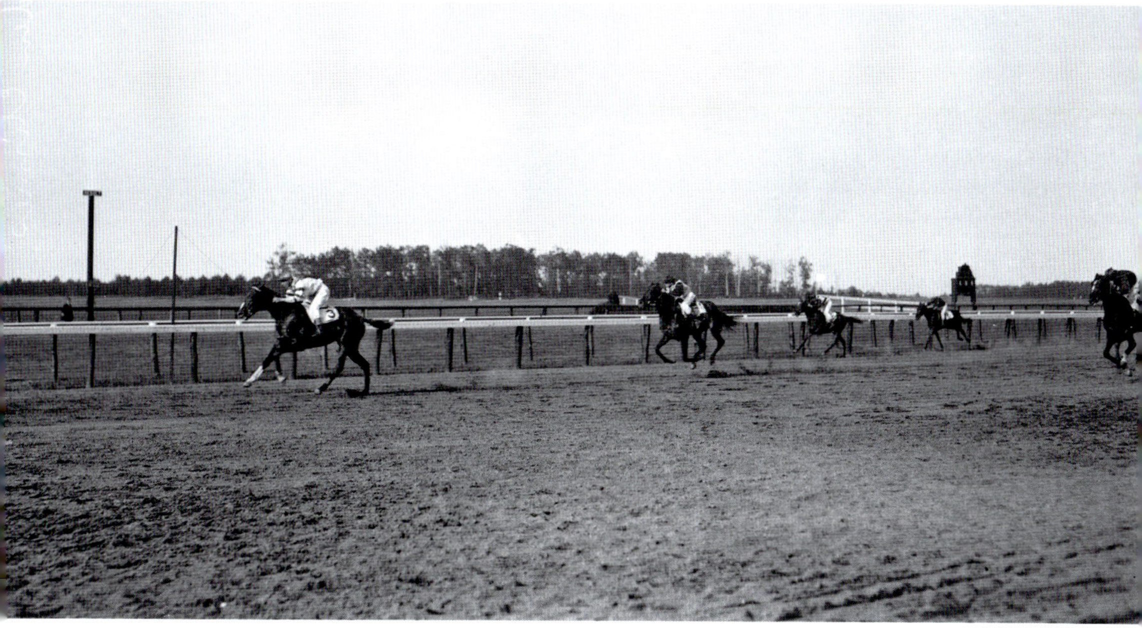

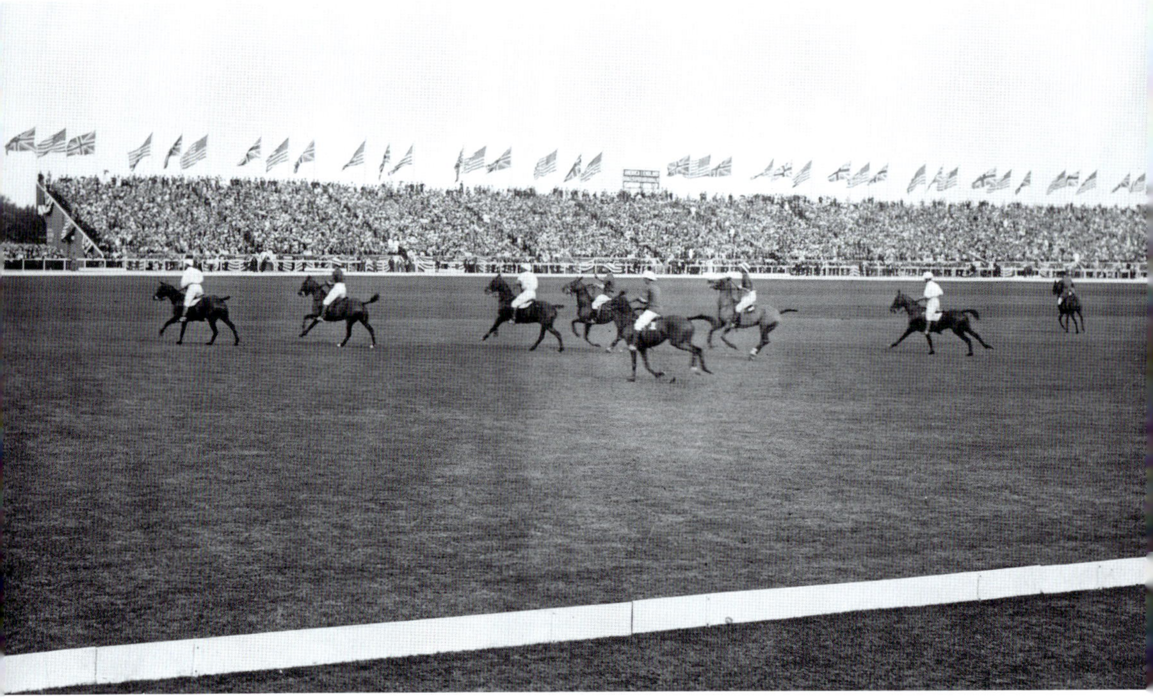

The Hempstead Plains was the perfect location for sporting events going back to the mid-seventeenth century. Sports such as polo require flat grassy surfaces. This image shows a polo match in June 1914 that was held at the international polo field, just off what is now Stewart Avenue and across from what is now Eisenhower Park.

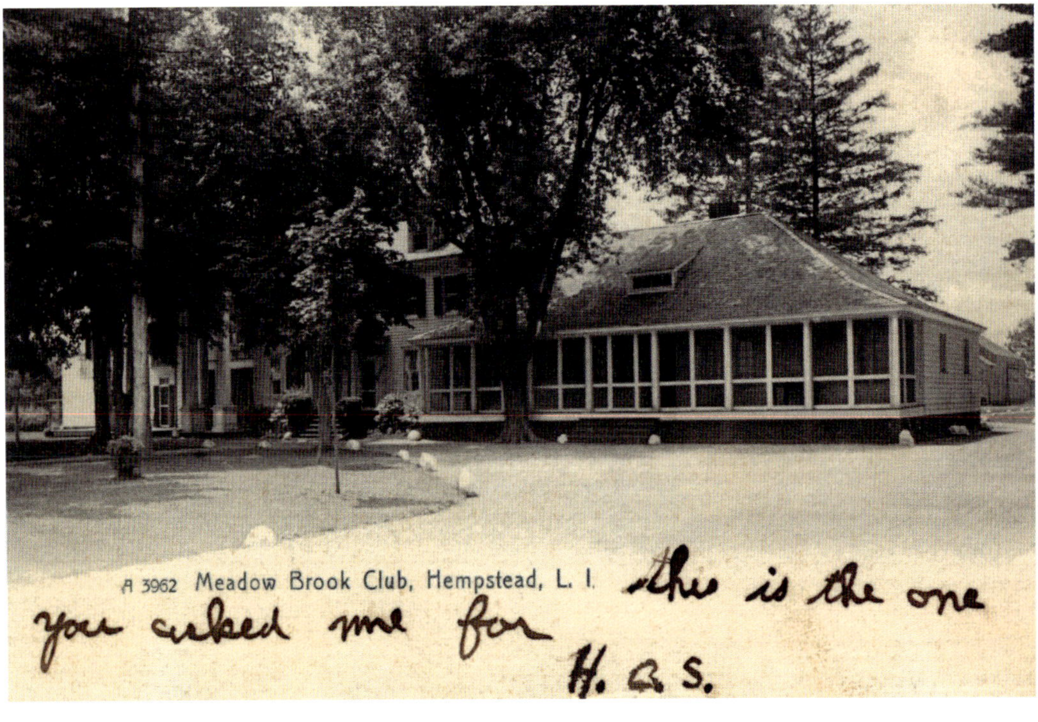

One of the buildings in the Meadow Brook Club complex *circa* 1906.

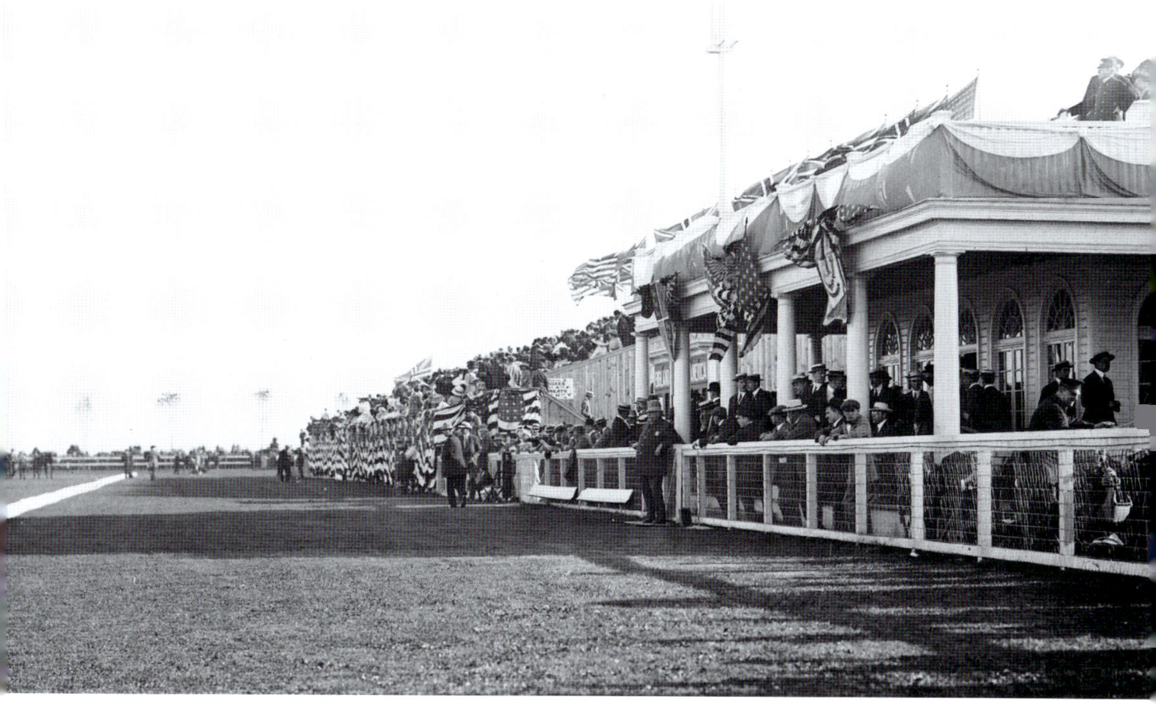

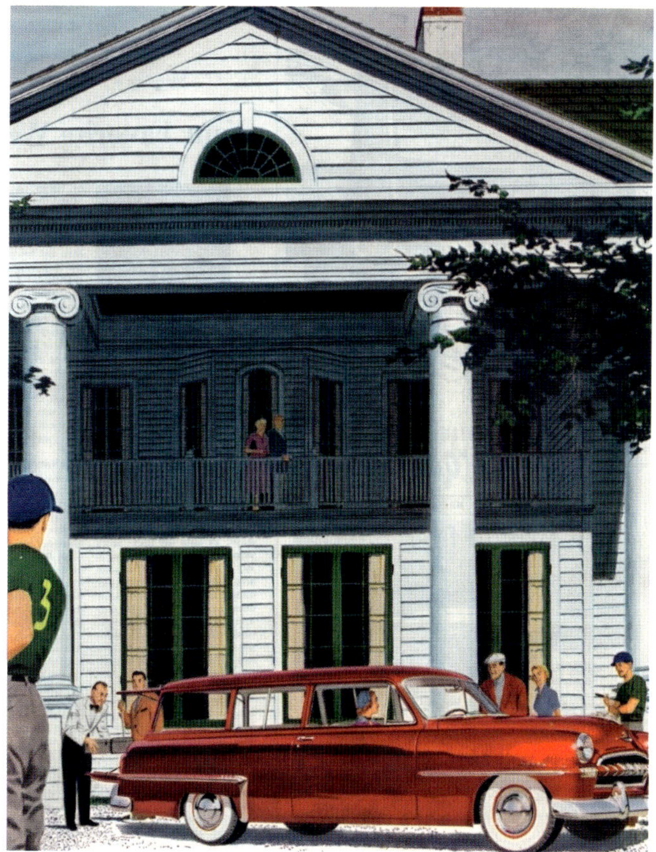

This was the clubhouse at the Meadow Brook Club. The earlier image dates to the first decade of the twentieth century and the later one is the clubhouse as it appeared around 1952. The polo part of the Meadow Brook Club still exists, on a field in Old Brookville near the CW Post college campus. The golf club branch of the Meadow Brook Club is in Jericho.

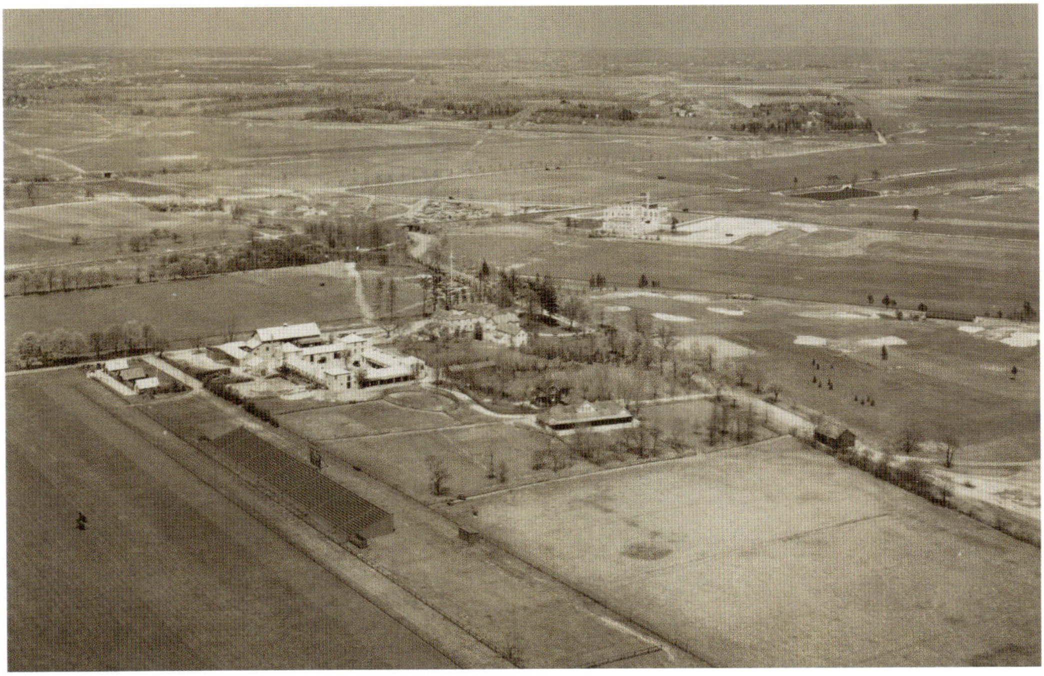

The Meadow Brook Club complex as seen from 700 feet in an aerial view taken in 1924, during the years of its heyday. Stands for a polo field are in the foreground at left. The small body of water was part of the Salisbury Golf Club course and was later expanded to become the lake at what is now Eisenhower Park. Note the flat expanse of the Hempstead Plains. Also in this image are the railroad tracks of the now defunct Central branch of the Long Island Rail Road, running just north of the pond, and the Long Island Motor Parkway running parallel to the tracks to the north.

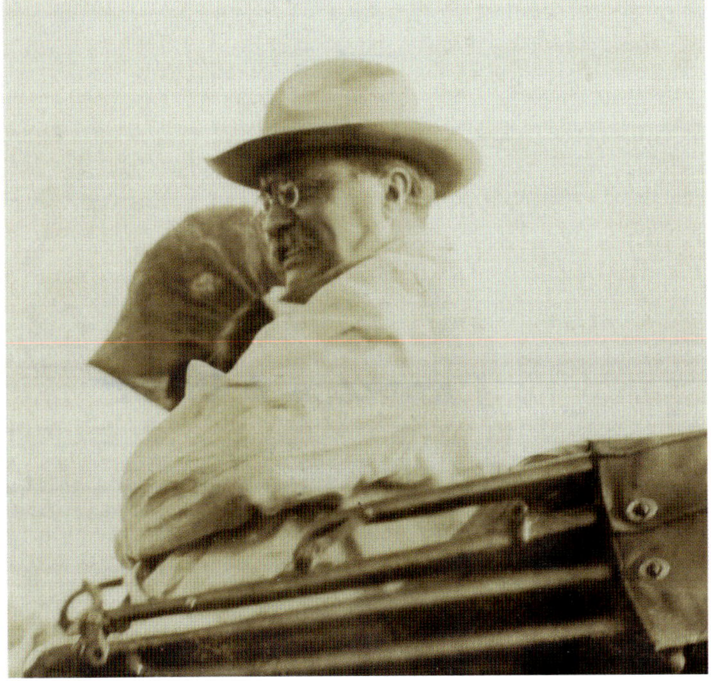

The polo matches invariably drew big crowds and many society names. In this instance, former president Theodore Roosevelt is seen watching a Meadow Brook match in 1911. Roosevelt was a member of the related Meadow Brook Hunt Club, which was headquartered adjacent to the polo field.

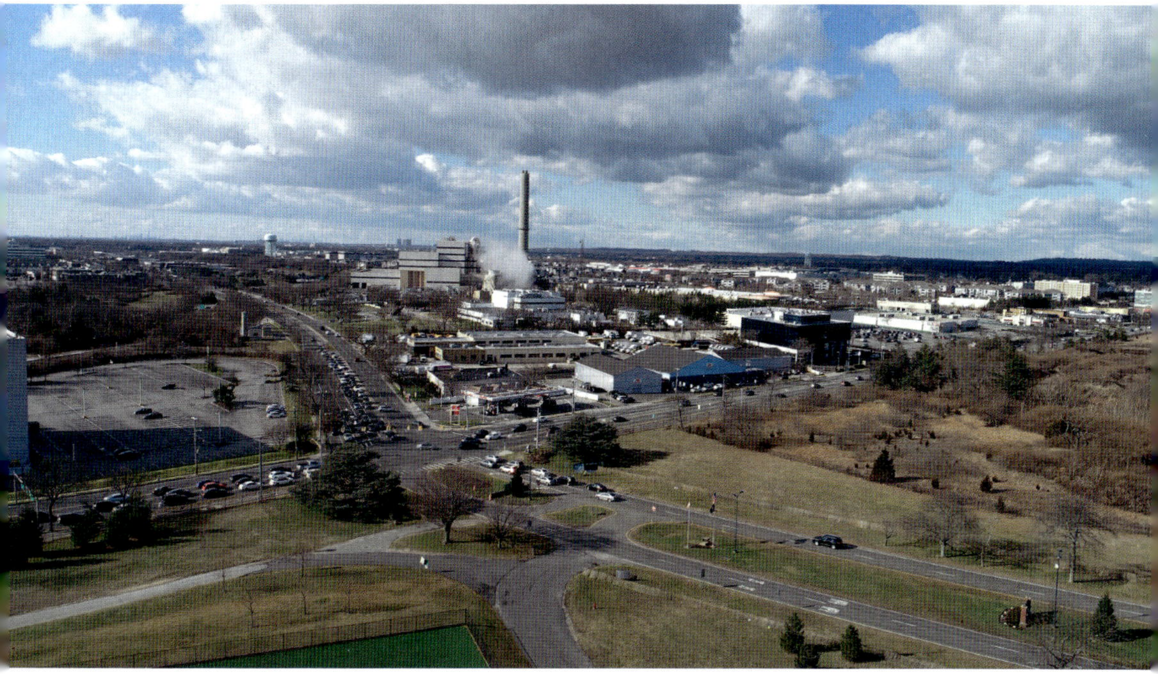

The area where the polo club was is wholly unrecognizable today. It is commercial, and fittingly includes a sports complex, albeit indoors.

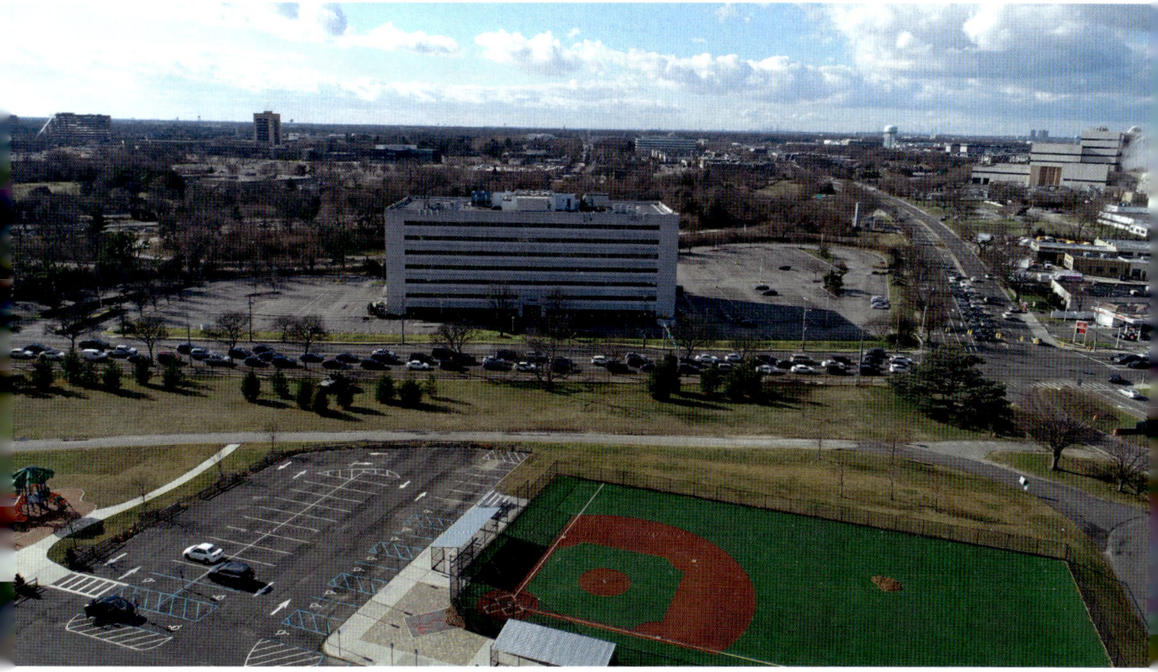

1600 Stewart Avenue stands where, during the late-nineteenth through mid-twentieth centuries, the famous Meadow Brook Club was located. As late as 1939, this hunting and sporting club owned all the land from Stewart Avenue south to Hempstead Turnpike, between Merrick Avenue to further west than where Merchants Concourse/Endo Boulevard is currently located.

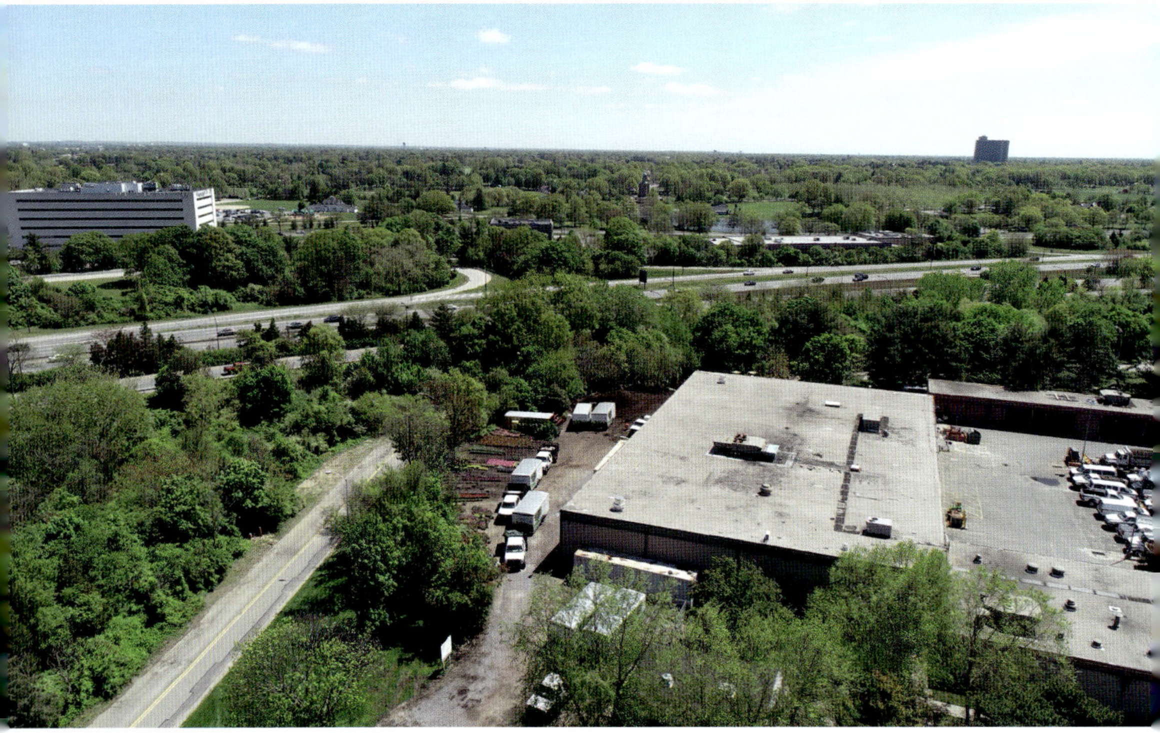

Looking east toward the Meadowbrook State Parkway and its ramps in spring and winter, which is where the Meadow Brook Club used to be located. The building in the background at left is MagnaCare, which fronts Merrick Avenue but whose address is 1600 Stewart Avenue.

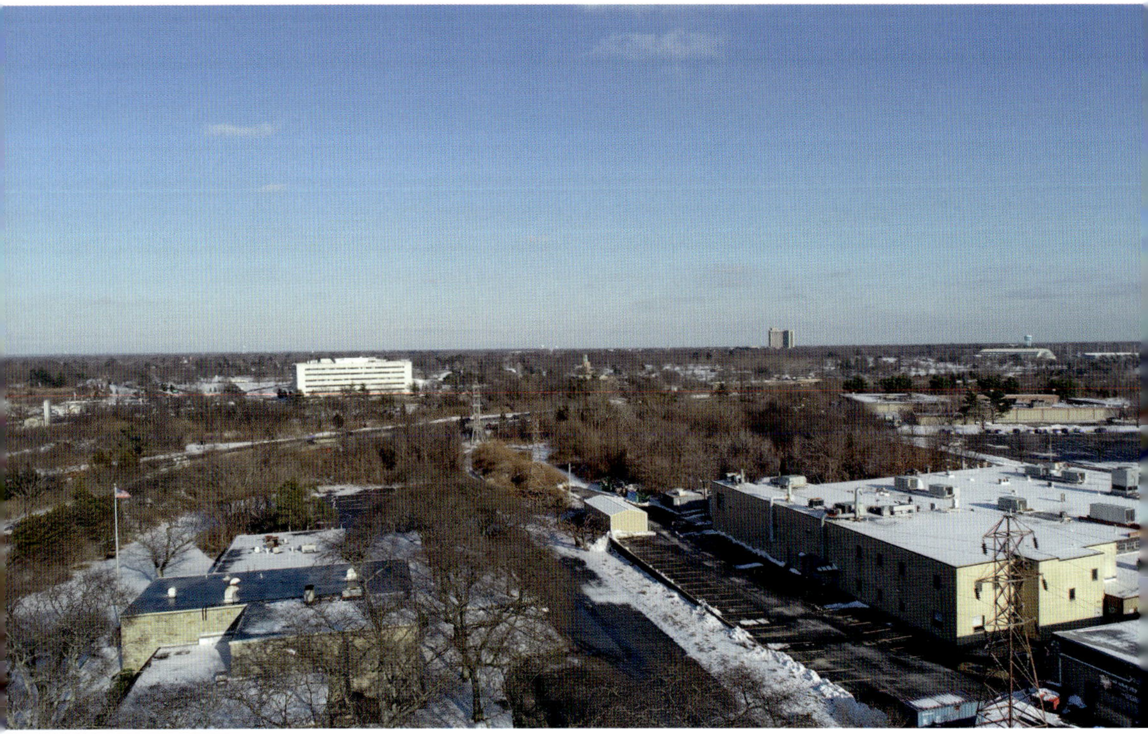

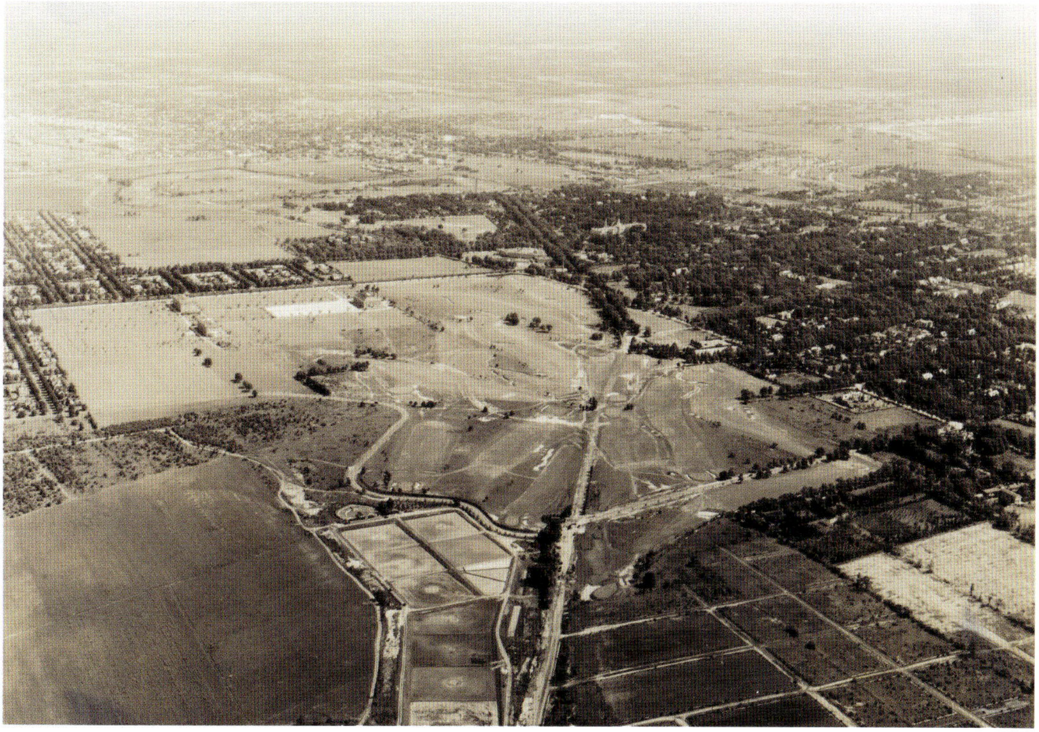

The Cherry Valley Country Club in Garden City as seen in 1936 from a height of 700 feet. The Hempstead Plains were ideal for golf courses, and there were a good many of them in the first half of the twentieth century.

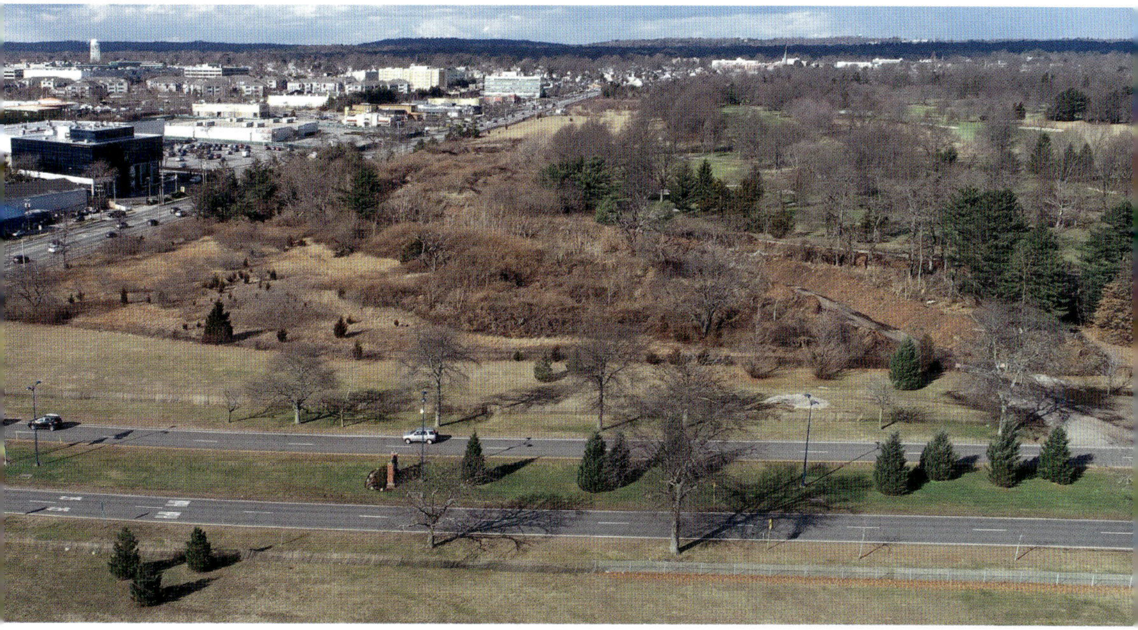

Eisenhower Park had its beginnings as the Salisbury Golf Club, *circa* 1916. It was originally owned by Joseph Lannin, who was also the owner of the Boston Red Sox. The park was created in 1944 after the land was obtained by Nassau County.

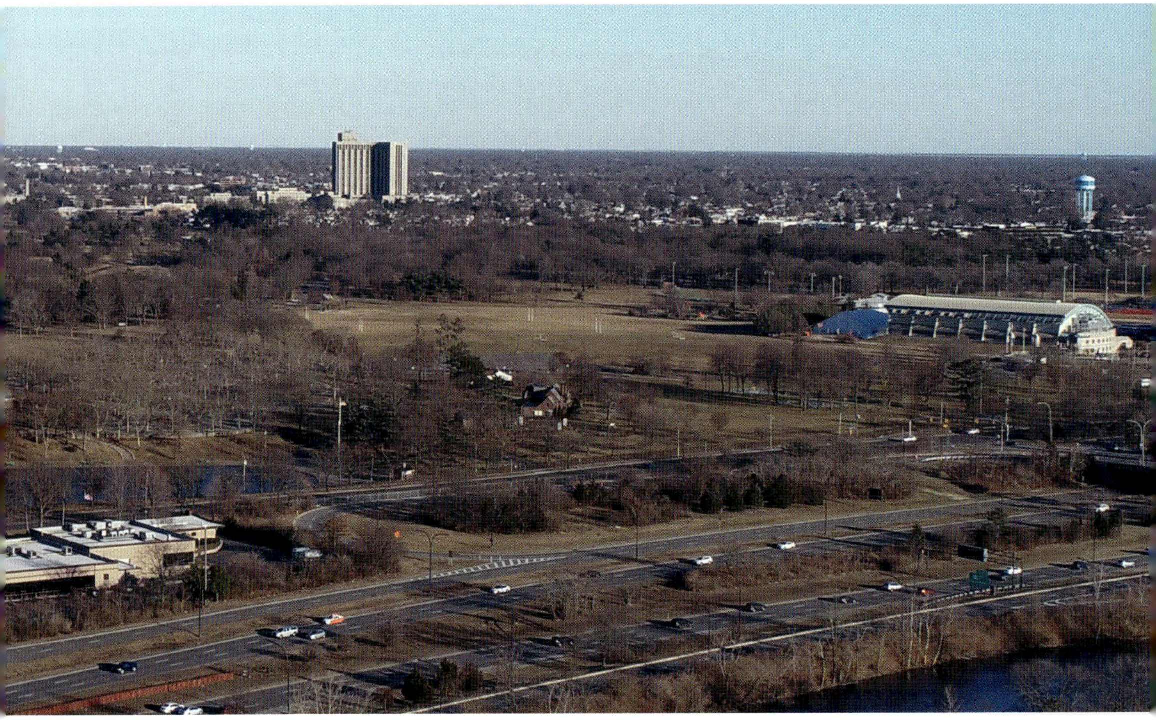

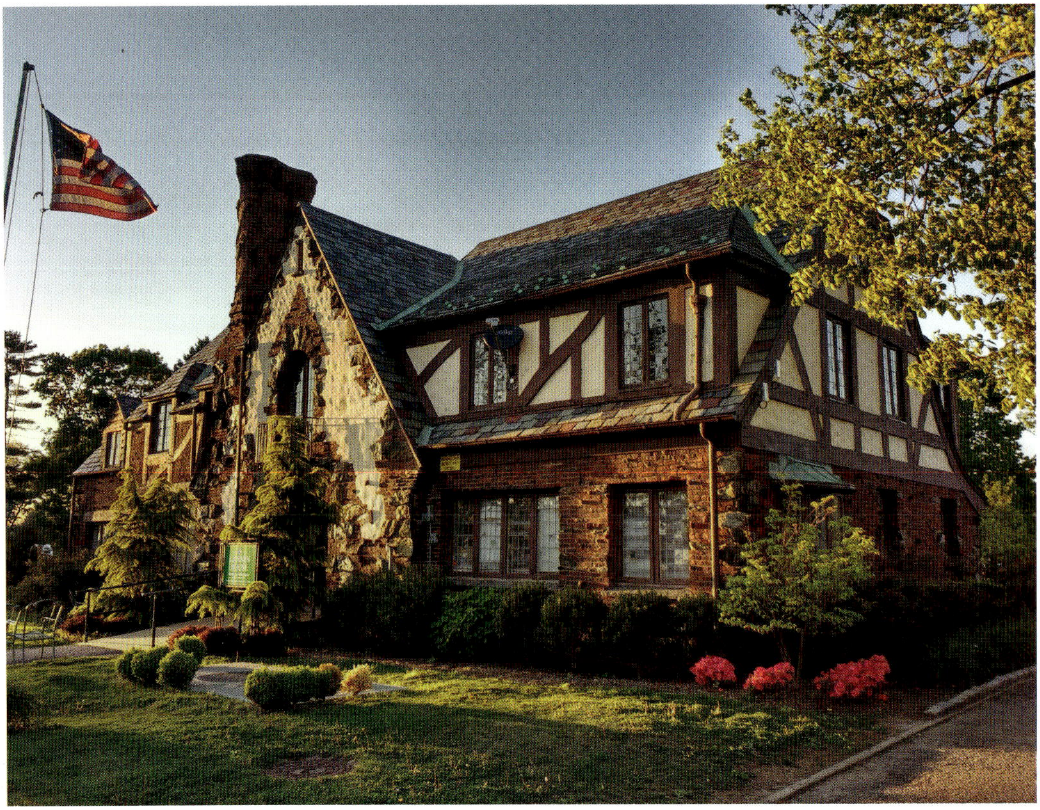

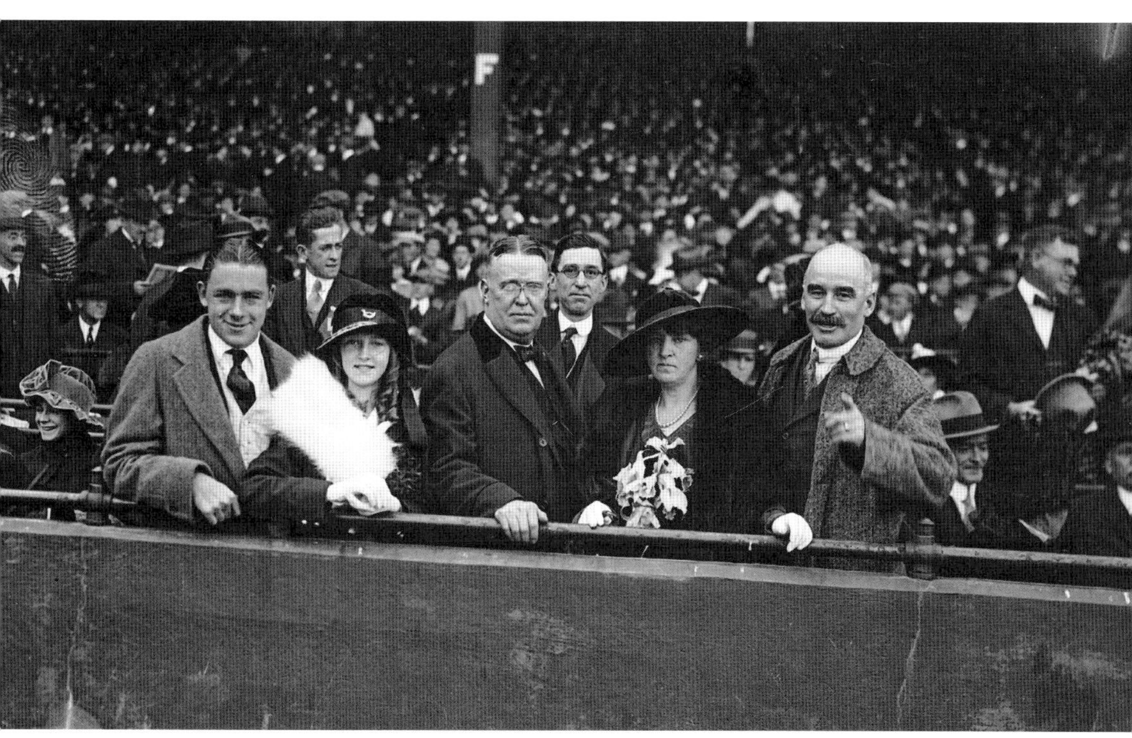

This image was taken at Fenway Park *circa* 1916. Dorothy Lannin is second from left and Joseph Lannin is at far right. Joseph Lannin also at one time owned the Roosevelt Flying Field.

Opposite page:

Above: At the center of this image is the Lannin House, which was built for Dorothy Lannin and her husband to replace an earlier and larger mansion that burned down while they were away on their honeymoon not long after the death of Dorothy's famous father.

Below: A ground-level view of the elaborately detailed Tudor-style Lannin House.

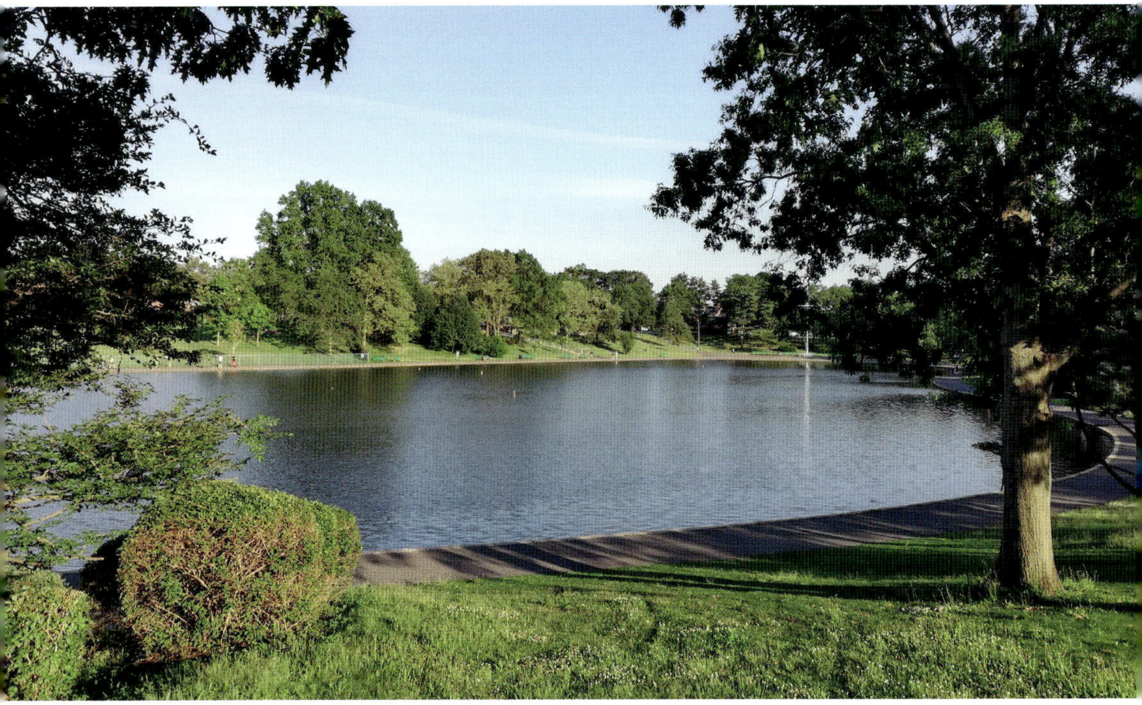

One of the most popular Eisenhower Park features is its lake, located on the western side of the park along Merrick Avenue. The lake originated as a smaller pond during the park's Salisbury Golf Club days between the 1910s and 1930s, and was enlarged and enhanced when the County took over the land. Also note the water body in the foreground; there was once a stream with several ponds along the way that ran north-south from just south of Stewart Avenue all the way to the Atlantic Ocean.

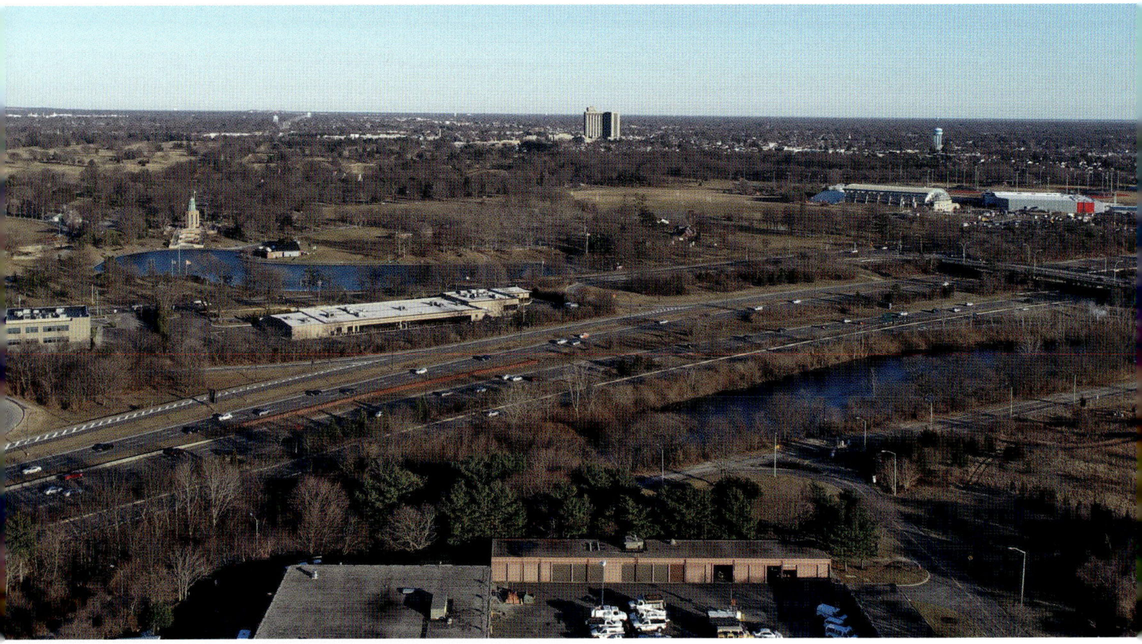

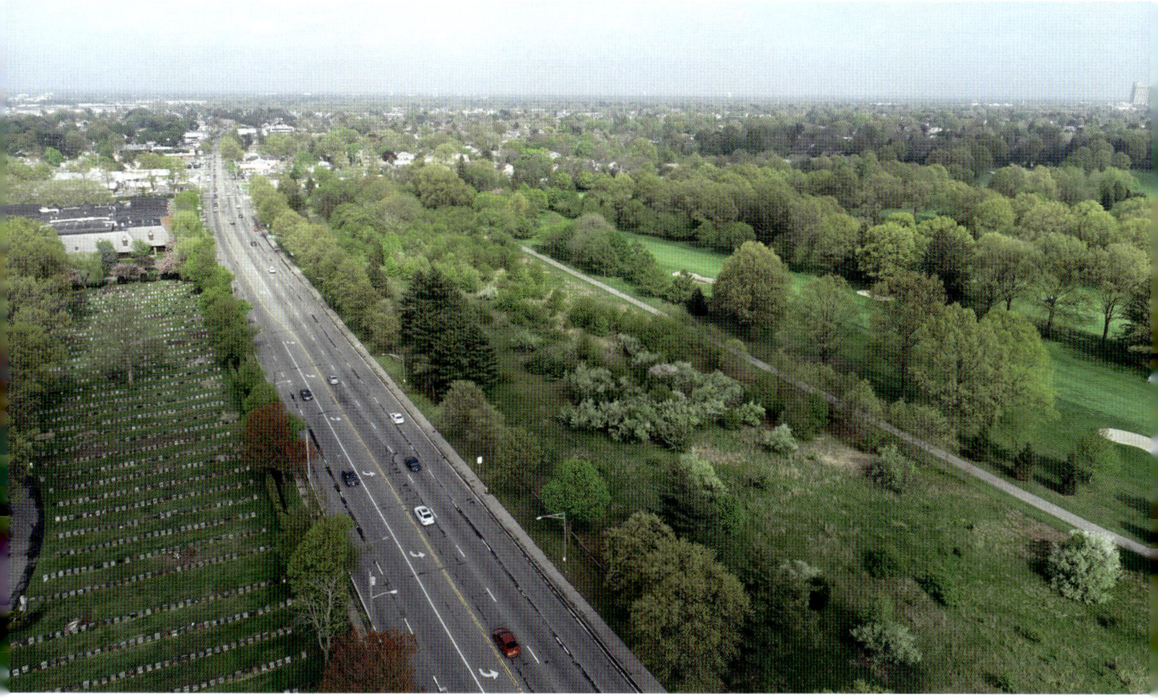

The Ladenburg Race Track (later the Meadowbrook Park Race Track), owned by Emily Ladenburg, was located east of what is now Eisenhower Park, among the trees toward the top right of the image. The site is now an East Meadow public school and its grounds.

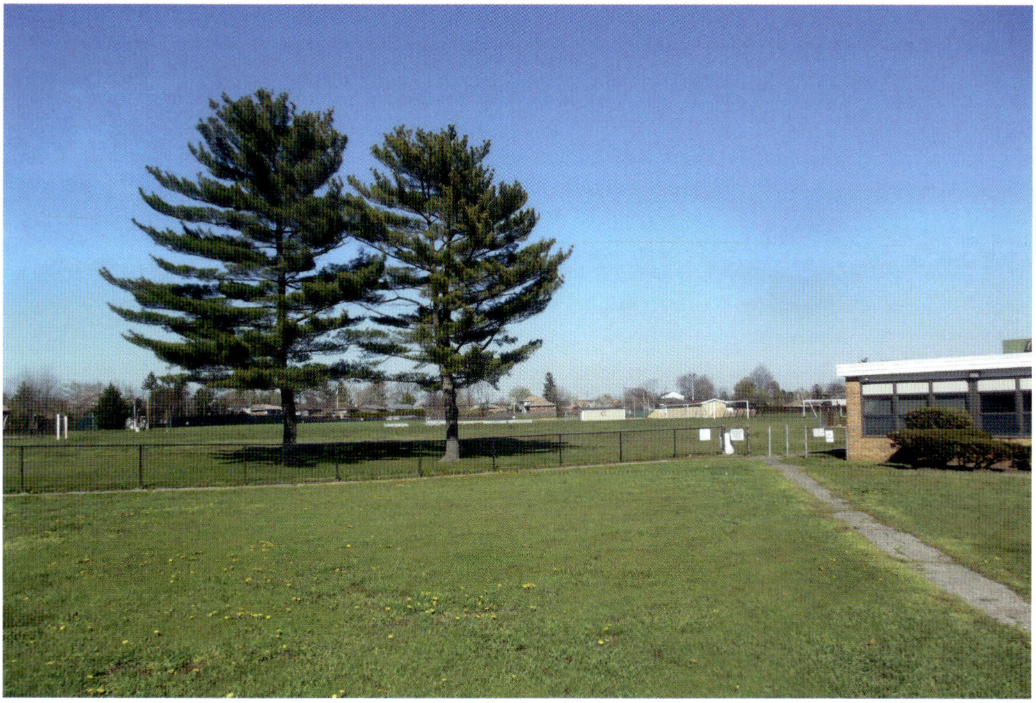

A ground-level view of the Ladenburg Park Track area today—still a park, but no more racing.

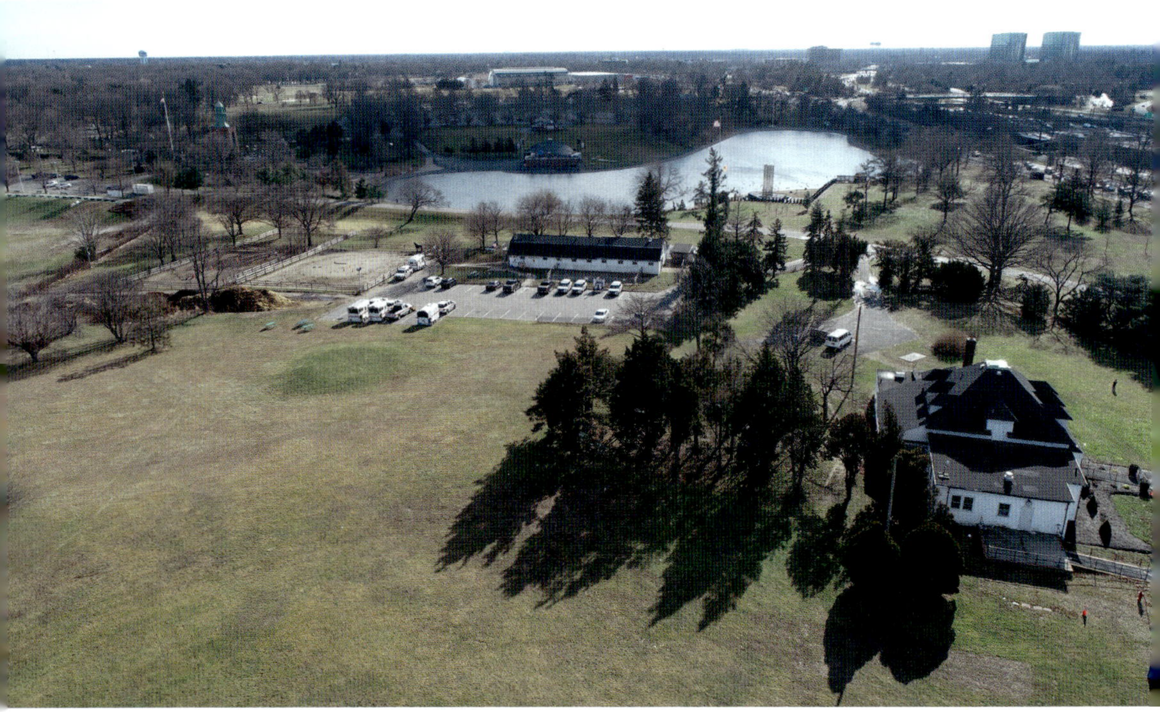

In Eisenhower Park, diagonally across the street from where polo horses used to run, the Nassau County Police Department has a large stable and an outdoor corral for their "fleet" of police horses.

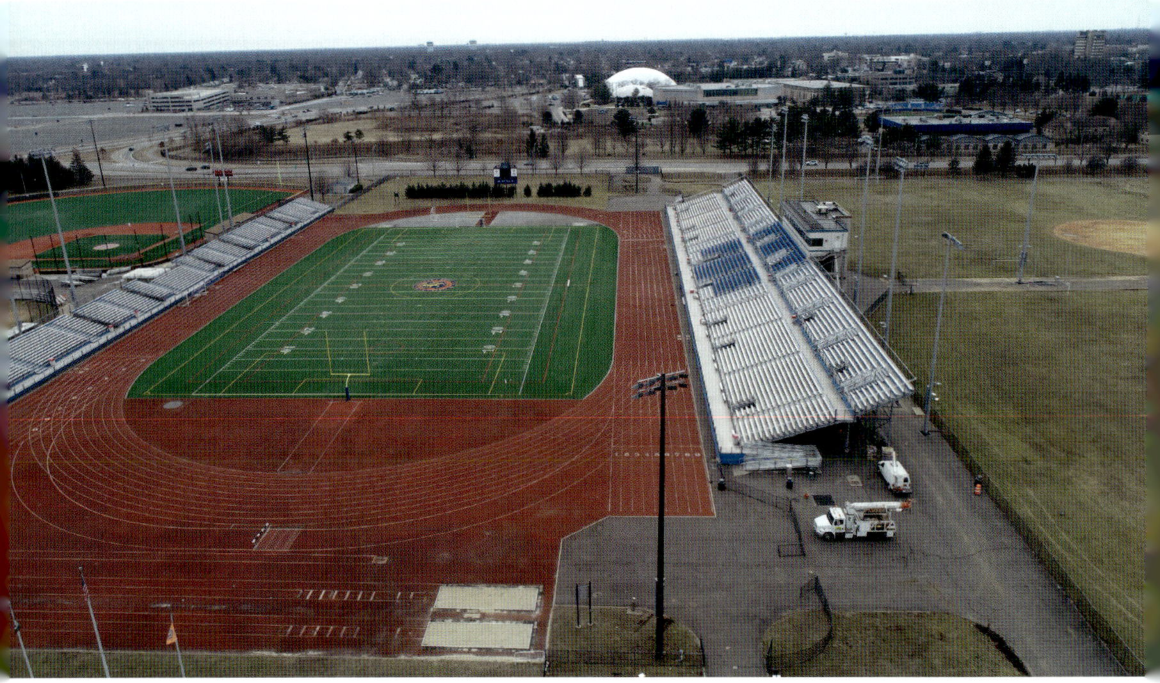

Above and opposite page: Sports and recreation are still a part of the Hempstead Plains' story today—the Mitchel Athletic Complex includes a football stadium and several baseball fields.

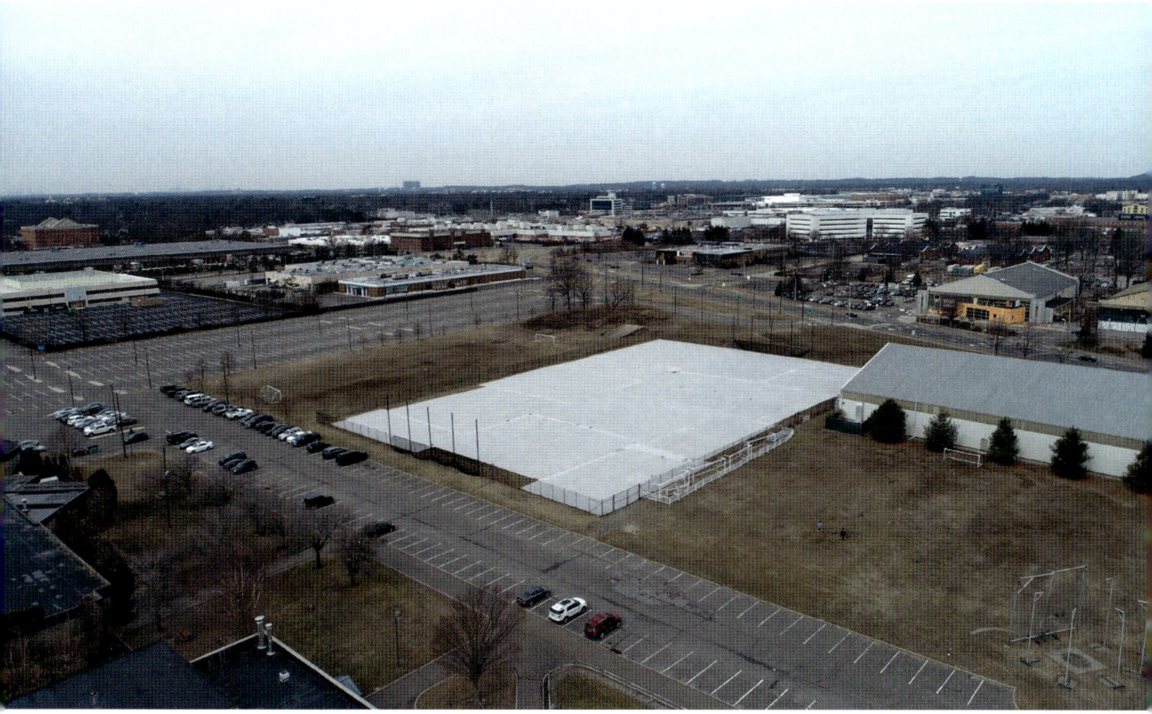

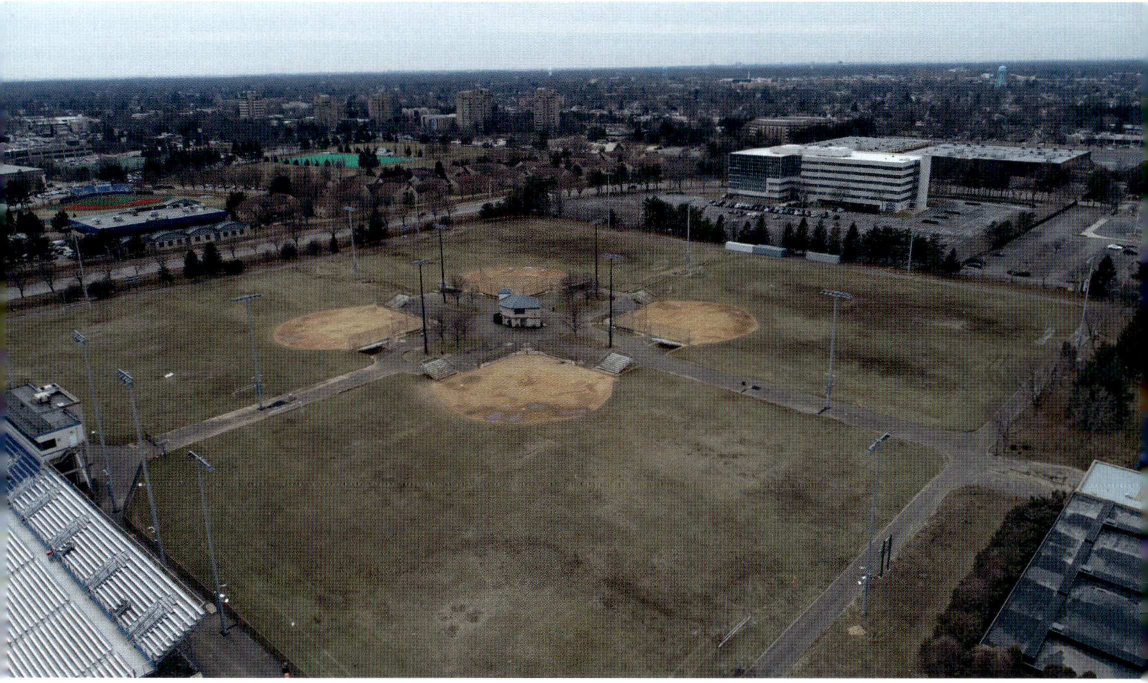

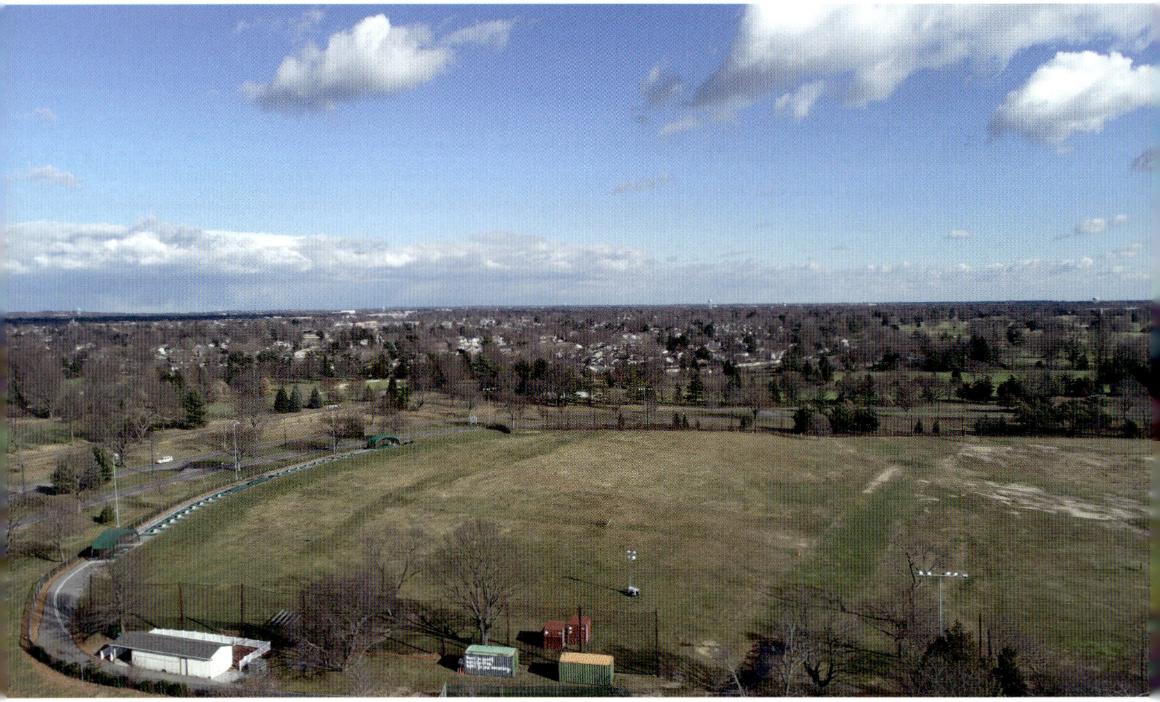

The driving range at Eisenhower Park is a popular year-round destination for serious and amateur golfers alike. Stewart Avenue used to cut through what is now the driving range before it was discontinued at the park entrance.

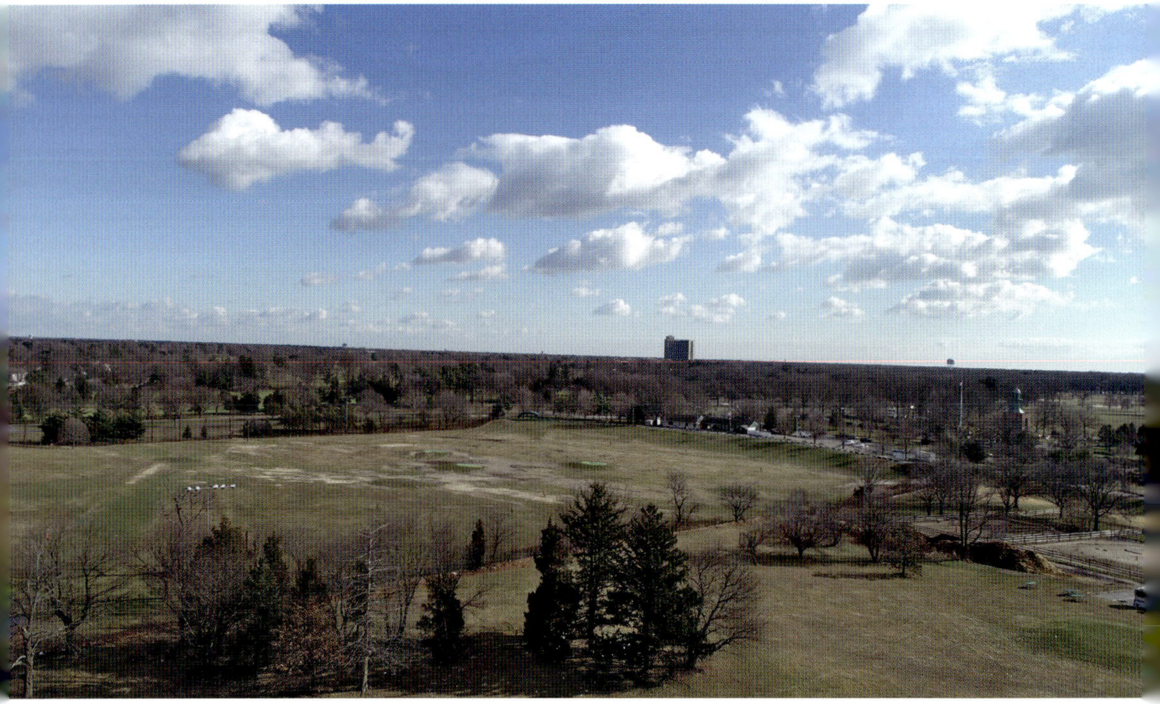

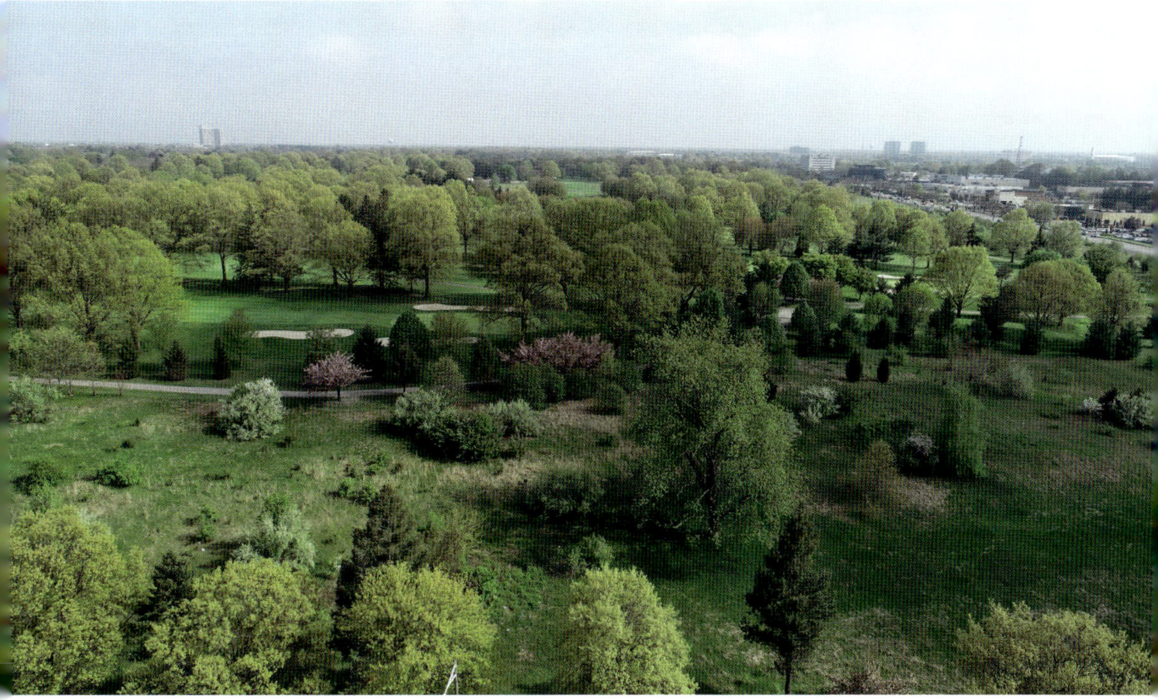

The Salisbury Club's courses were redesigned and incorporated into the new Salisbury Park (later Eisenhower Park). The northern reaches of Eisenhower Park are occupied by the very challenging Red Course, a golfer's delight. Remnants of the Hempstead Plains can be seen just south of Old Country Road, and north of the course itself. Because its golf courses are part of the park, Eisenhower Park is a total of 930 acres, 90 acres larger than Manhattan's Central Park.

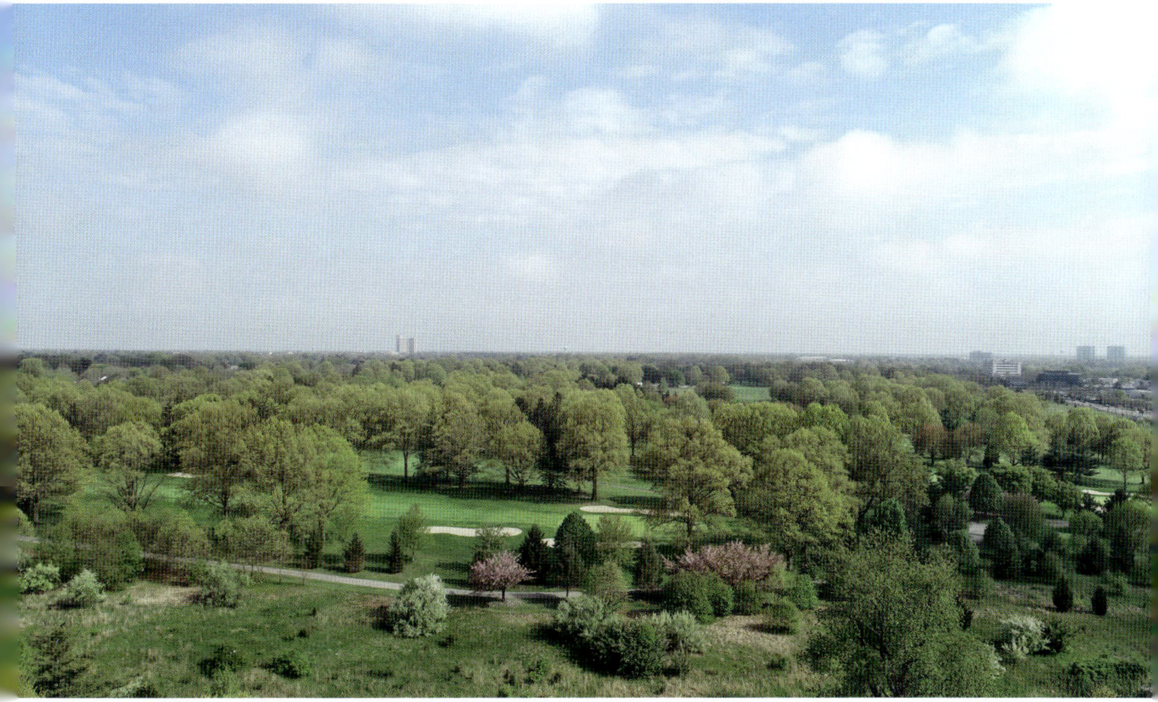

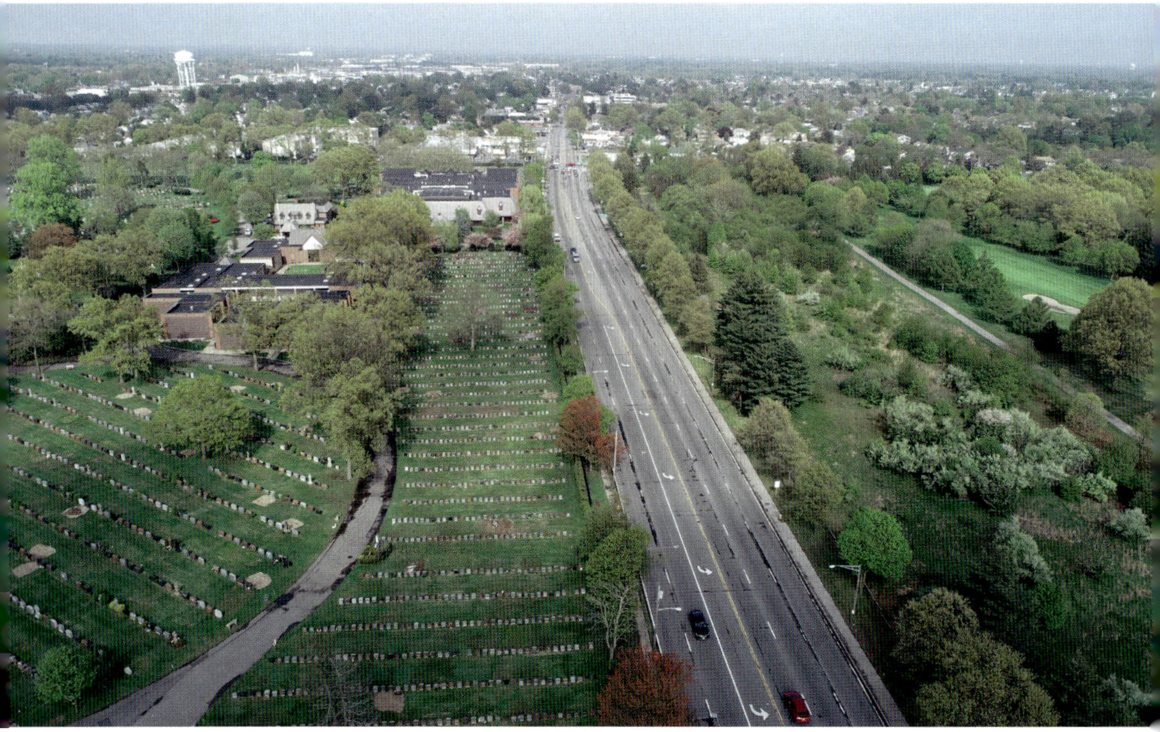

Old Country Road comprised more than a third of the 1909 and 1910 Vanderbilt Cup Race Course, between Garden City and Hicksville. The road back then was not nearly as wide as it is today. At top, looking east along Old Country from just east of Post Avenue in Westbury, and at bottom looking west.

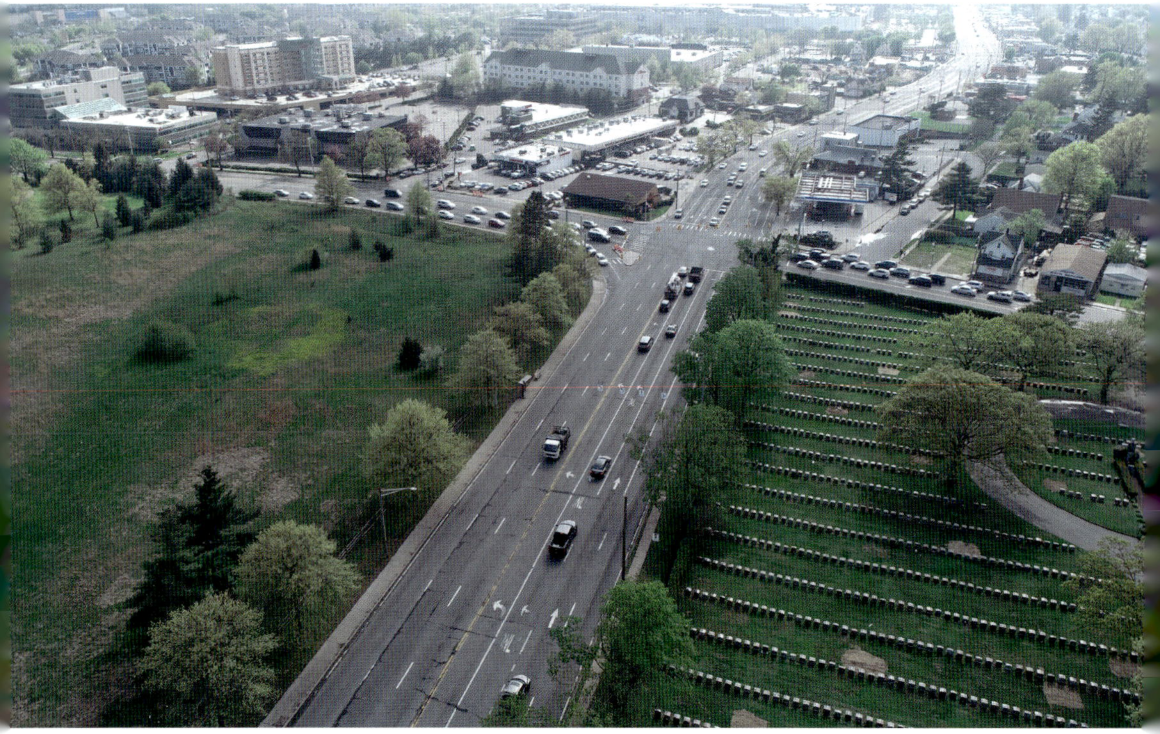

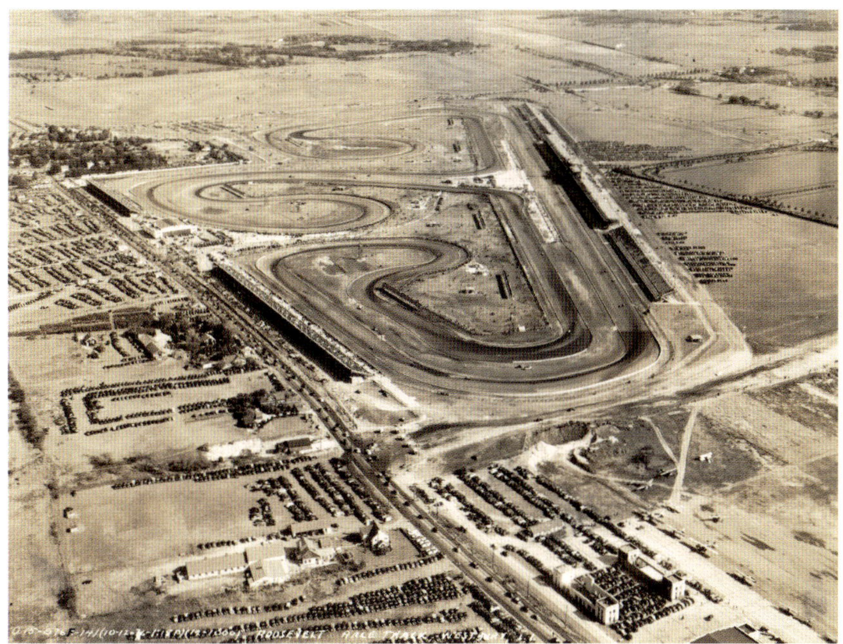

This 1936 aerial shows the newly completed Roosevelt Raceway in the foreground. The photograph was taken on the day of the Vanderbilt Cup Race, and cars can be seen on the track.

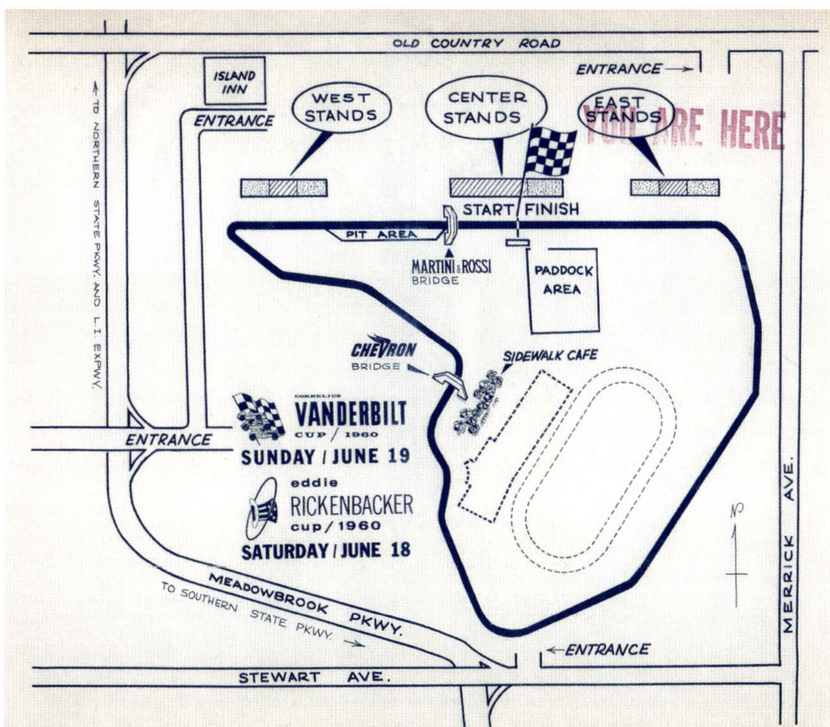

A map of the racecourse and surrounding area from the program of the 1960 Vanderbilt Cup Race, a direct descendant of the Vanderbilt Cup Races held by William K. Vanderbilt in the early years of the twentieth century on local roads in Westbury and adjacent villages.

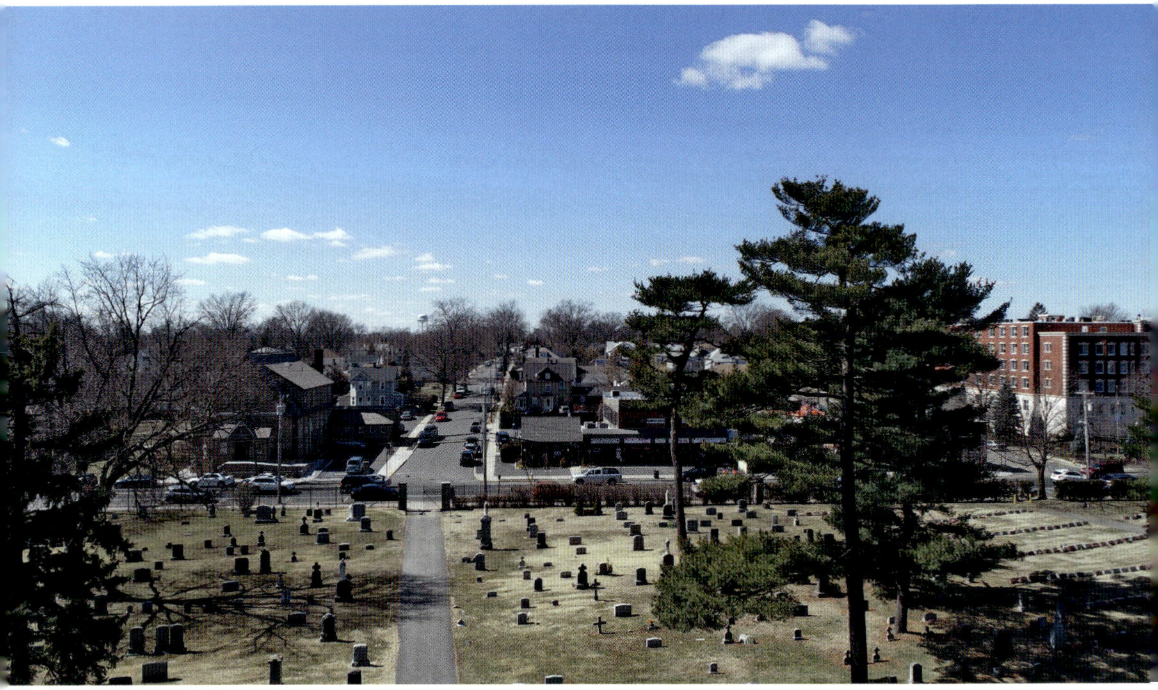

The famous race car driver Henri Fournier was on his way back from a visit to the Meadow Brook Club in 1901, and had just passed the St. Brigid Church and cemetery heading north when his car was hit by an oncoming train at what was then the Post Avenue at-grade crossing. It was the first car-train crash in the United States.

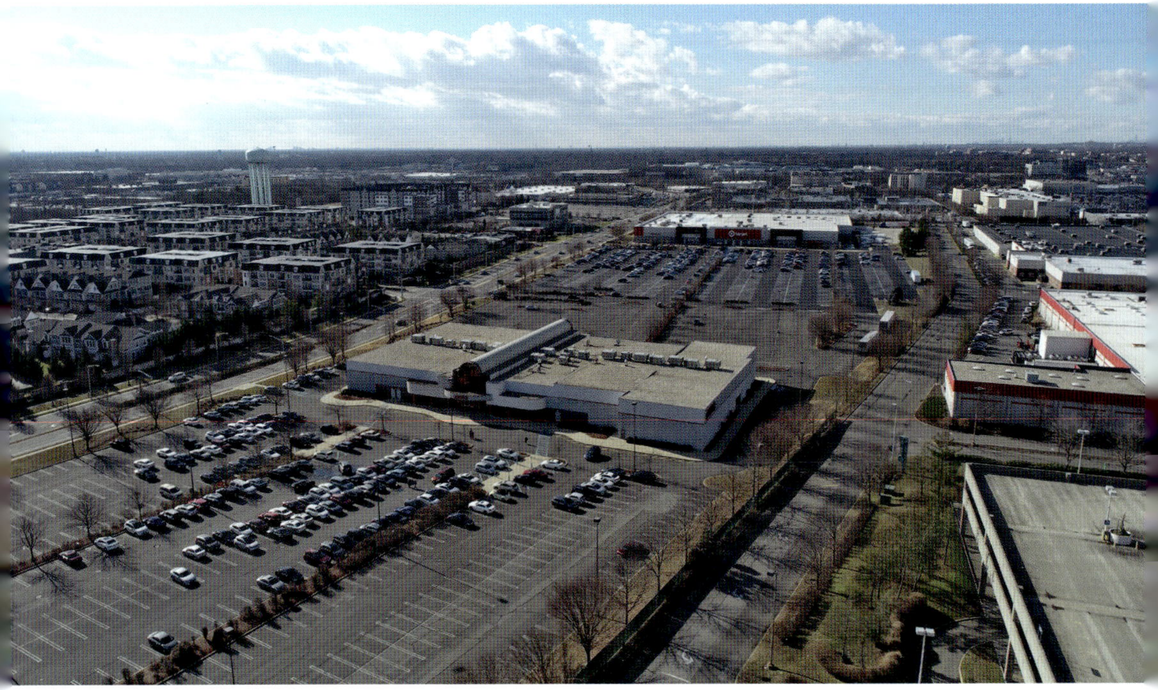

Roosevelt Raceway enjoyed decades of prosperity before it closed in 1988. The area, seen in this view, was eventually developed into retail and housing.

3

THE CRADLE OF AVIATION

Aviation may have been born in North Carolina with the Wright Brothers' first flight in 1903, but it grew up on the Hempstead Plains a few years later, thanks largely to an upstate New York motorcycle manufacturer named Glenn H. Curtiss (1878-1930). A flight in a dirigible in 1904 peaked Curtiss' interest in flying. By 1909, Curtiss was building his own planes and had won trophies for flight records, including a prize for achieving an average of 47 miles per hour over more than 10 miles. He also flew 142 miles from Albany to New York, and really made a name for himself. When Curtiss moved his aviation operations from upstate, he chose the Hempstead Plains as the perfect locale for his base of operations. He made the first Long Island flight from Mineola in 1909, a 25-mile trip that stunned the locals. Before long, there were several flying fields on the Plains, east of Mineola, including the Hempstead Plains Airfield *circa* 1911 (which would eventually become Roosevelt Field). A 1910 air meet at Belmont Park was a momentous occasion that brought together many of the best flyers of the time, and fired the Long Islanders' imaginations. During the 1910s, it became a common sight for residents of Mineola, Westbury, and Hempstead to spot an airplane in the sky. Aviation left its cradle for good in May 1927, when Charles Lindbergh successfully took off from Roosevelt Field, heading for France on the first transatlantic nonstop flight, beating out several others also vying for the honor, including the explorer (and later admiral) Richard Byrd. Both Curtiss and Lindbergh are memorialized in roads with their names in East Garden City and Uniondale, as is Earl Ovington, a pioneer who piloted the country's first airmail flight in 1911, carrying a sack of mail from Garden City to Mineola.

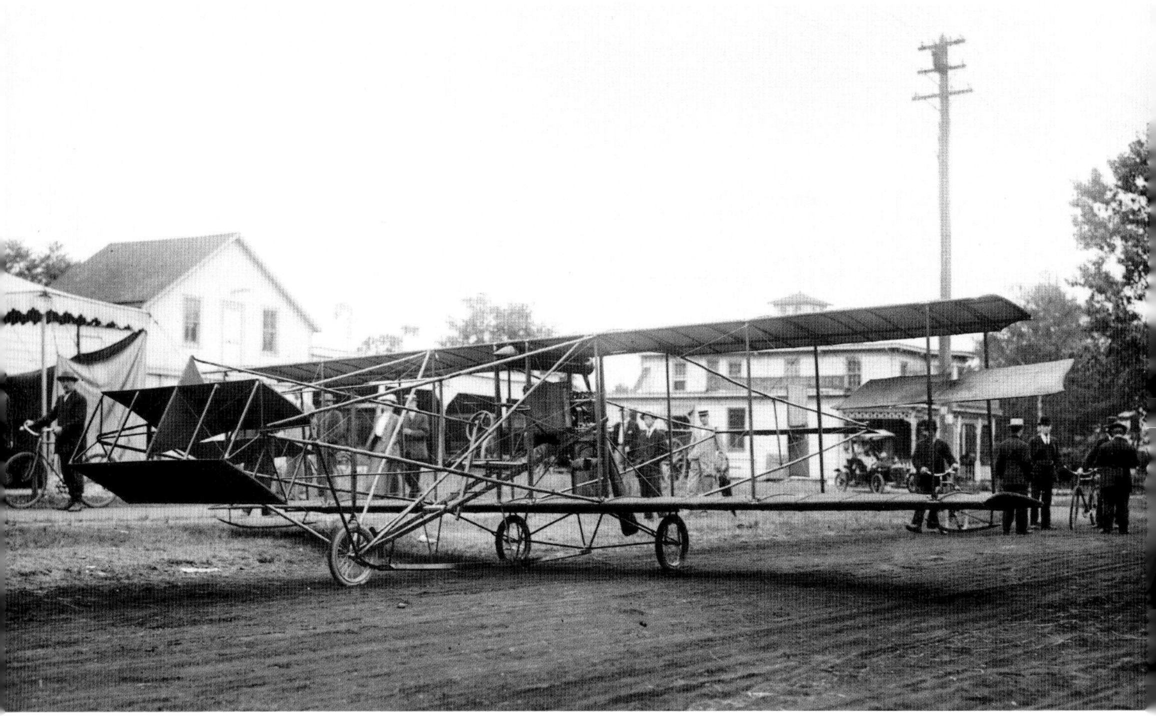

Aviation grew up on the Hempstead Plains. This image shows a Herring-Curtiss flying machine at Mineola *circa* 1909. Mineola was the site of the first flying field on the Hempstead Plains. Note the proximity to homes and businesses.

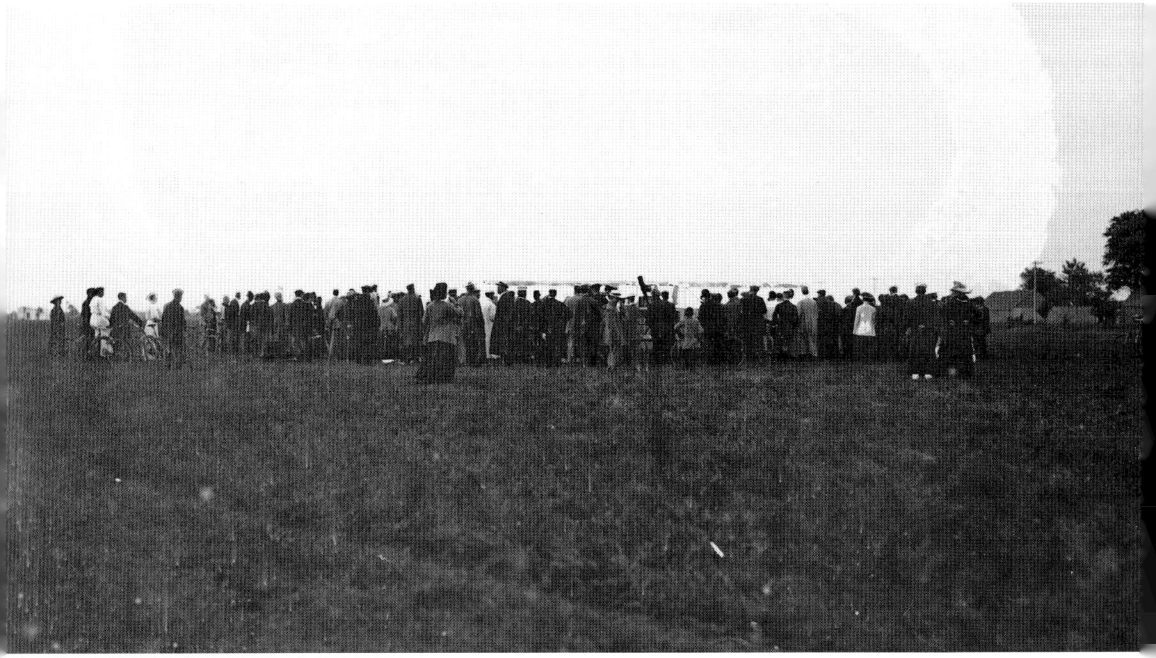

A crowd of spectators gathers around Glenn Curtiss and his flying machine in Mineola *circa* 1909.

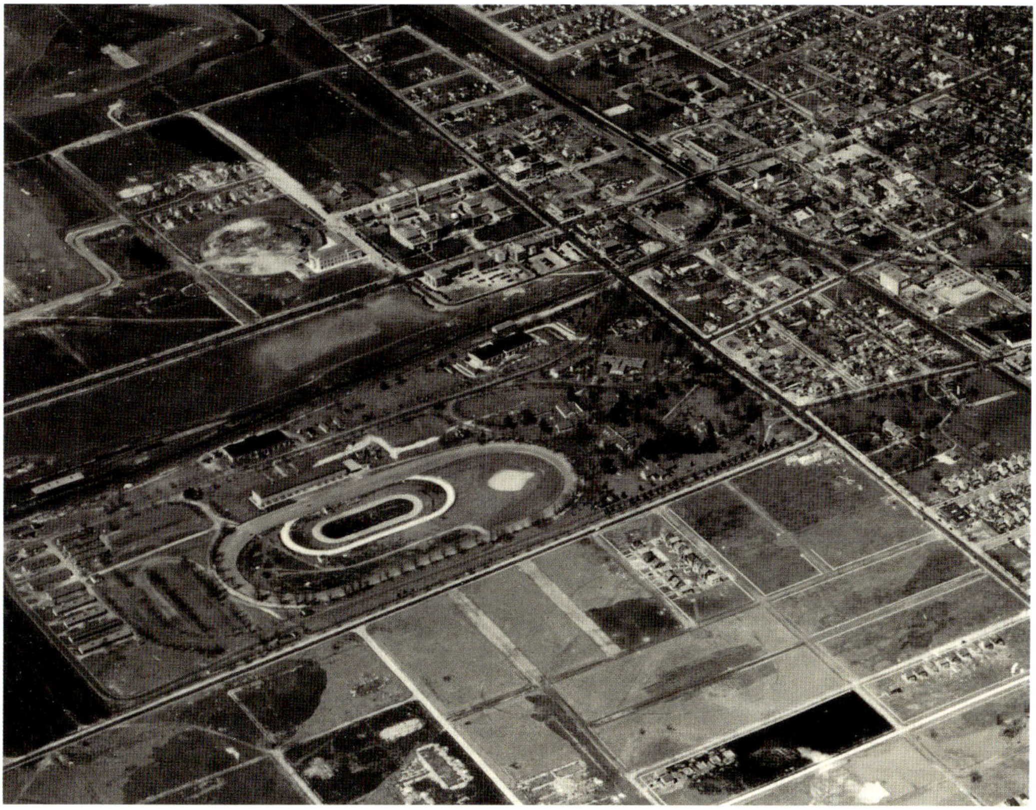

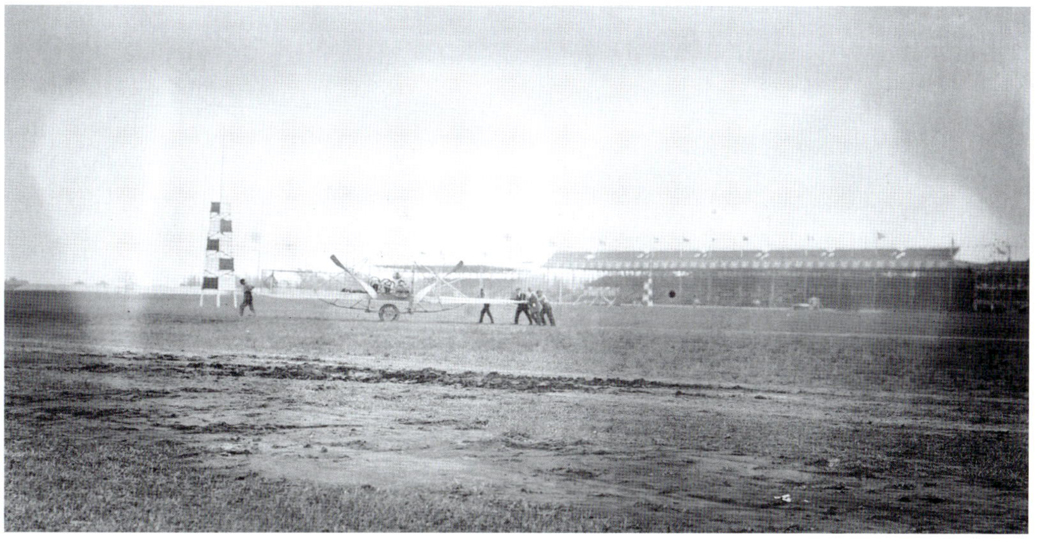

The first flight on Long Island (not counting an earlier flight that took place in Brooklyn in 1908) took place near where the County courthouses are now located, seen in this aerial view from 1931 (elevation 5,000 feet) when the Nassau County Agricultural Fair was located at that spot; that flying field was long gone by this time, but others flourished further east until the 1950s.

In 1910, an aviation meet was held at Belmont Park, attracting many of the day's premier aviators, including the Wright Brothers.

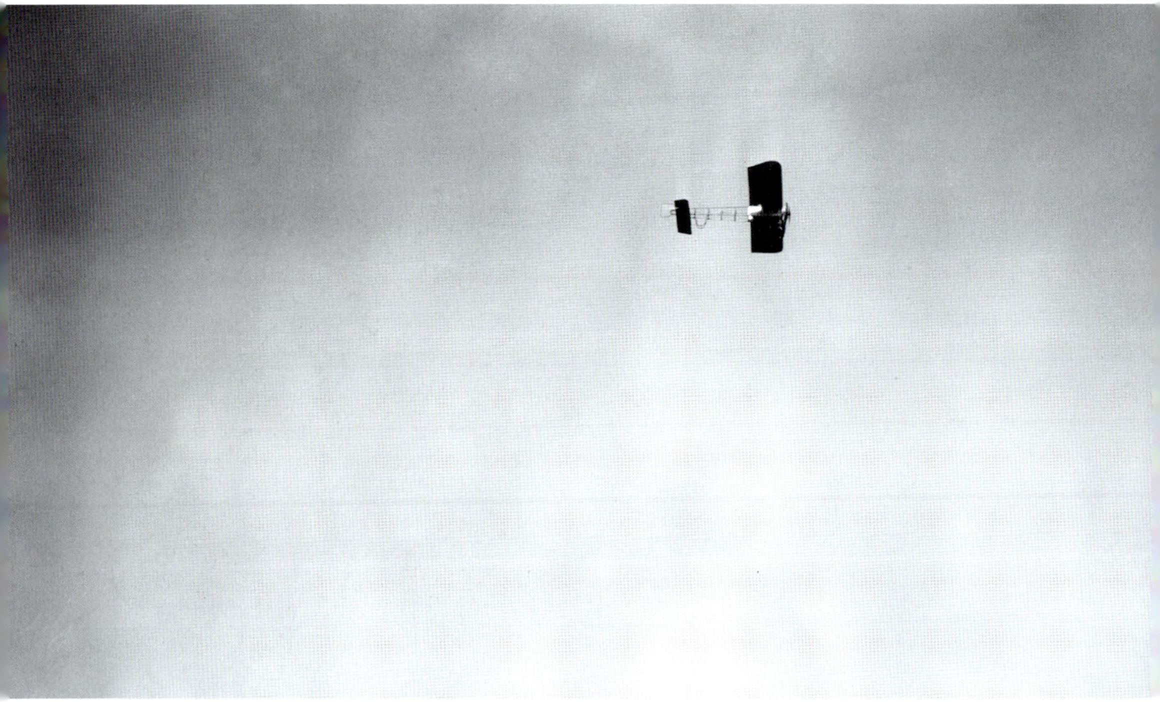

Clyde Murvin Wood flying his plane over the international polo tournament at Meadow Brook in June 1913.
It was a quick flight from the nearest flying fields to the north and west to get to Meadow Brook.

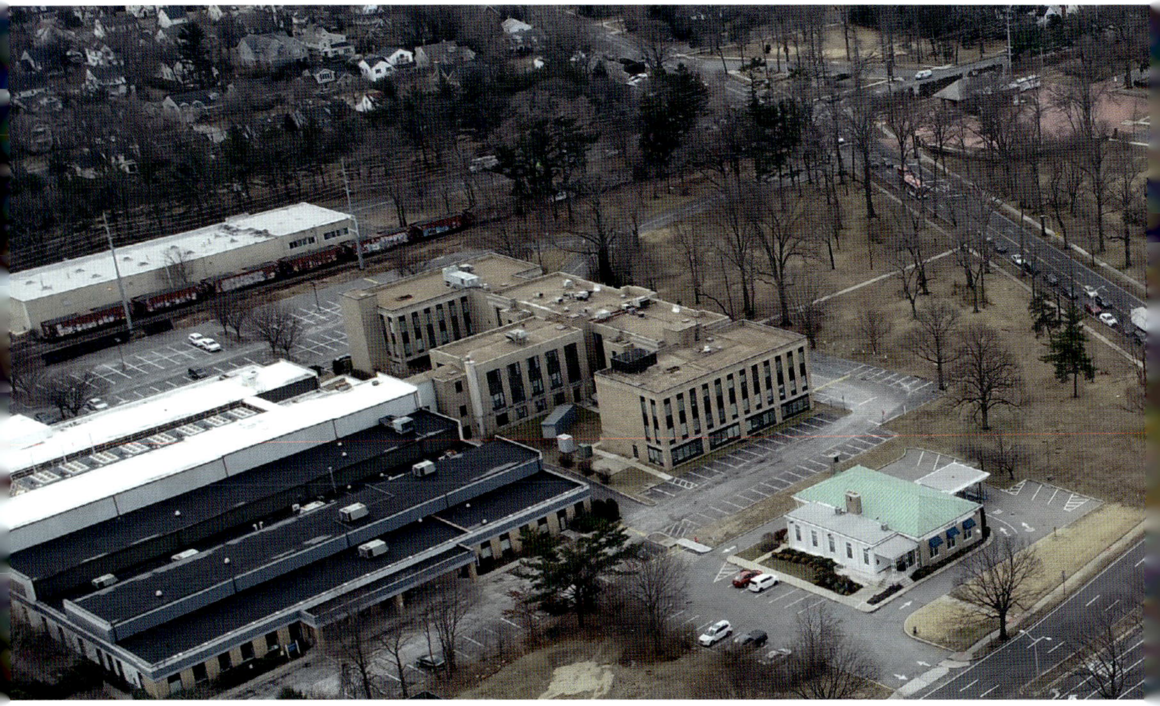

In December 1917, the Garden City Company sold the Curtiss Engineering Company 20 acres at the corner of Clinton
and Stewart Avenues. On this plot of land, Glenn Curtiss had an airplane research and manufacturing facility built.

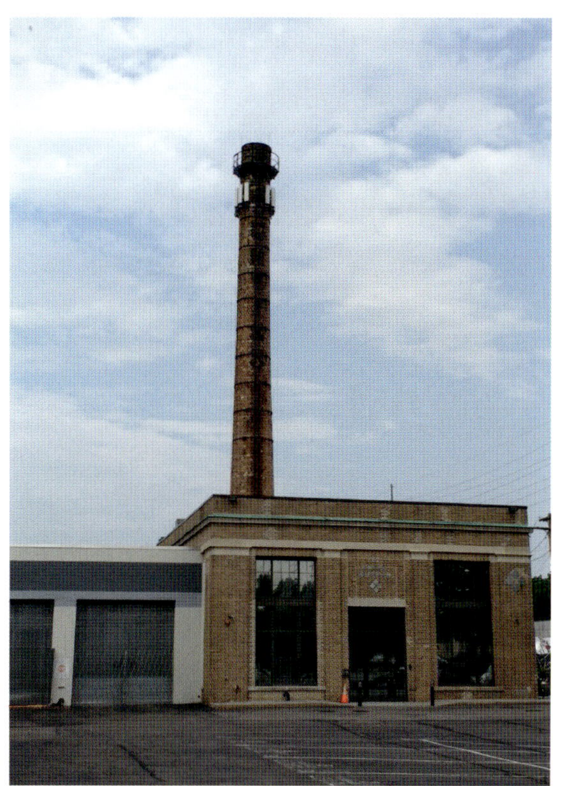

The original main Curtiss building still stands today, as does the old smokestack behind the building. As of 2019, the building housed a Nassau BOCES operation.

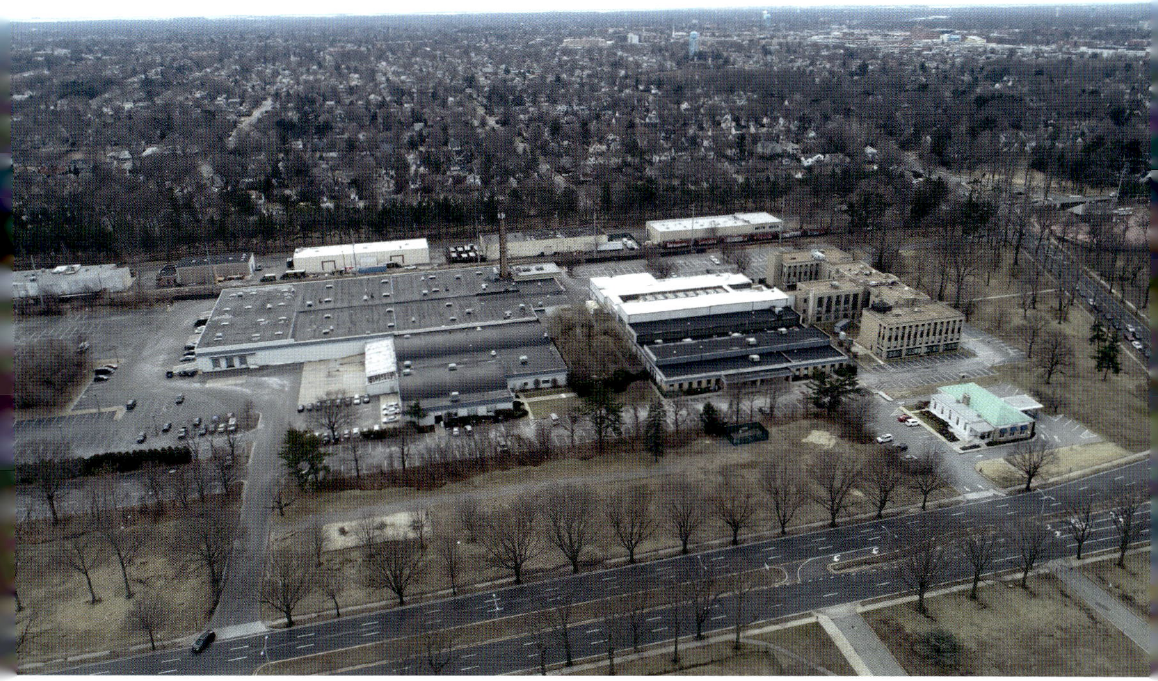

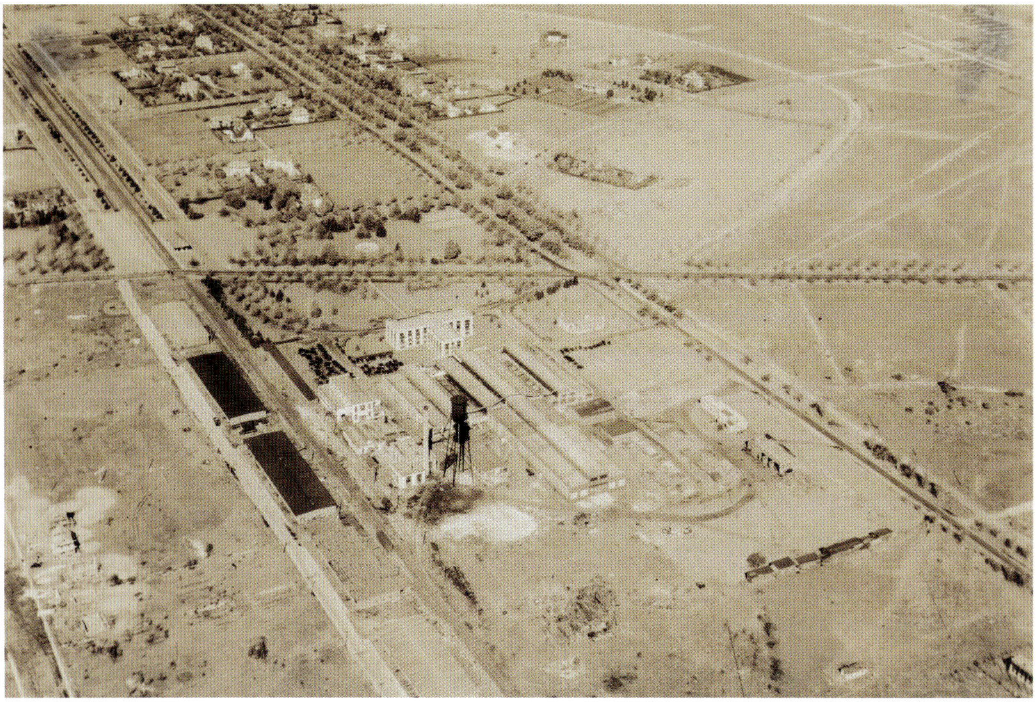

This 1928 aerial view taken from 800 feet up shows the Curtiss factory complex. The Curtiss Flying Field, used to test its planes, was to the northeast of the factory.

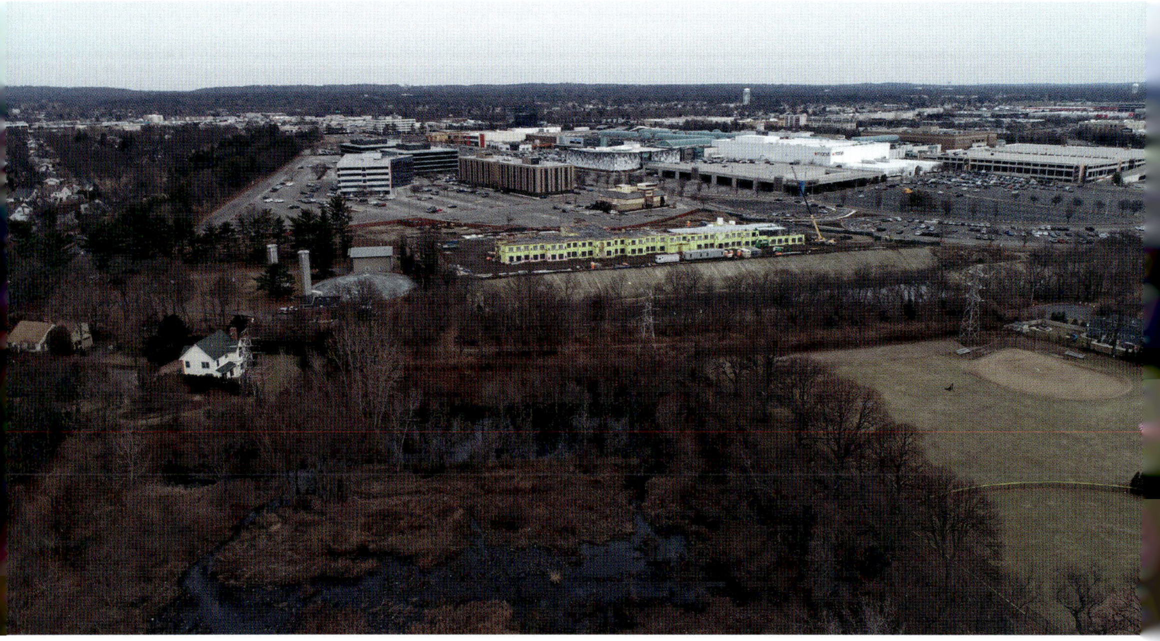

The Curtiss Flying Field became part of Roosevelt Field, which eventually spanned from Clinton Road all the way east to Post Avenue, from Old Country Road south to the Long Island Motor Parkway, with notches cut out of the southern limits for the Old Westbury Country Club and the Meadow Brook polo field.

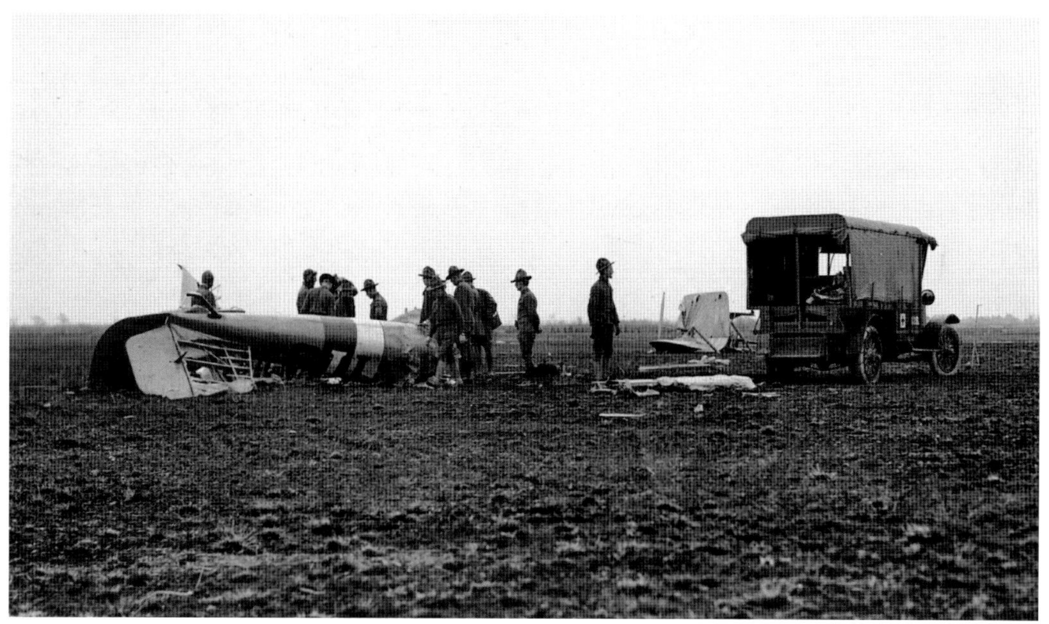

When two student aviators—at the government airfield that was soon to become Hazelhurst Field—took a plane into the air without permission, it ended in tragedy. On May 5, 1917, Ransom Merritt, twenty-three years old, and Anthony Spileno, twenty-five years old, decided to take a joyride in a $12,000 L. W. F. biplane they were wheeling to a gasoline tank. Merritt, at the wheel, lost control, but amazingly, it remained in the air for thirty-five minutes before it crashed to the ground, killing both men. Astonishingly, neither man had ever flown a plane before.

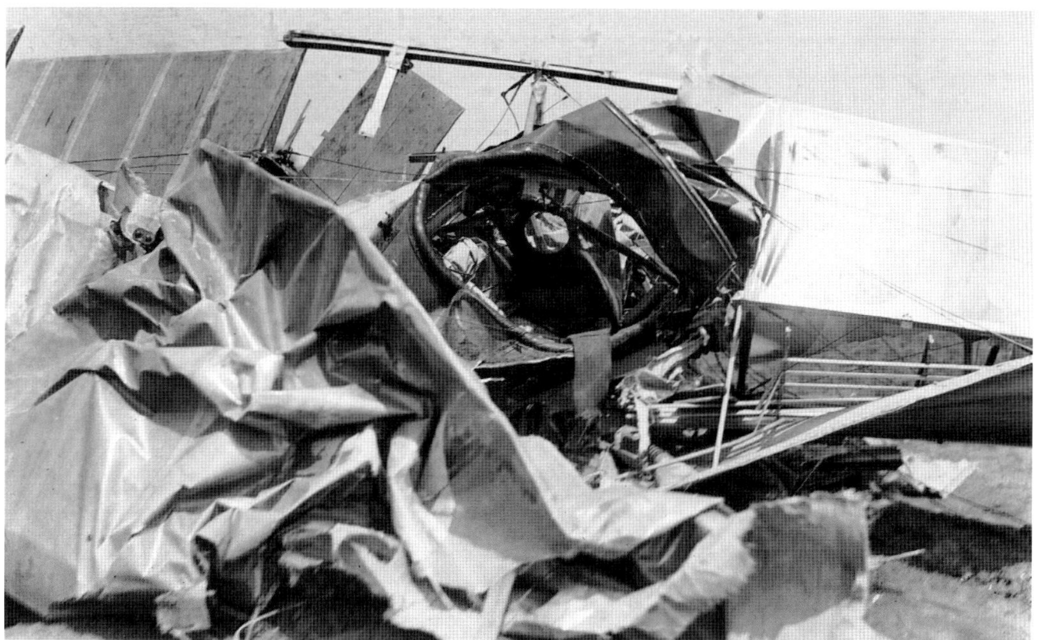

This image shows the mangled pilot seat of the Merritt/Spileno wreck at the future Hazelhurst Field. Rumors that Merritt had taken the plane aloft in an attempt to commit suicide were not proven. According to Captain J. W. Butts, who was in command at the airfield, Merritt had flown as a passenger and was eager to become a pilot and go to France to fight in the war effort.

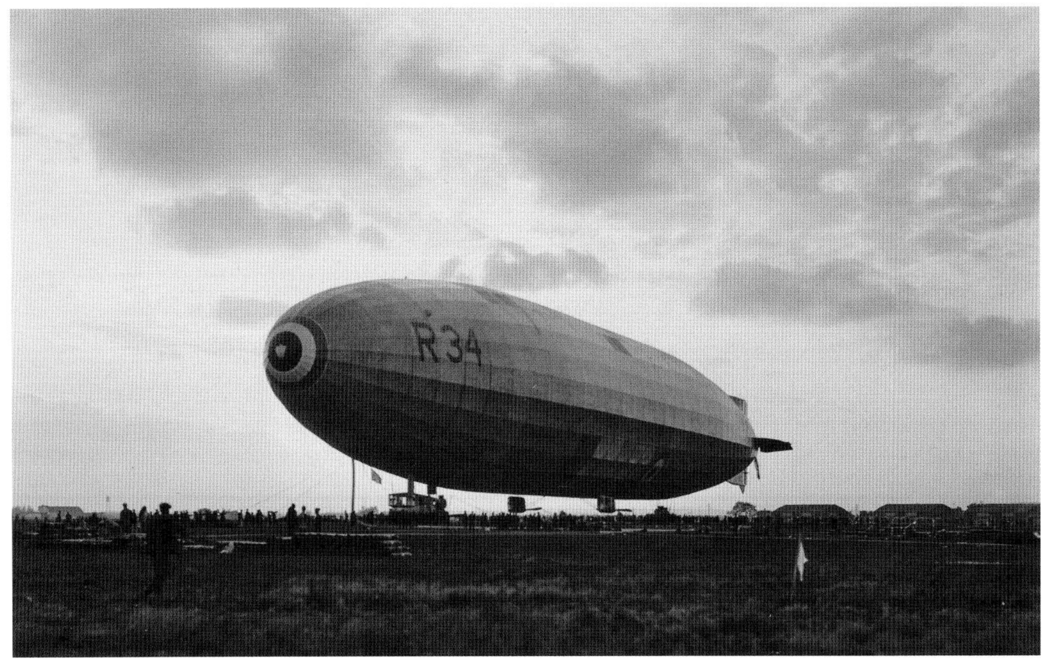

The British dirigible R-34, which arrived at Roosevelt Field on July 6, 1919, to much fanfare after a successful transatlantic flight.

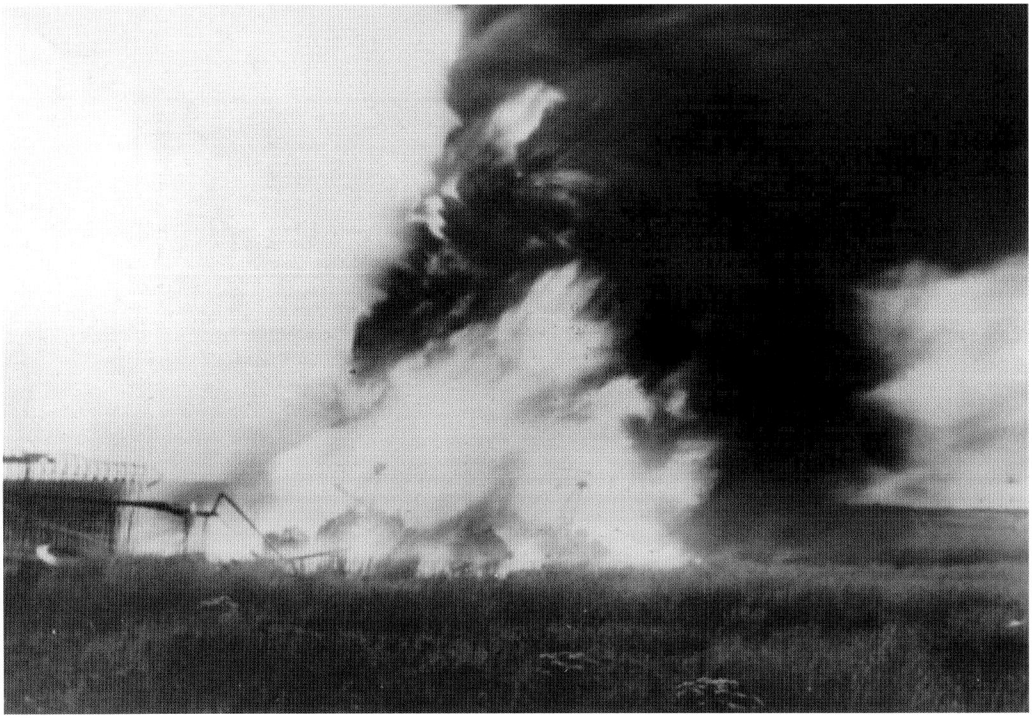

Captain Rene Fonck's Sikorsky airplane in flames after it crashed at Roosevelt Field on September 21, 1926, during Fonck's attempt to become the first to fly across the Atlantic, months before Lindbergh actually accomplished it. The radio operator and mechanic were killed in the crash, but Fonck and his alternate pilot escaped.

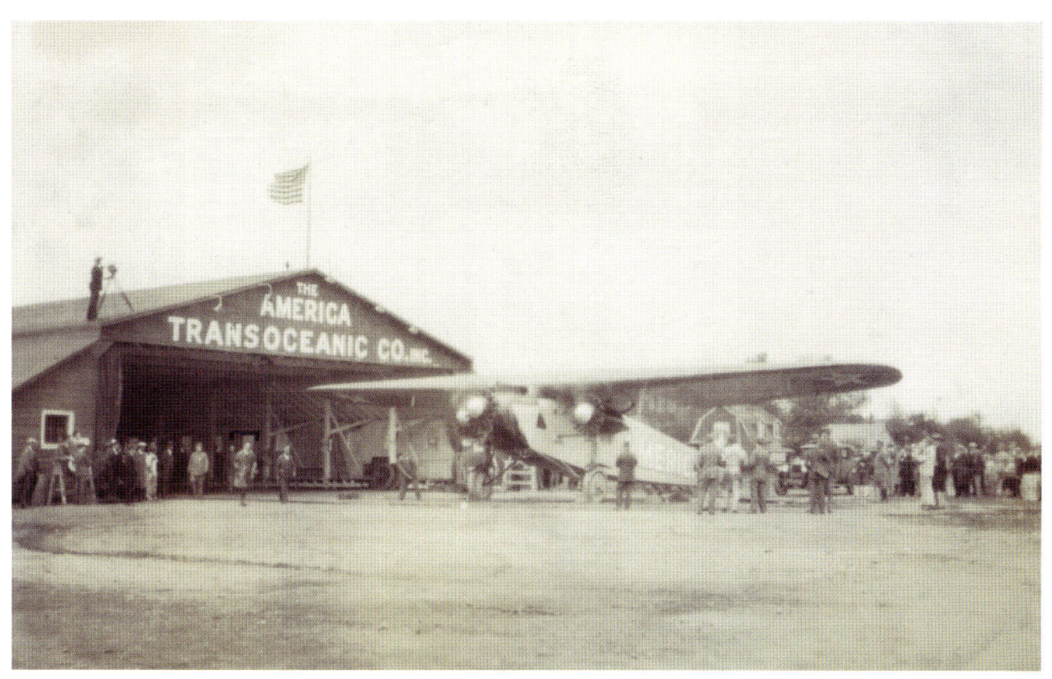

Transatlantic flight hopeful Commander Richard E. Byrd emerges from a hangar at Roosevelt Field and walks toward his plane, the America, May 15, 1927. Byrd was not quite ready in time to make the attempt before Lindbergh.

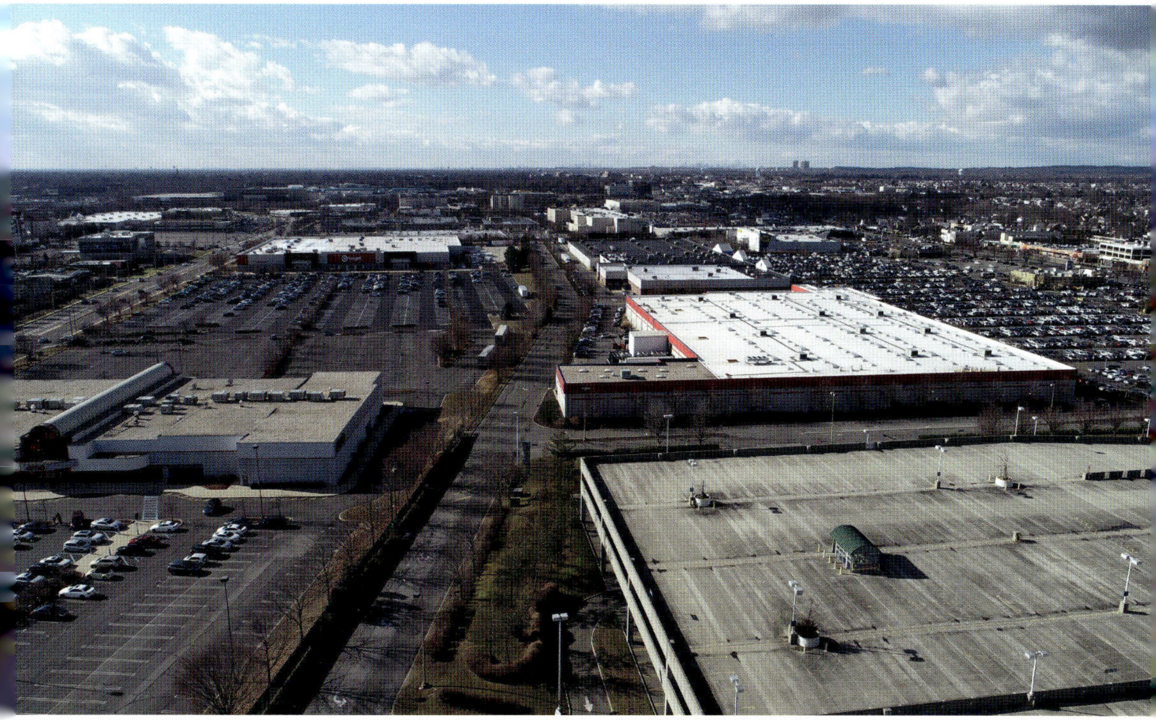

A view looking west from roughly the spot where Charles Lindbergh's plane, The Spirit of St. Louis, took off the morning of May 20, 1927. Back then, much of what is in this image was part of the airport known as Roosevelt Field.

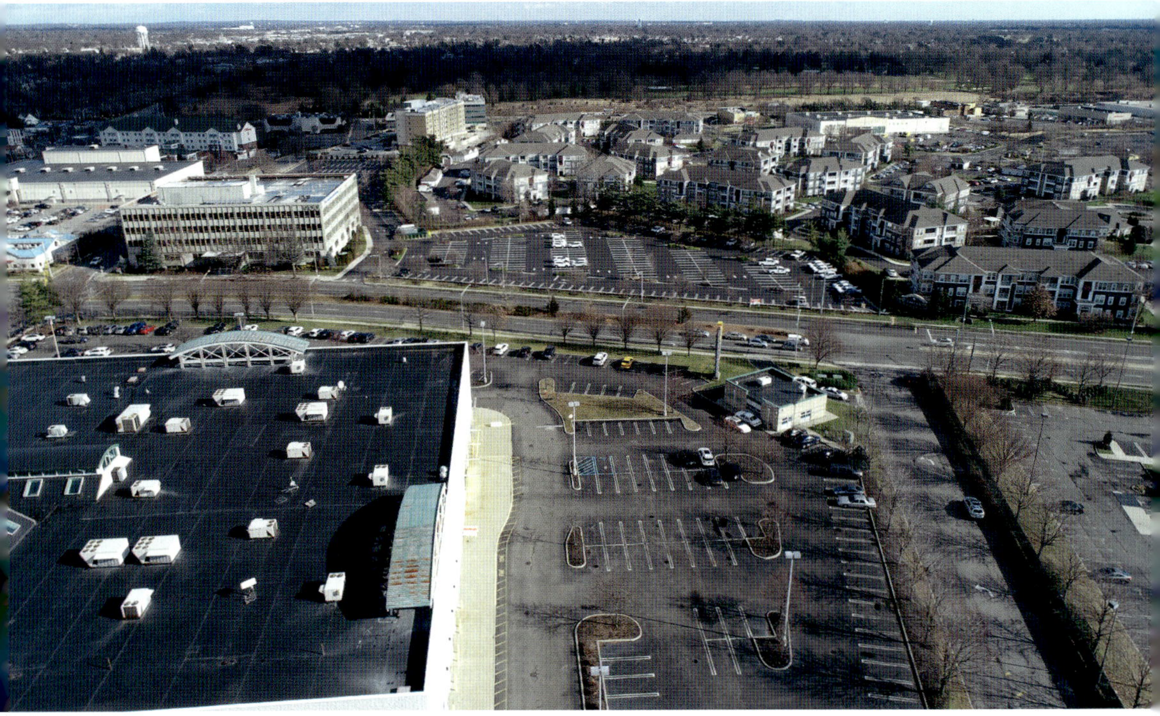

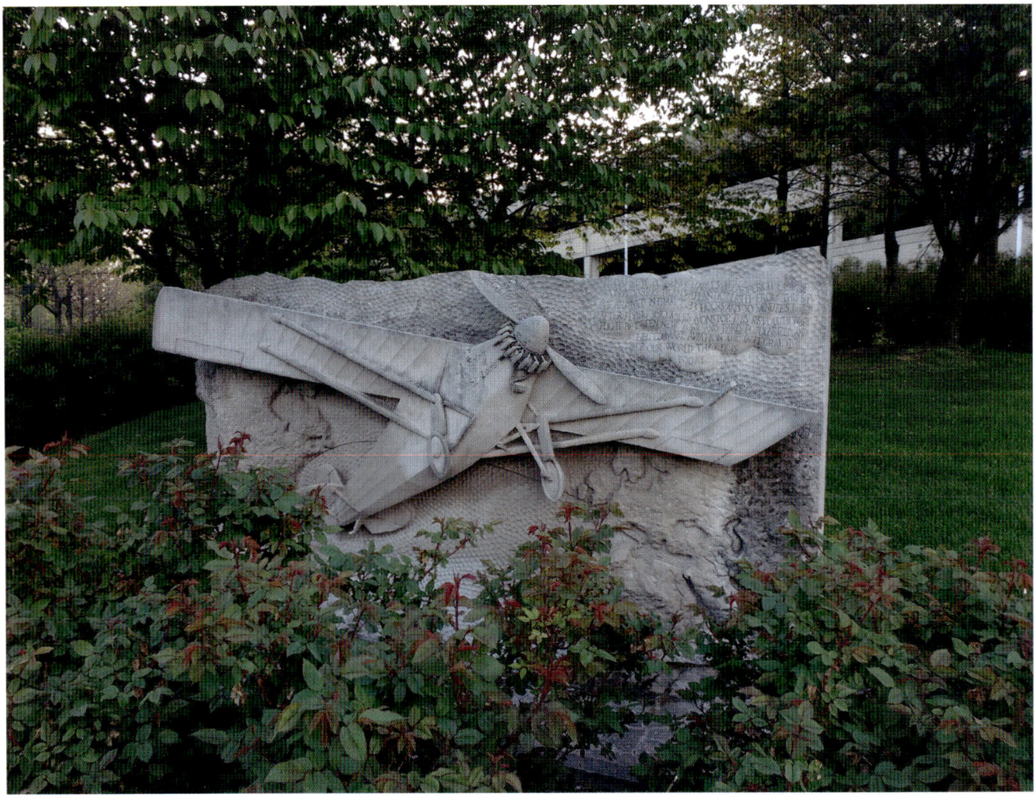

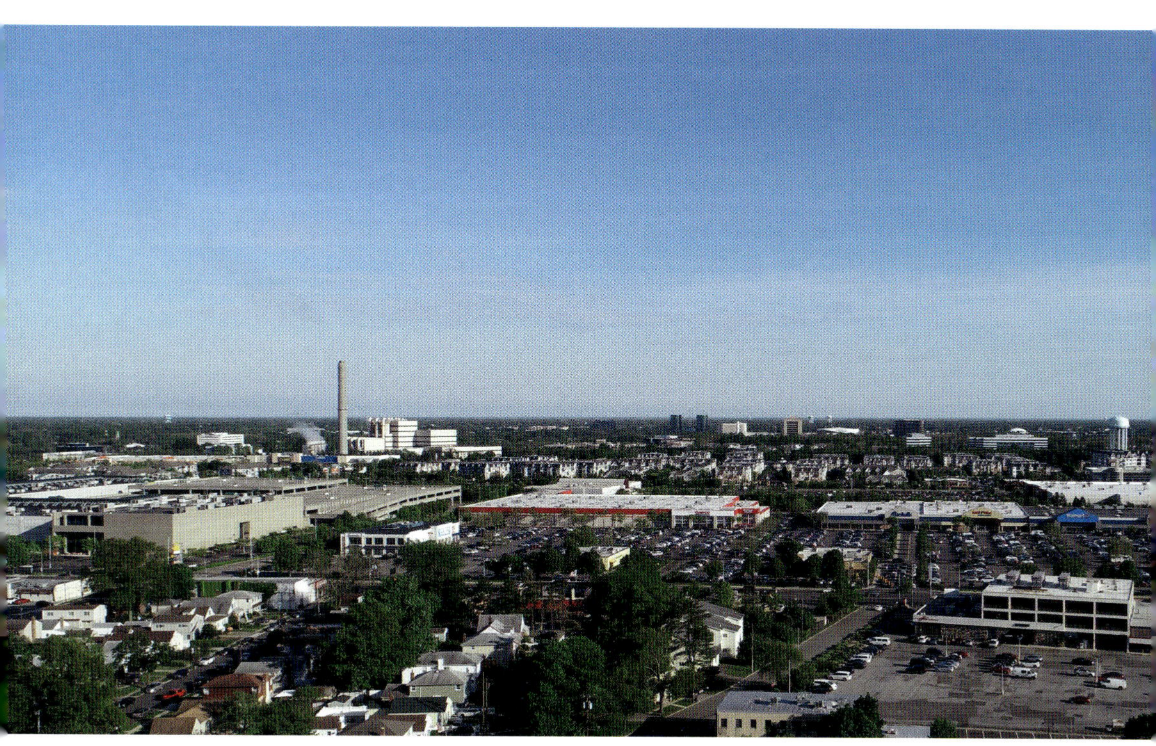

Looking south at the Roosevelt Field area today. Those who lived in southern Carle Place and Westbury back in 1927 had a clear view to the airfield.

OPPOSITE PAGE:

Above: A view looking east from the spot where Lindbergh's plane became airborne.

Below: A stone marker was placed to commemorate the spot where Lindbergh's plane lifted off the ground in 1927.

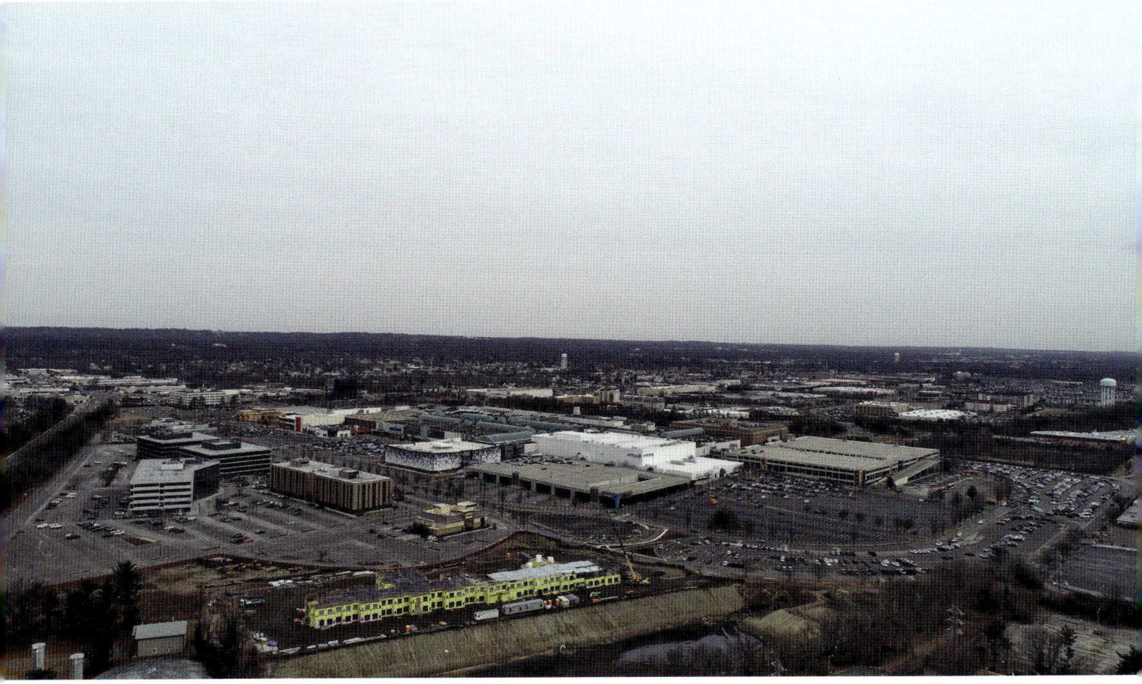

Two views of the Roosevelt Field shopping center from the southwest, from what was once Camp Mills.

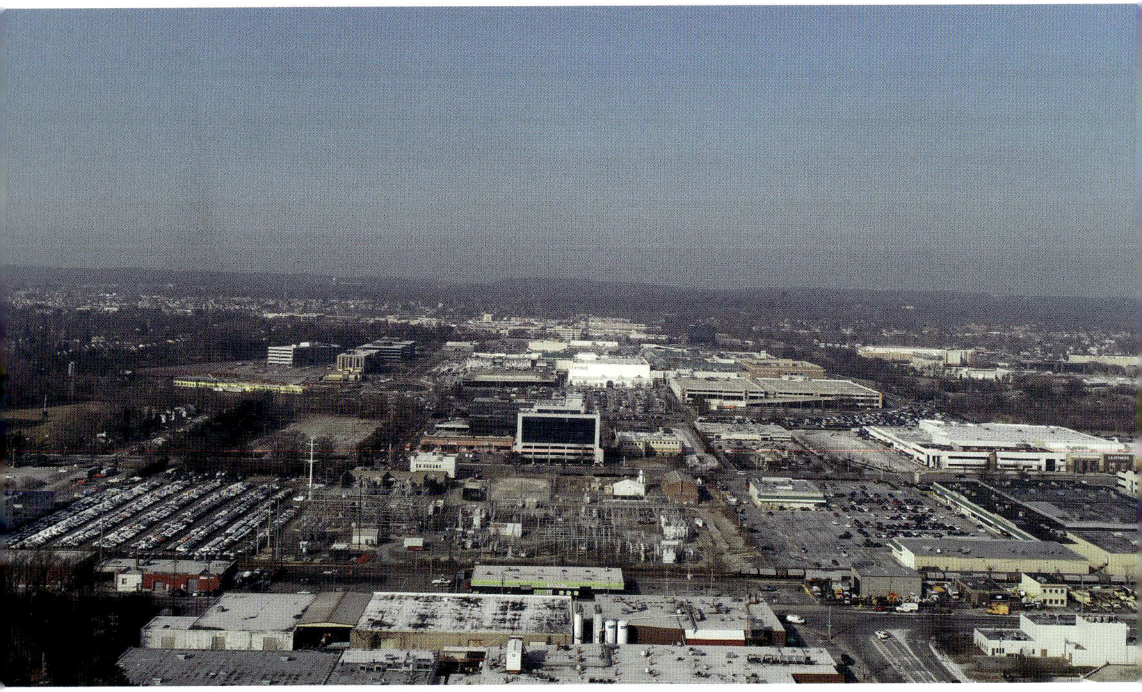

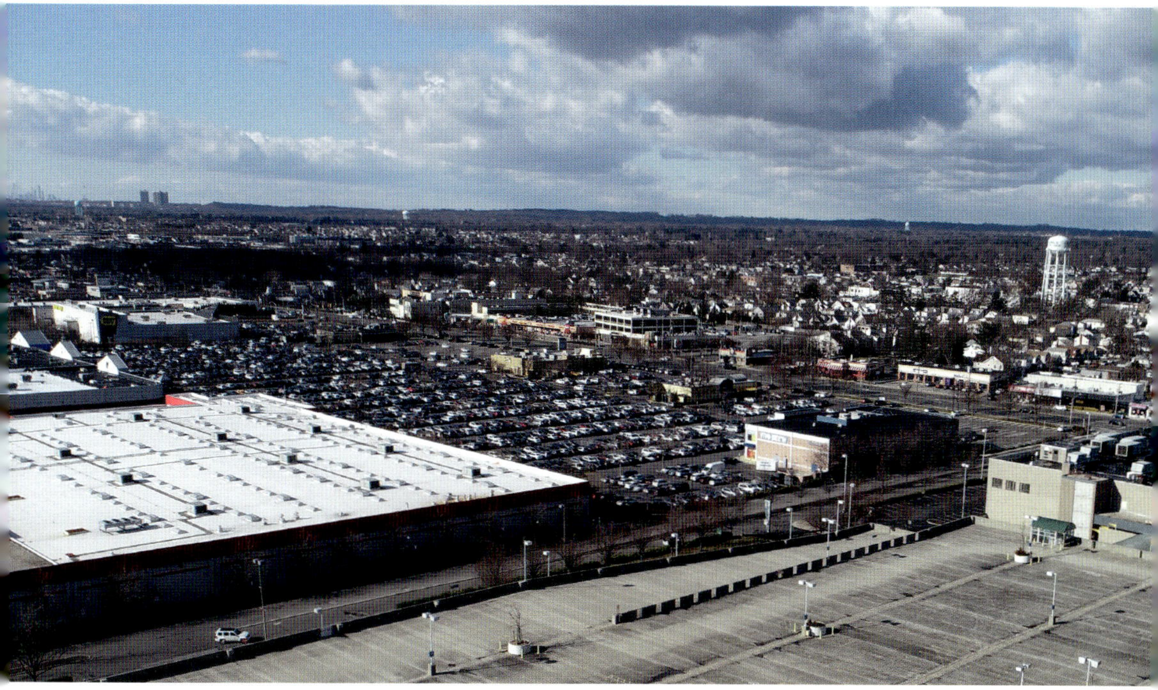

Much of what was once the flat runways of Roosevelt Field is now the flat parking lots of all the retail that replaced the airport.

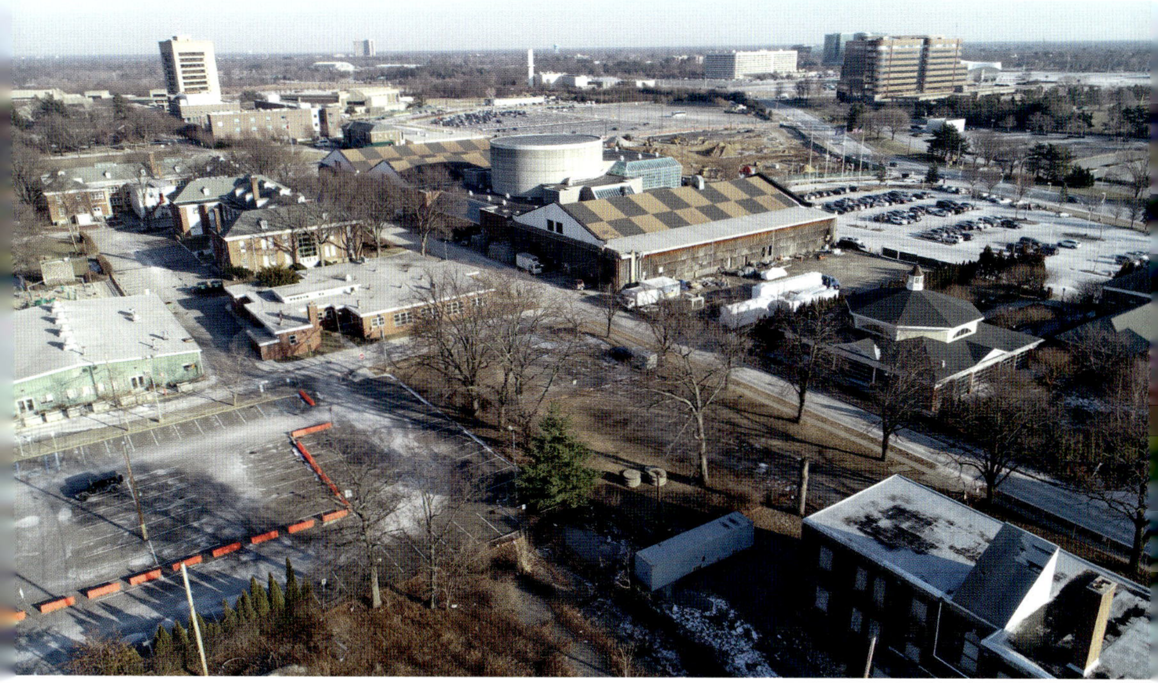

Above and next page: Views of the Cradle of Aviation Museum, which was born from the remains of an old airplane hangar, and highlights the history of aviation with an accent on the role the Hempstead Plains played in the growth of the industry.

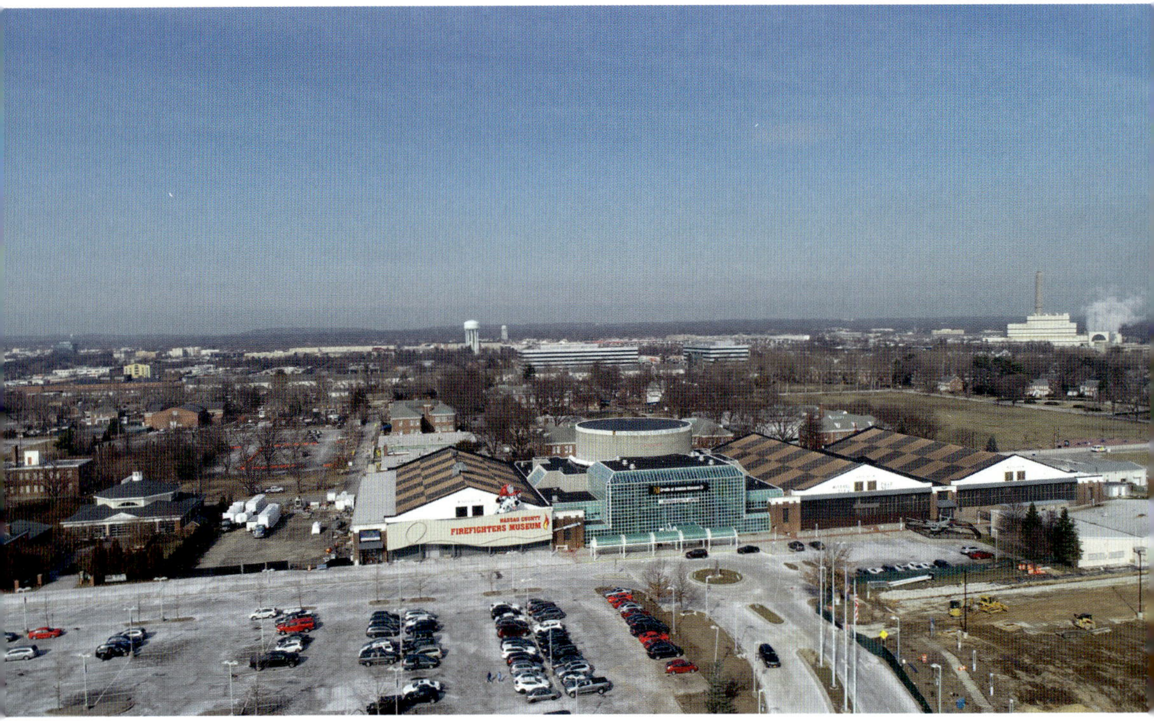
NASSAU COUNTY
FIREFIGHTERS MUSEUM

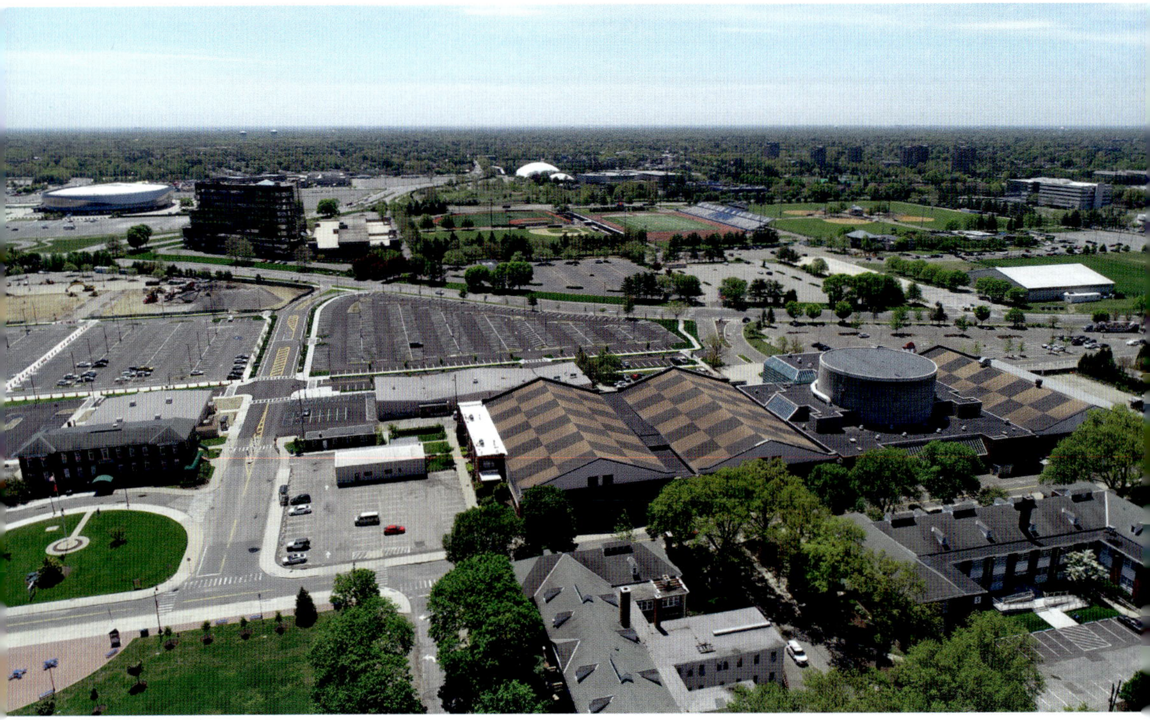

4

MILITARY MIGHT

Civilian aviation on the Hempstead Plains was put on hold for the most part for a few years once the United States entered World War I in 1917. Hazelhurst Field, on the site of the older airfield known as the Hempstead Plains Airfield, was opened as an Army airfield, and then to its south Hazelhurst II, more commonly known as Flying Field #2. Hazelhurst was renamed Roosevelt Field in 1918 after the death of former president Theodore Roosevelt's son, Quentin, whose plane was shot down while he was fighting the Germans in France. Flying Field #2 was renamed Mitchel Field after former New York City mayor John Purroy Mitchel, who died in a training accident in Louisiana in 1918.

But World War I era aviation did not mark the start of military activity on the Hempstead Plains; the great flatlands had been used for army camps since the days of the Civil War and Camp Winfield Scott (opened 1861), which was located near the intersection of today's Eleventh Street and Washington Avenue in Garden City. During the Spanish-American War, Camp Black was also located in Garden City (for five months in 1898), and a sign on Stewart Avenue just east of Clinton Road commemorates the camp. With the American entry into World War I, an army camp was quickly built just west of Flying Field #2, again in Garden City. Named Camp Mills, it was begun in haste in the summer of 1917, and closed not long after the war ended.

While Mitchel Field remained an air base for more than forty years after the war ended, Roosevelt Field returned to civilian duties in 1919. World War II once again brought Mitchel Field a renewed sense of purpose, but Roosevelt Field closed in 1950 and was fully developed soon after. It was simply becoming too difficult to maintain airfields in the middle of an increasingly crowded Nassau County. Mitchel Field closed in 1961, but it took several years for the area to be developed, and even today, parts of the area remain almost untouched. Many of Mitchel Field's remnants are still present today either as repurposed buildings or abandoned places.

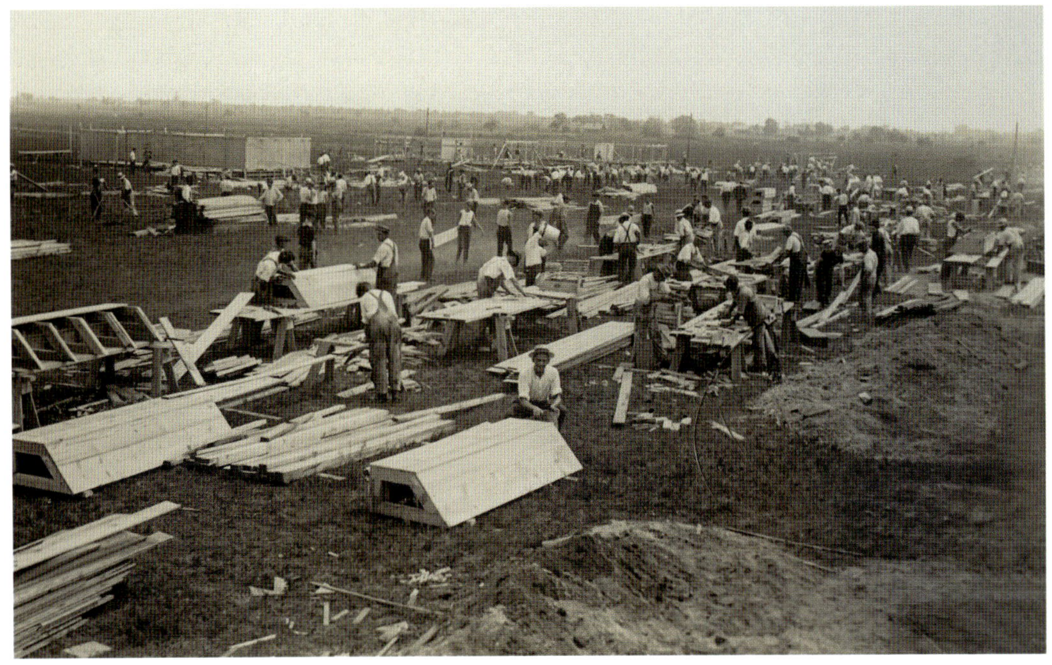

Upon the United States' entry into World War I, Camp Mills was built west of Oak Street and south of the railroad tracks of the Central Branch of the LIRR. This photo taken in August 1917 shows some of the 1,500 men who worked on the construction of Camp Mills so it could open in time for the arrival of the Rainbow Division (which included the 69th Regiment of the NY National Guard), where they would train before being sent overseas to the battle front in France.

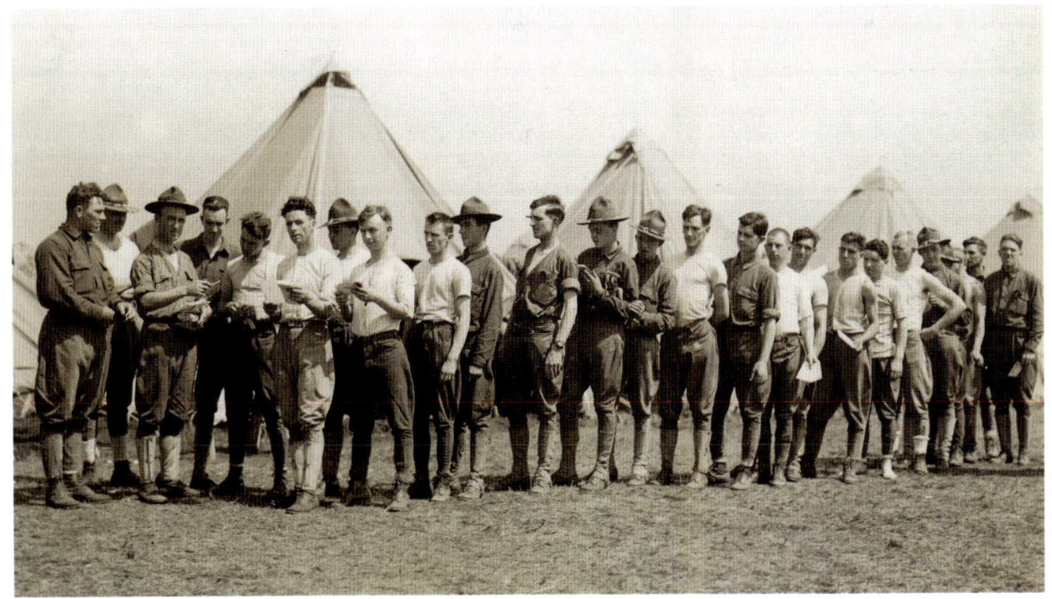

This photo, probably from summer or fall 1917, shows the distribution of the daily mail at Camp Mills. In this image, twenty-five members of the old 69th Regiment of the New York National Guard, which became the 365th Regiment, eagerly await news from home.

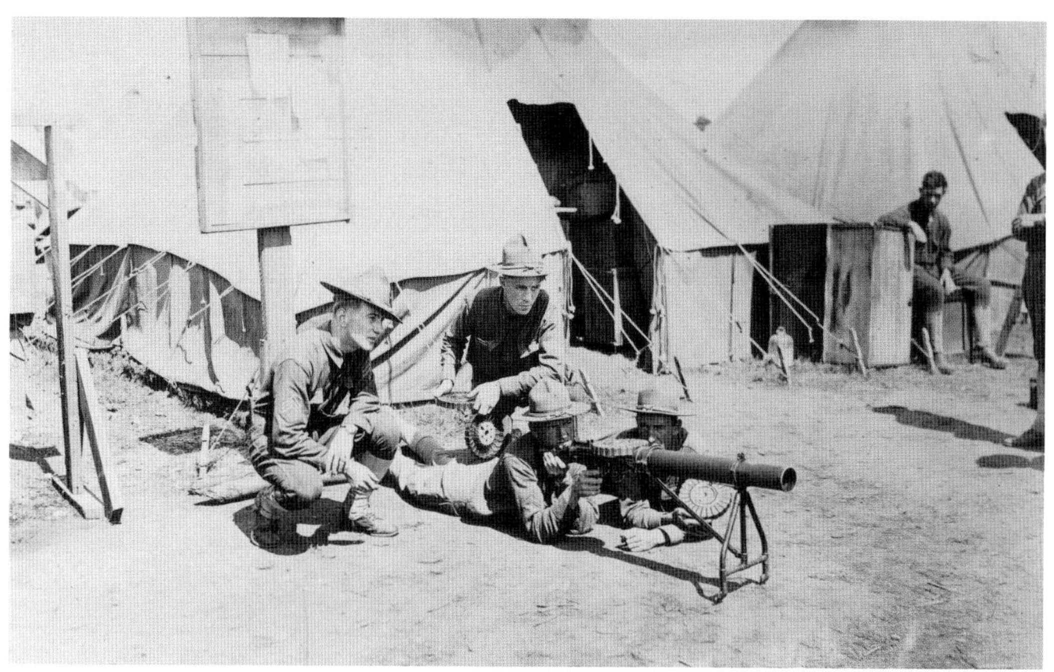

A Lewis machine gun squad in a drill at Camp Mills, 1918. The gun included a 47-cartridge magazine and could fire up to 600 rounds per minute. Originally designed in 1911 in the United States, the gun was adopted first by Belgium and in 1917 by the United States Army.

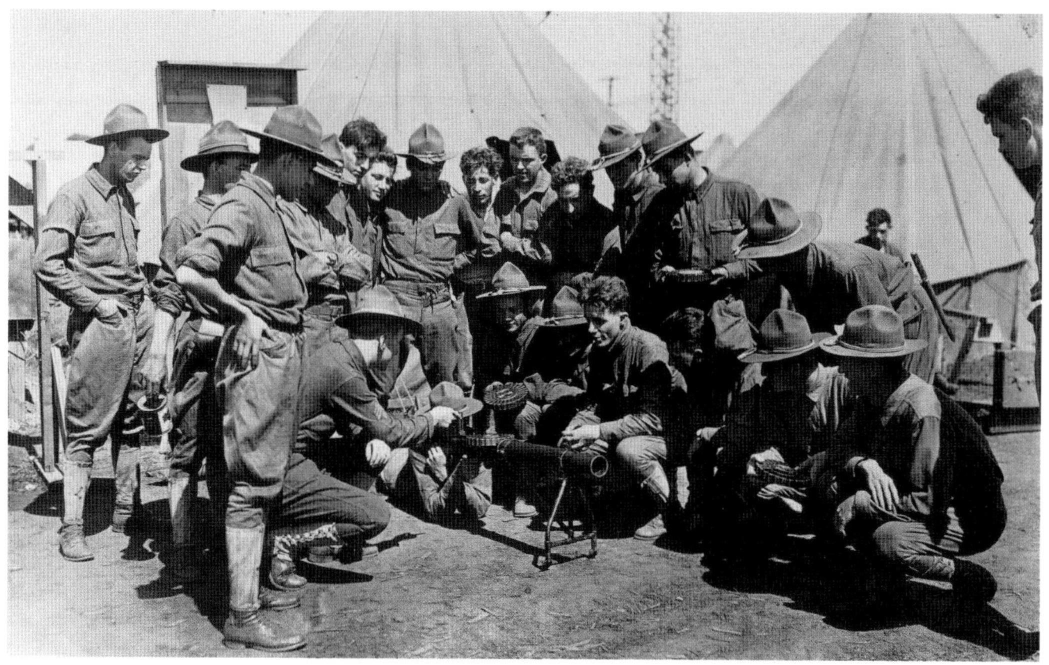

From the close crowding depicted in this Camp Mills photo, no rounds are about to be fired quite yet. Three soldiers can be seen holding additional cartridges. In times of war, training camps are of vital importance in weapons training. Once shipped overseas, there would be no time for learning as most troops went straight to the battle front.

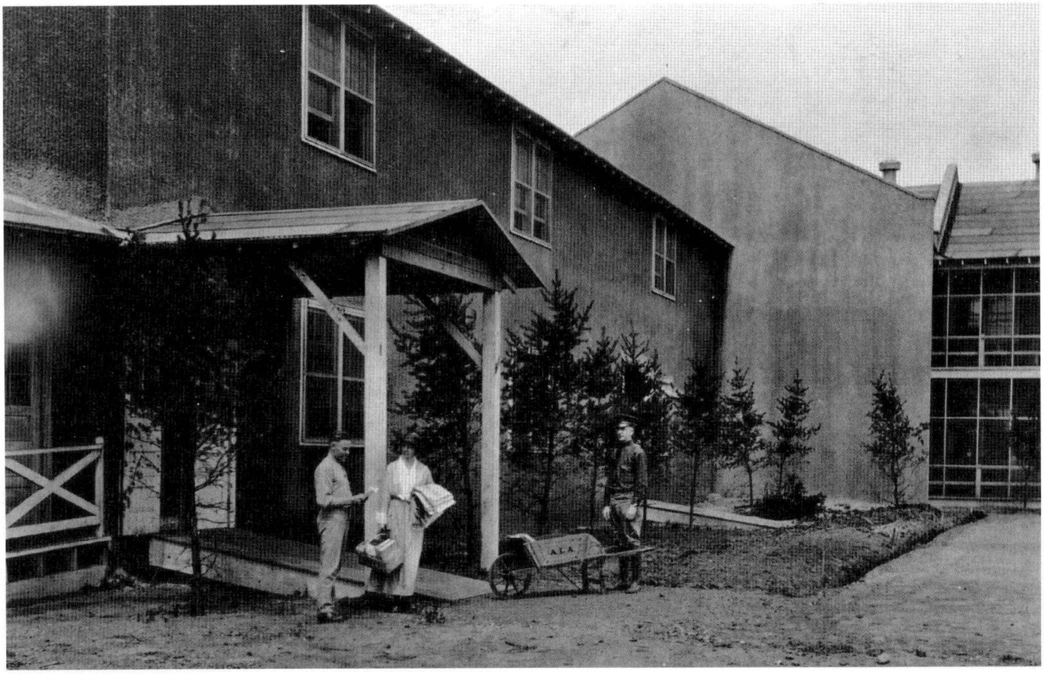

The American Library Association visiting the Camp Mills base hospital to lend books to soldiers. Note the initials "A. L. A." on the wheelbarrow. In the days before radio or television, books were the main source of entertainment for those who were laid up with nothing else to do.

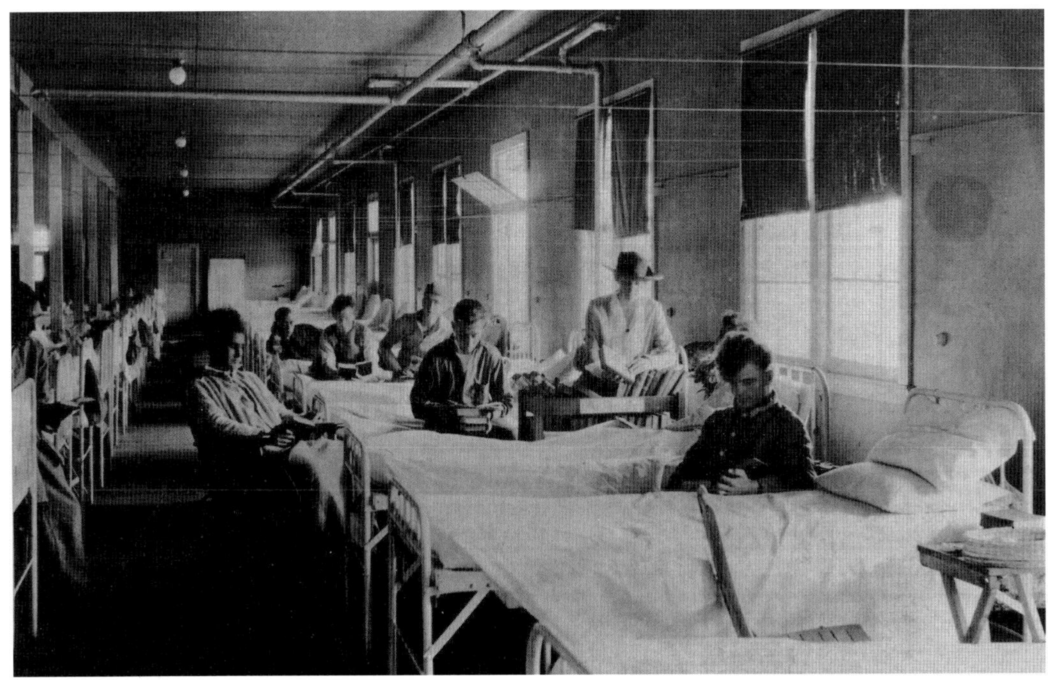

A fascinating glimpse of the American Library Association's library service staff visiting soldiers in the base hospital at Camp Mills and offering a selection of books to borrow. Among the most popular books in 1918 were Willa Cather's *My Antonia* and Booth Tarkington's *The Magnificent Ambersons*.

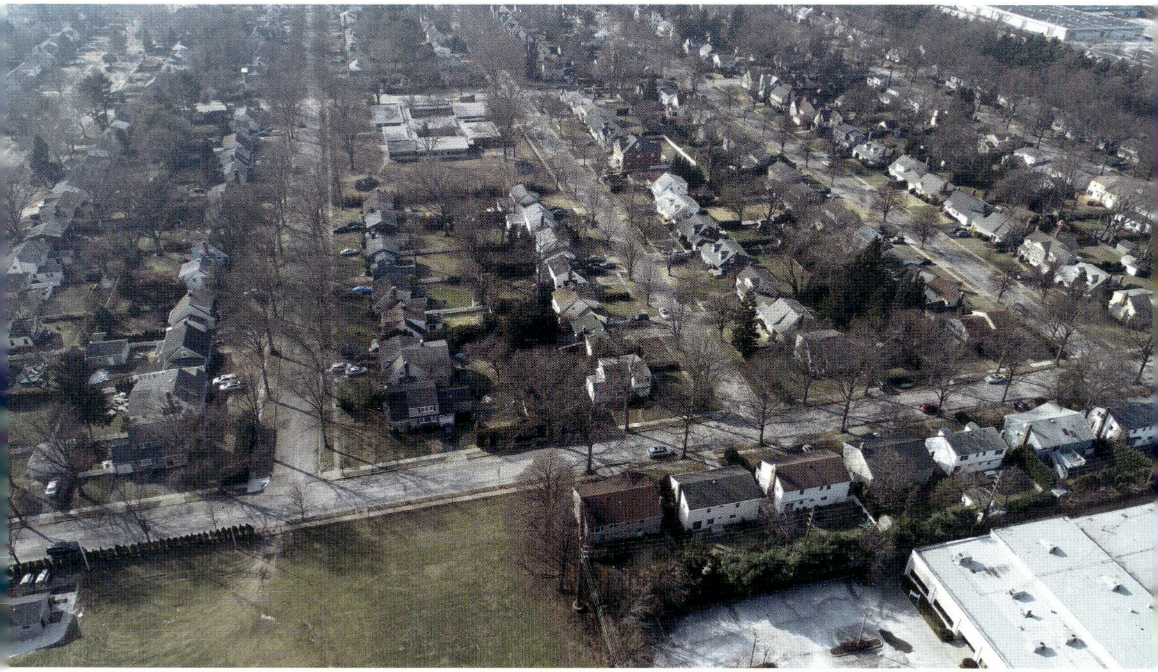

Much of what was once Camp Mills is now a residential neighborhood with private homes that were built starting in the 1920s when the last remnants of the old camp were demolished.

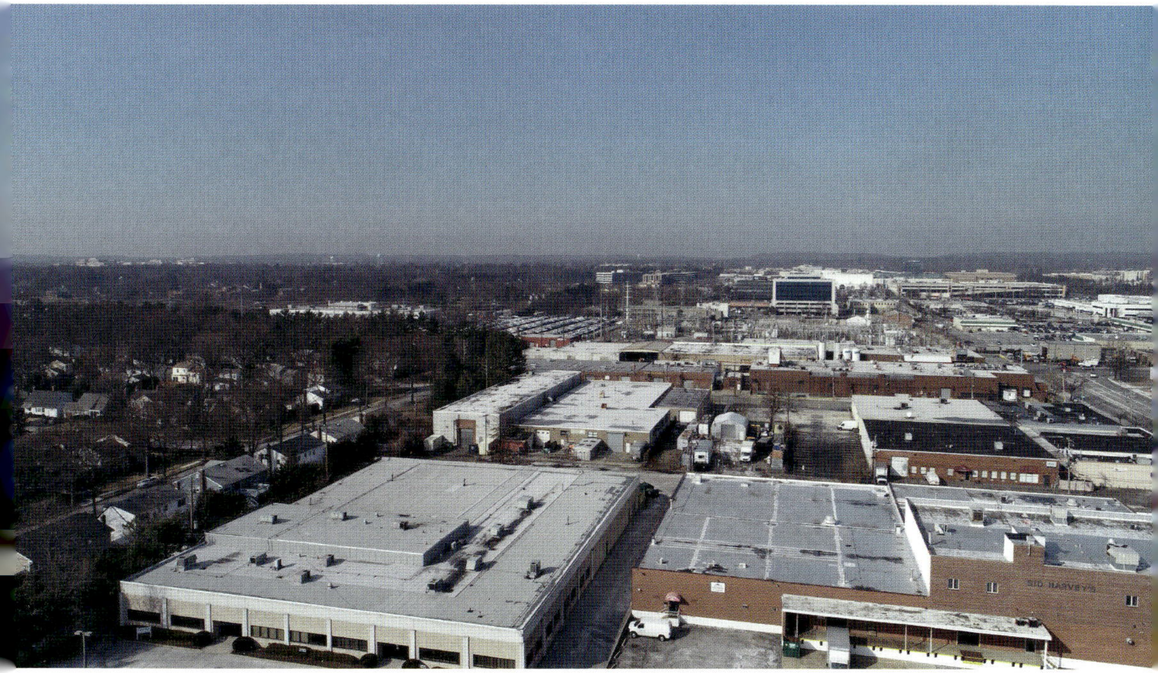

The eastern section of what was once Camp Mills is now filled with low rise industrial buildings that line Oak Street. The parcel of land was owned by "Merillon Estates" after it was decommissioned.

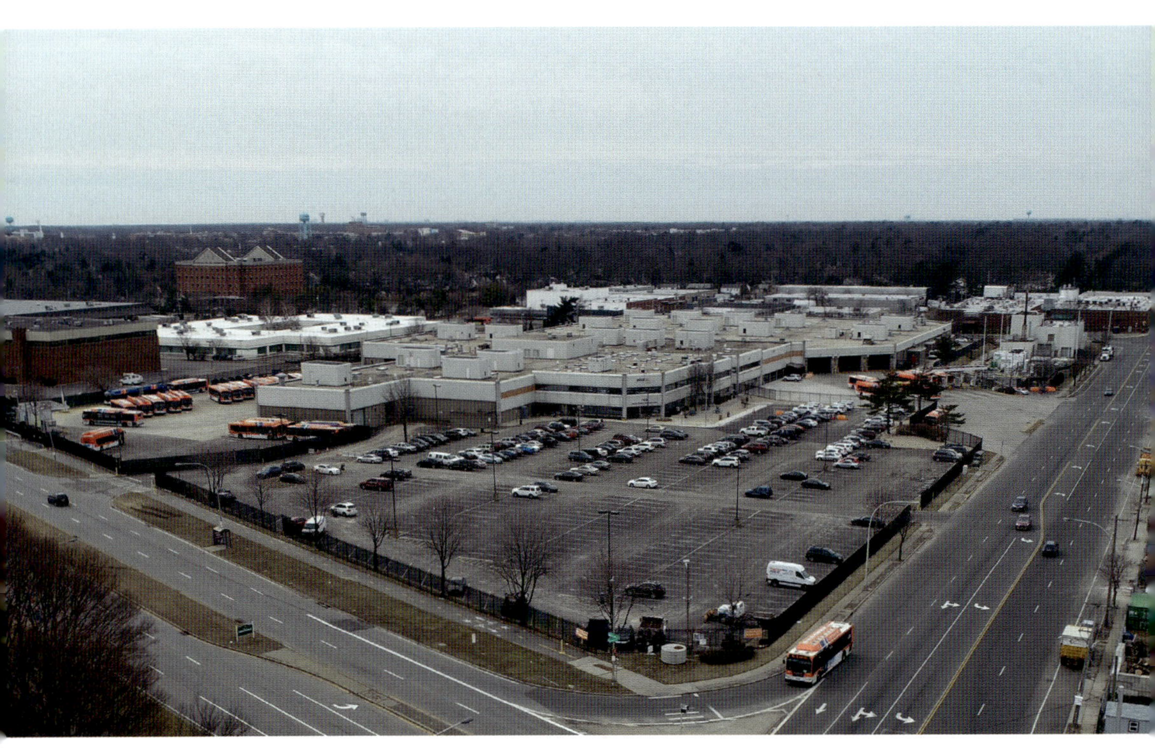

Looking west from Quentin Roosevelt Boulevard and Commercial Avenue toward the site of Camp Mills, which was west of Oak Street, just beyond the buildings in the foreground.

OPPOSITE PAGE:

The Stewart School is on the site of the Salvation Army Hotel, which served Camp Mills.

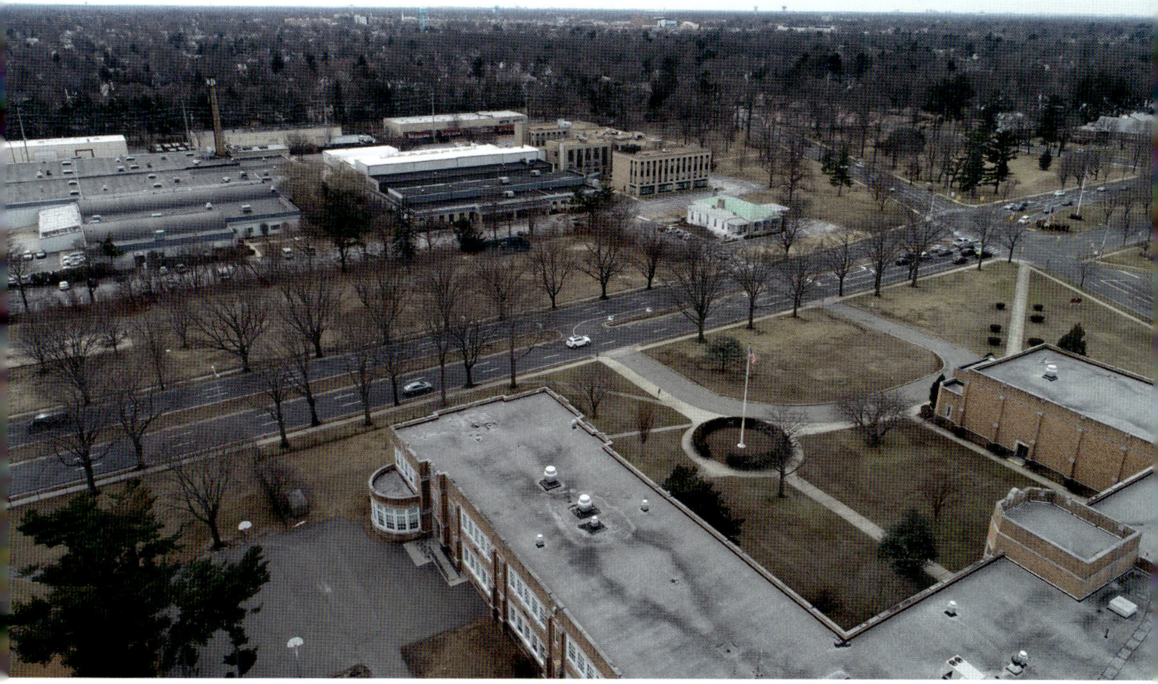

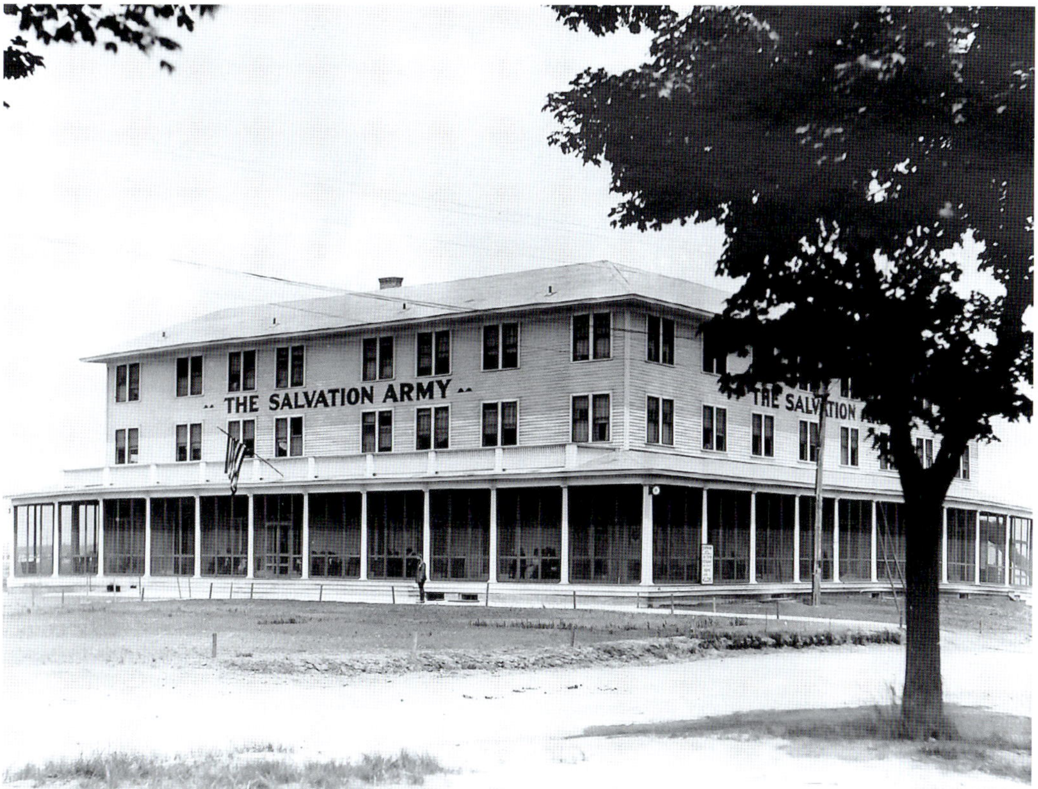

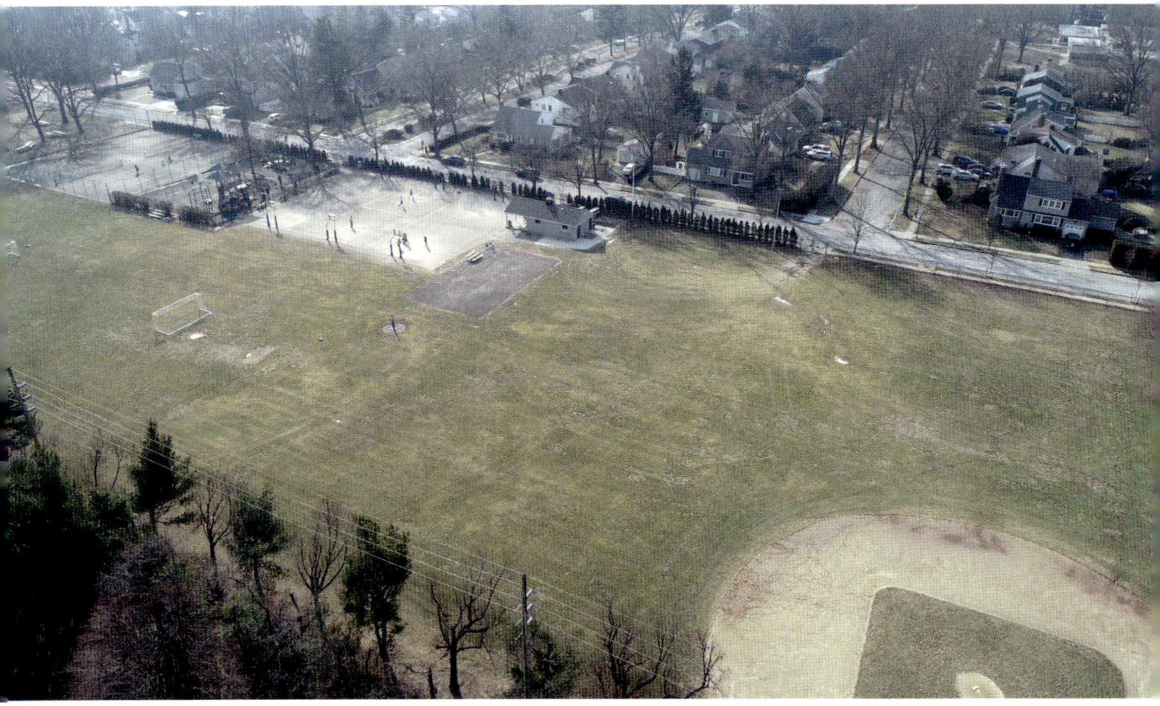

This sports field on Grove Street is the largest parcel of flat grassy land in what was once entirely flat, grassy Camp Mills.

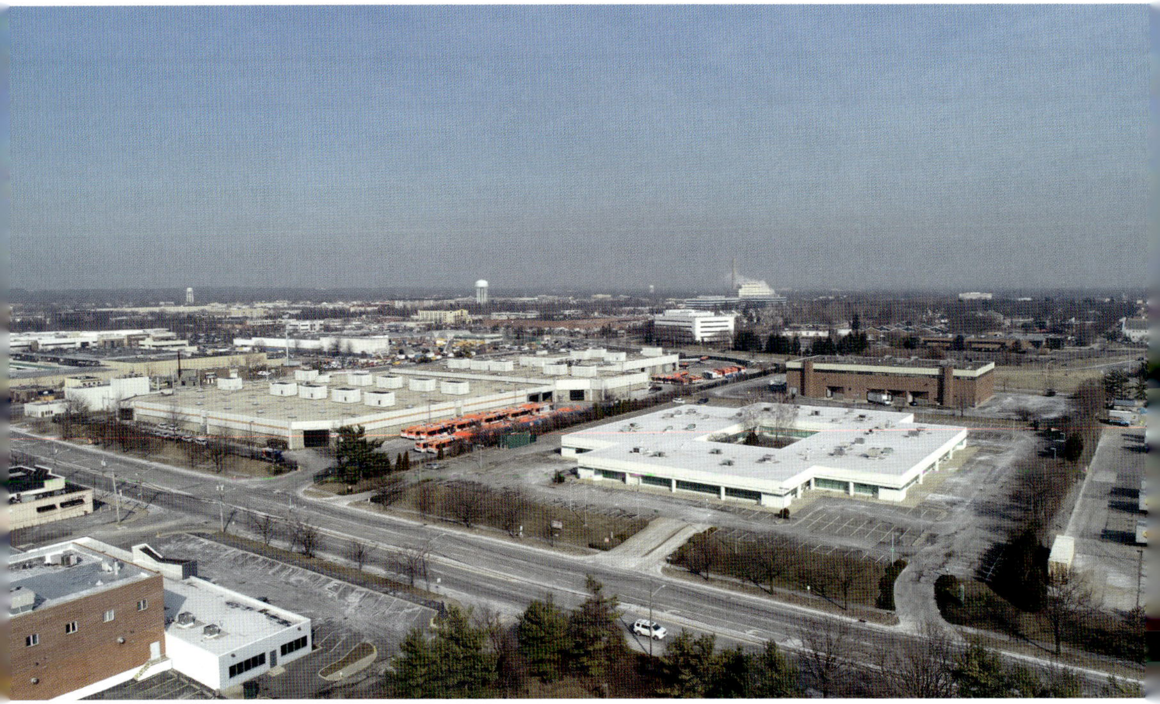

Across Oak Street from Camp Mills was the western end of Mitchel Field (first known as Aviation Field No. 2) part of which is now occupied by the headquarters of Nassau Inter-County Express (NICE buses).

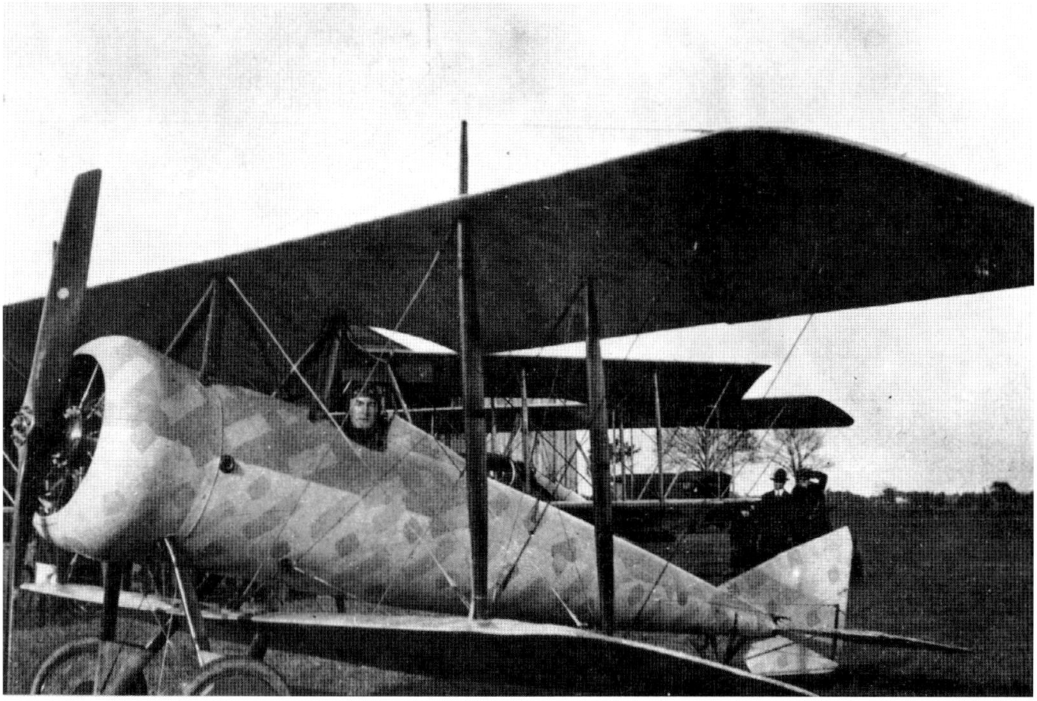

The Berckman Speed Scout plane, designed by brothers Maurice and Emile Berckman, was painted with "camouflage in the form of a light green and blue background upon which square and oblong spots of many colors were placed are arranged at regular intervals, on the body and surfaces," per *Aerial Age Magazine* of 1917. This photo, taken at Hazelhurst Field, dates to 1917.

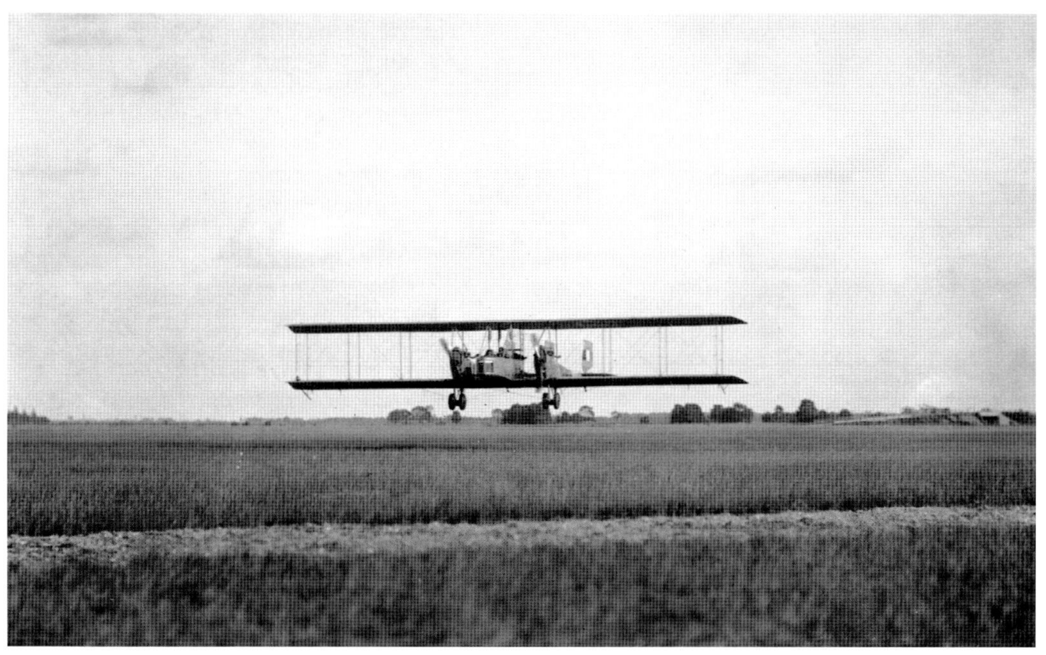

This view shows an Italian Caproni airplane taking off from Hazelhurst Field.

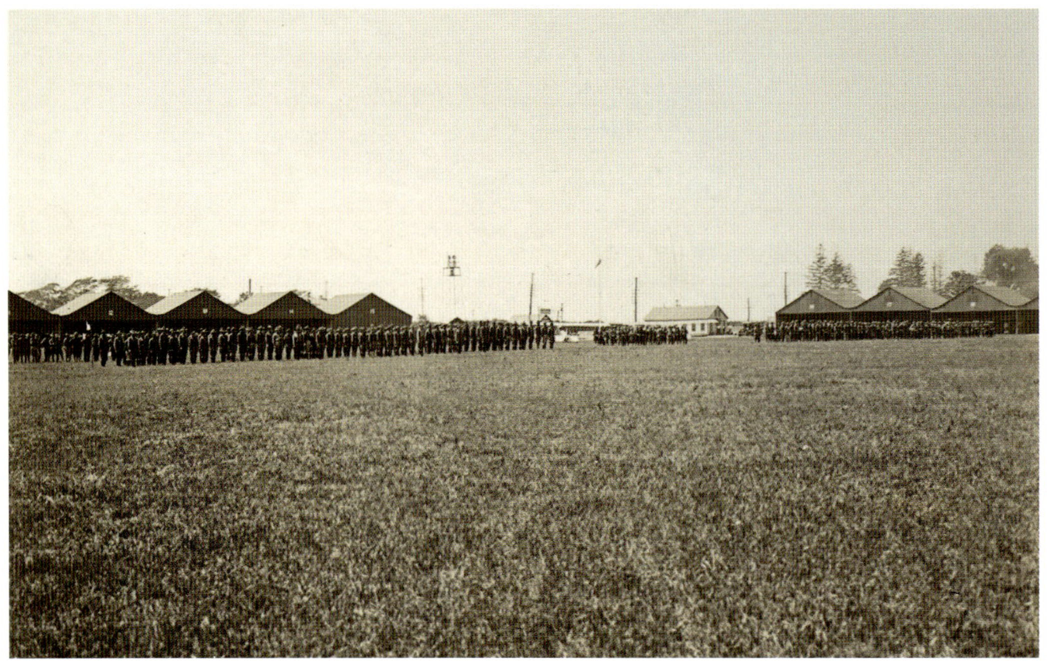

Muster at the Hazelhurst Aviation Field on July 31, 1917. Hangars numbered 11 through 18 are visible in this image. The flat expanse of the Hempstead Plains made this area ideal for a flying field with no alterations to the terrain necessary other than the addition of runways.

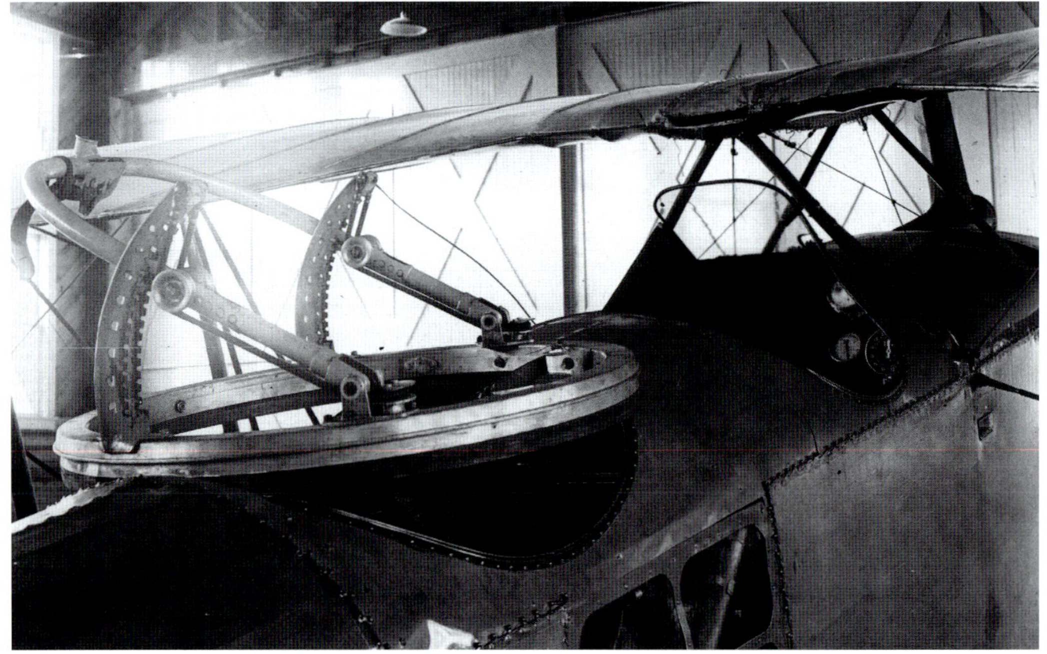

Taken January 5, 1918, this photograph shows a machine gun mounting on a Breguet airplane at the future Hazelhurst Field. Founded in 1911, the French company made dozens of different aircraft before merging with another company in 1971. Their wartime planes included several generations of bombers and fighters. The most popular wartime plane was the Breguet 14, first developed in 1916.

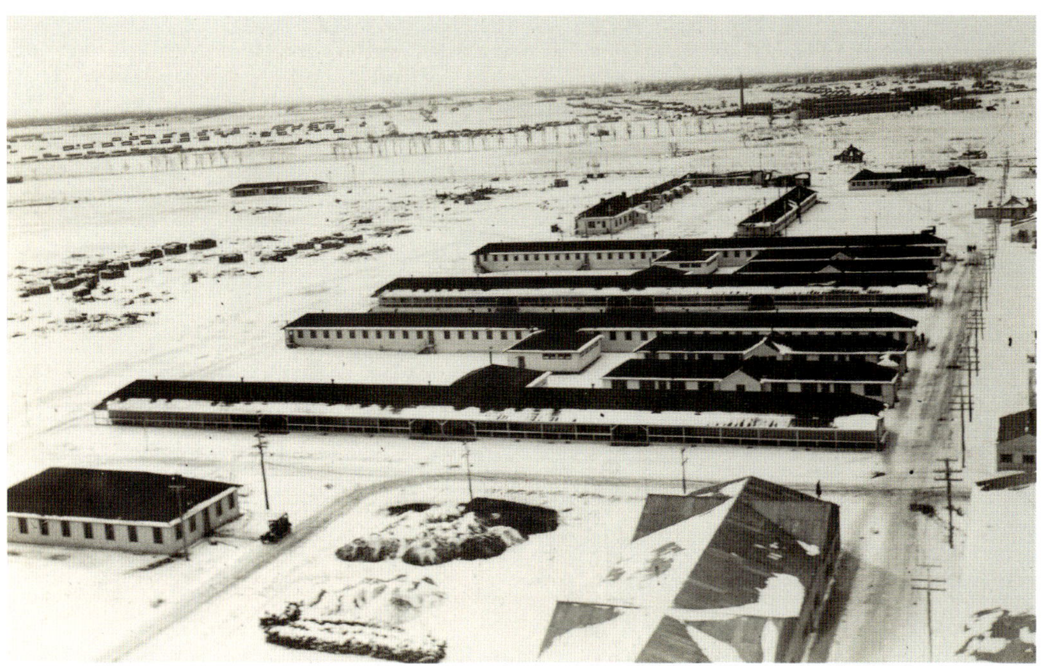

Looking south from the water tower at the western end of Hazelhurst Field in January 1918. Also visible are the railroad tracks and the smokestack of the Curtiss Engineering Corporation.

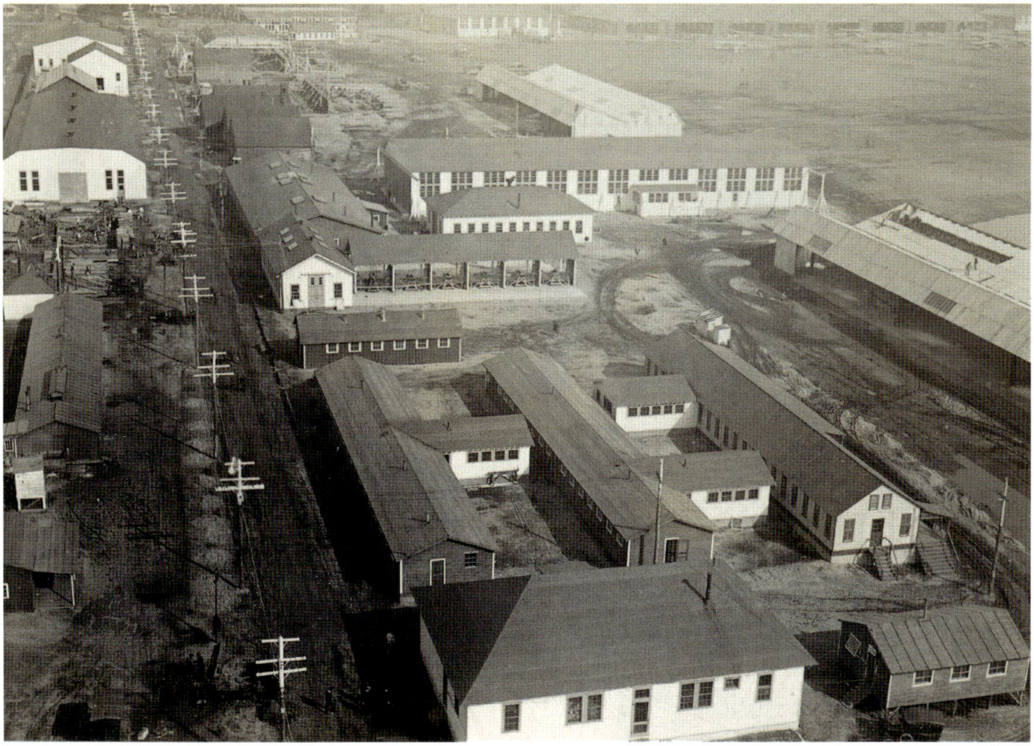

An aerial view of the future Hazelhurst Field in late 1917. Note the airplanes and hangars in the background.

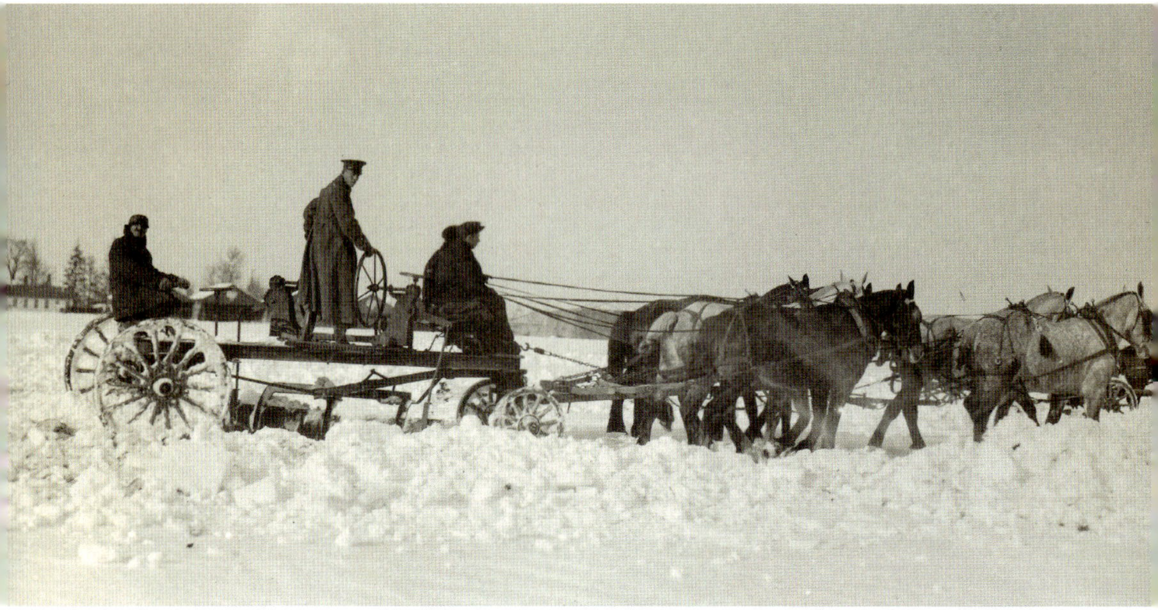

Much like today, a snowstorm could wreak havoc on the ability to fly. This photo was taken on November 6, 1917, and shows a crew clearing the runway at the future Hazelhurst Field.

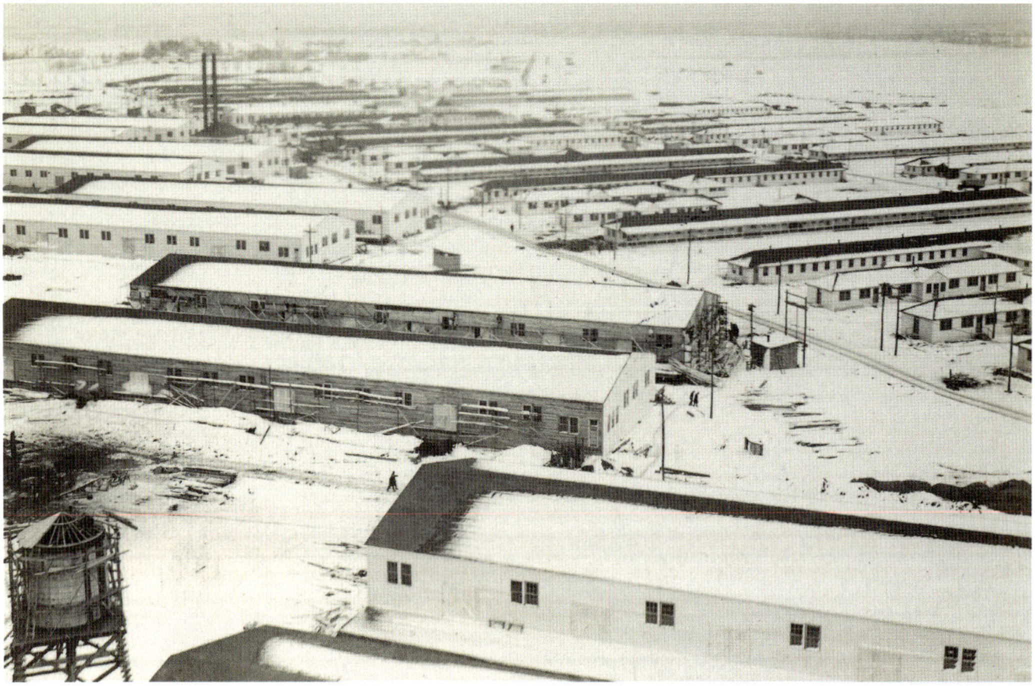

An aerial view of Aviation Field #2, later to become Mitchel Field, in December 1917.

Opposite above: Soldiers training at Mitchel Field during World War II. From the official Office of War Information caption: "On the rifle range members of the airbase squadron learn to fire the snubnose Thompson sub-machine gun. The highest degree of proficiency in the use of these firearms is attained in the intensive training program."

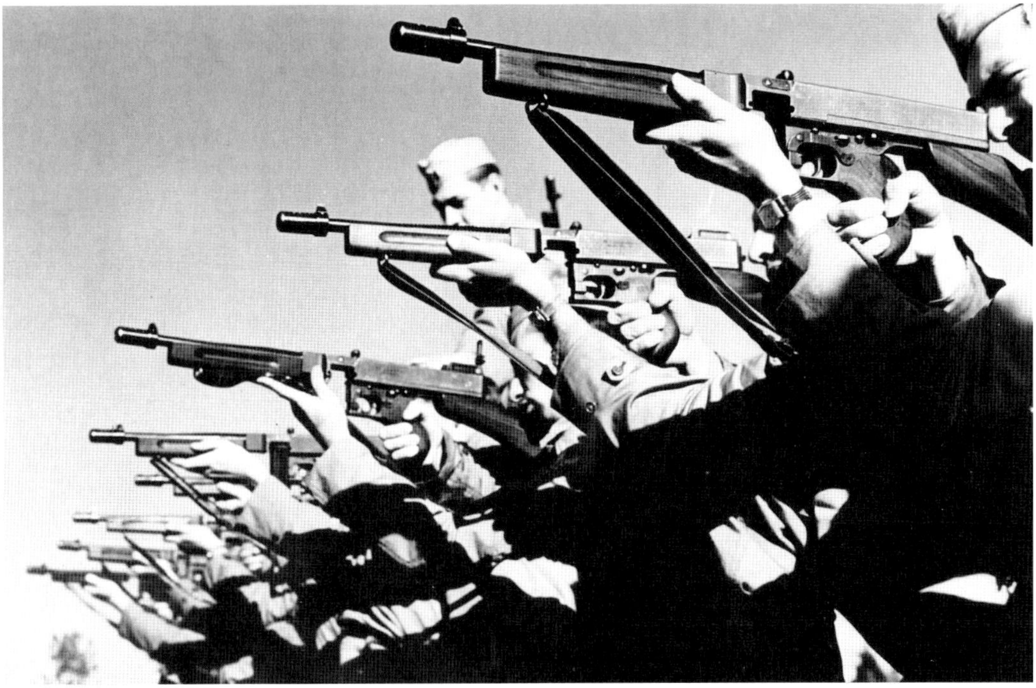

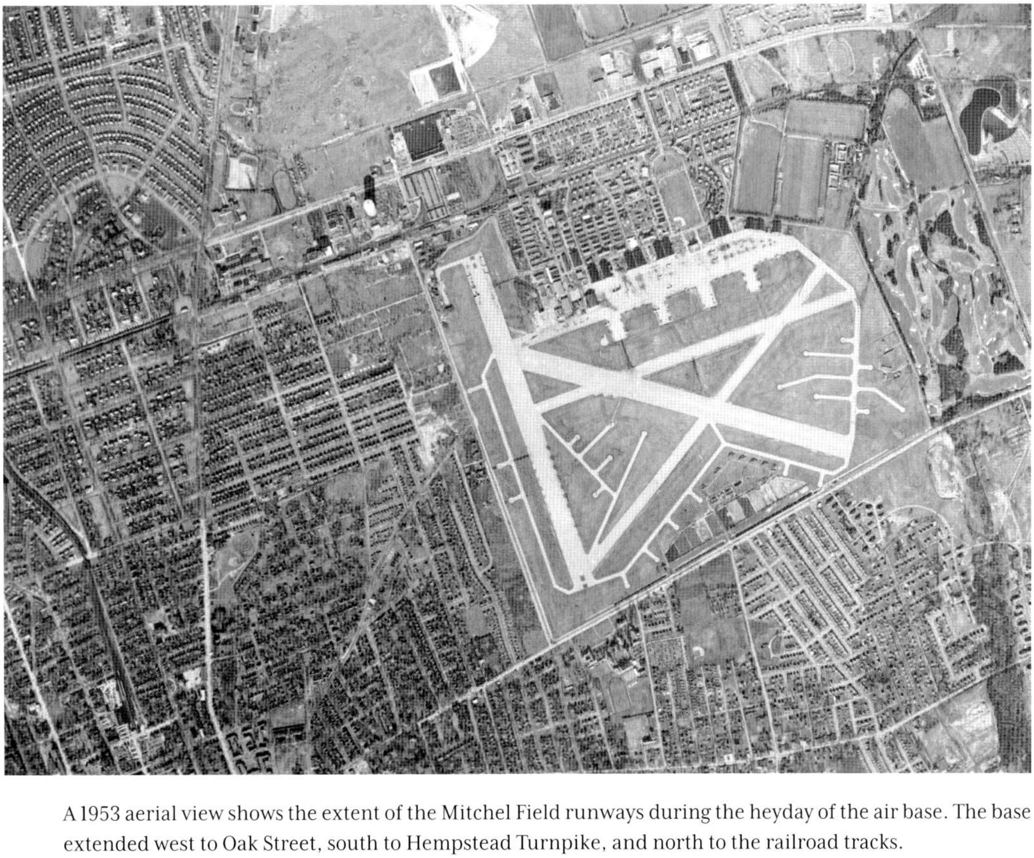

A 1953 aerial view shows the extent of the Mitchel Field runways during the heyday of the air base. The base extended west to Oak Street, south to Hempstead Turnpike, and north to the railroad tracks.

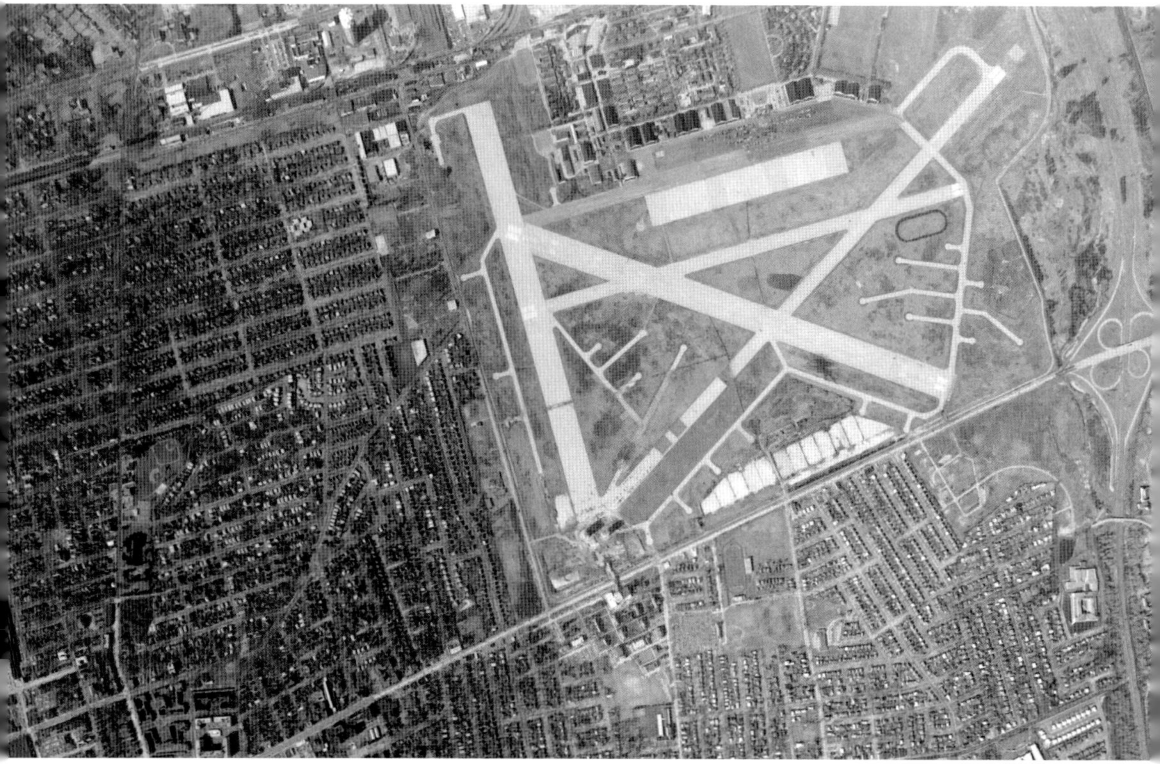

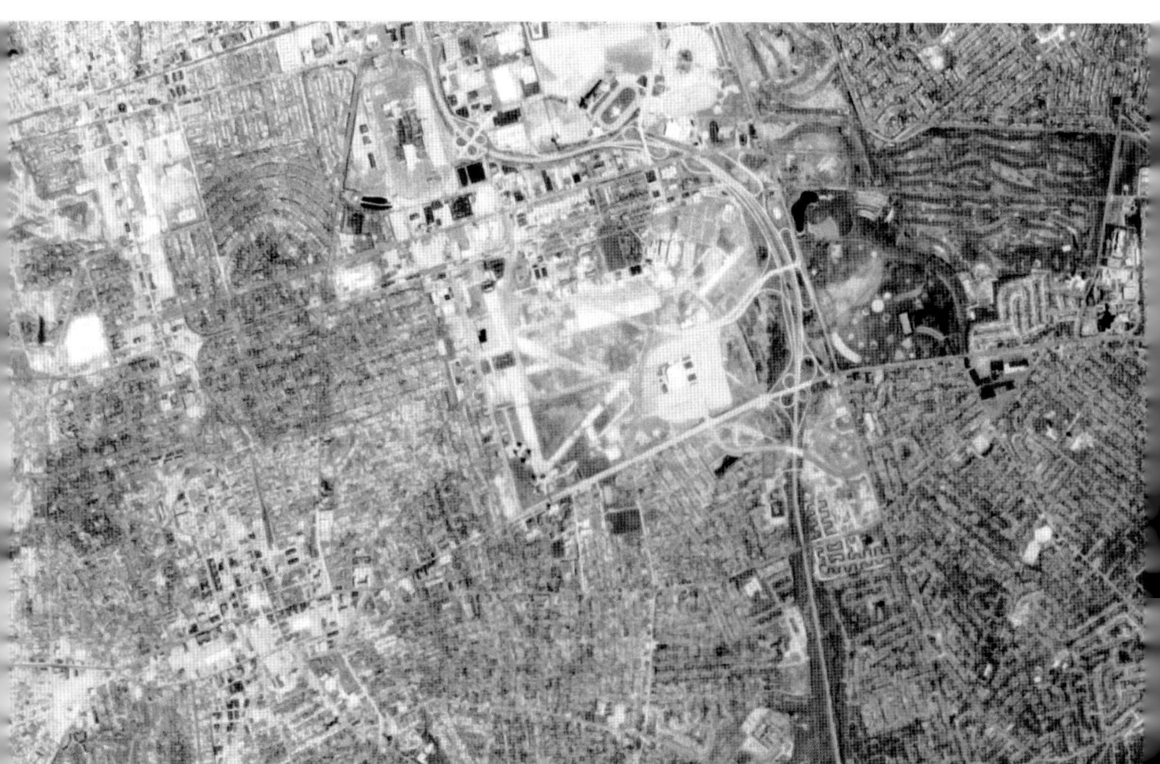

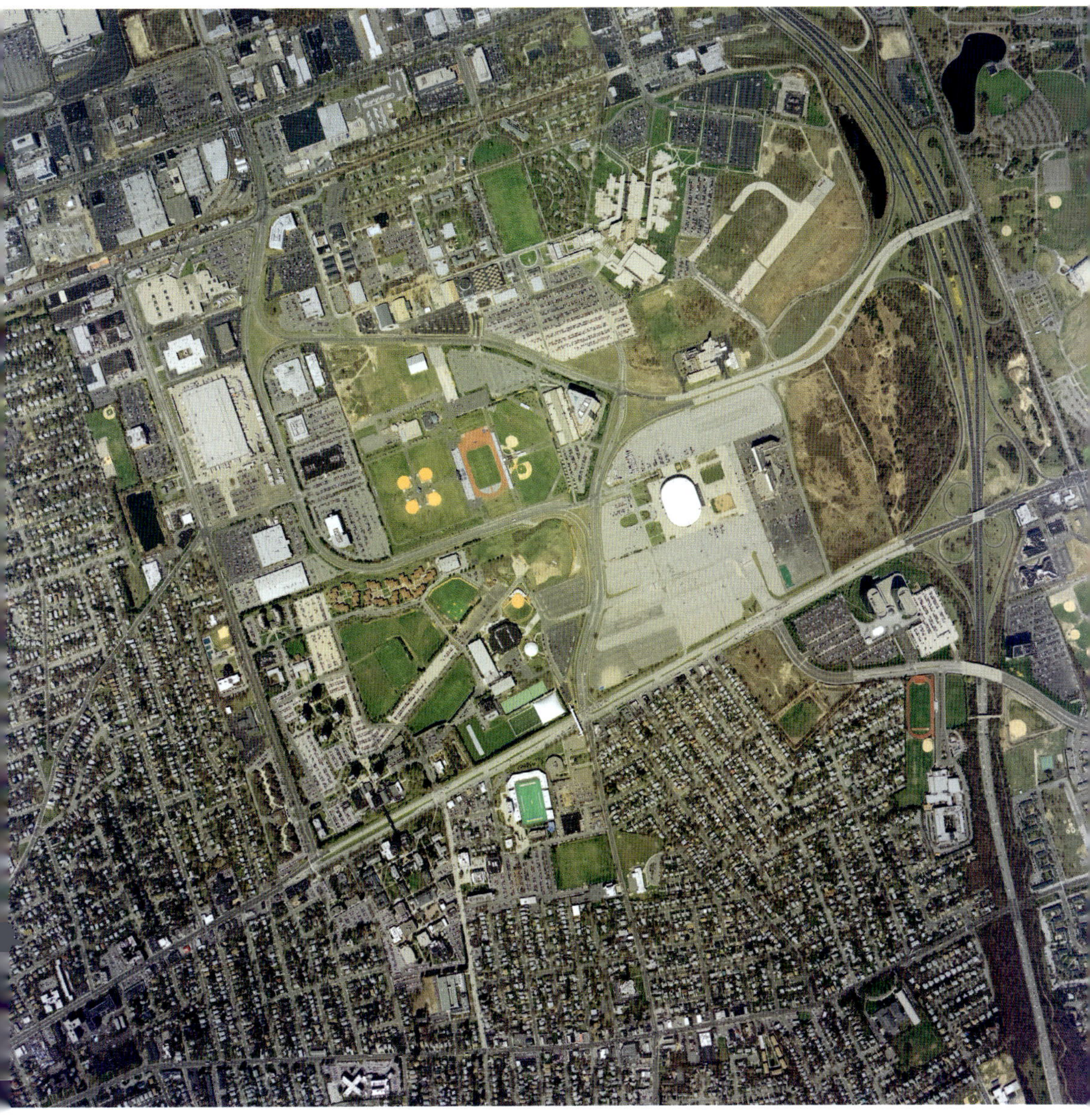

This USGS aerial from 2002 shows the Mitchel Field area as development of the former air base continued over the years.

Opposite page:

Above: In 1966, a few years after Mitchel Field closed, the runway system was still entirely intact.

Below: A 1981 aerial view shows the Mitchel Field area development well under way, with the Nassau Coliseum built.

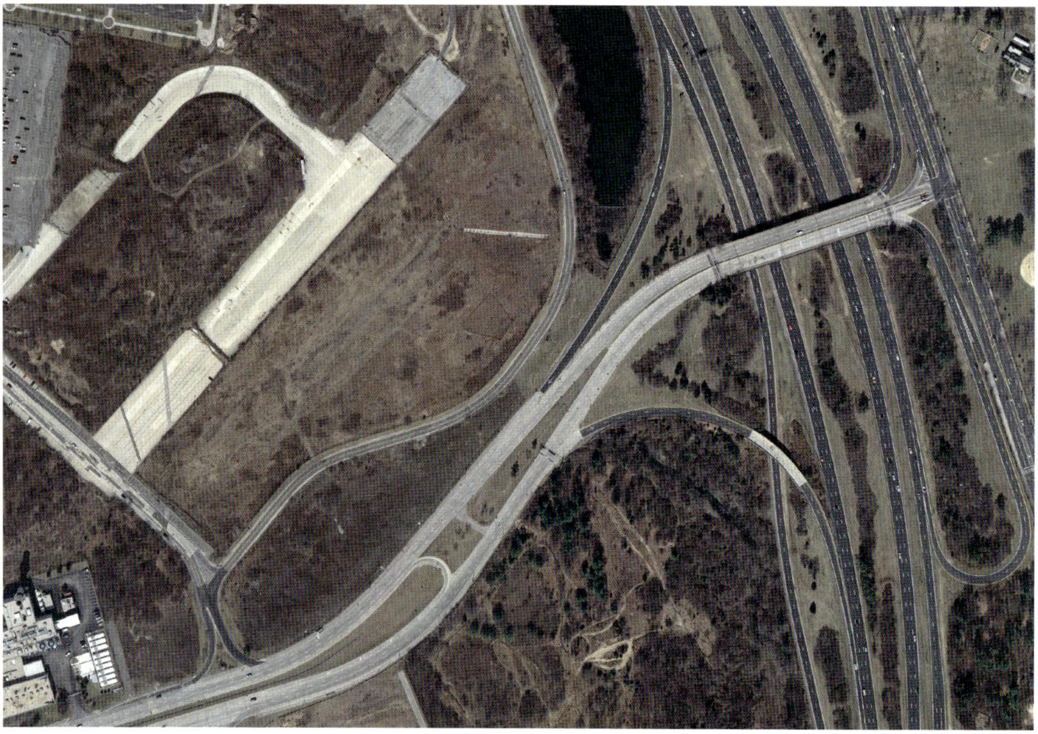

A closeup view of the remnants of the Mitchel Field runway in 2007.

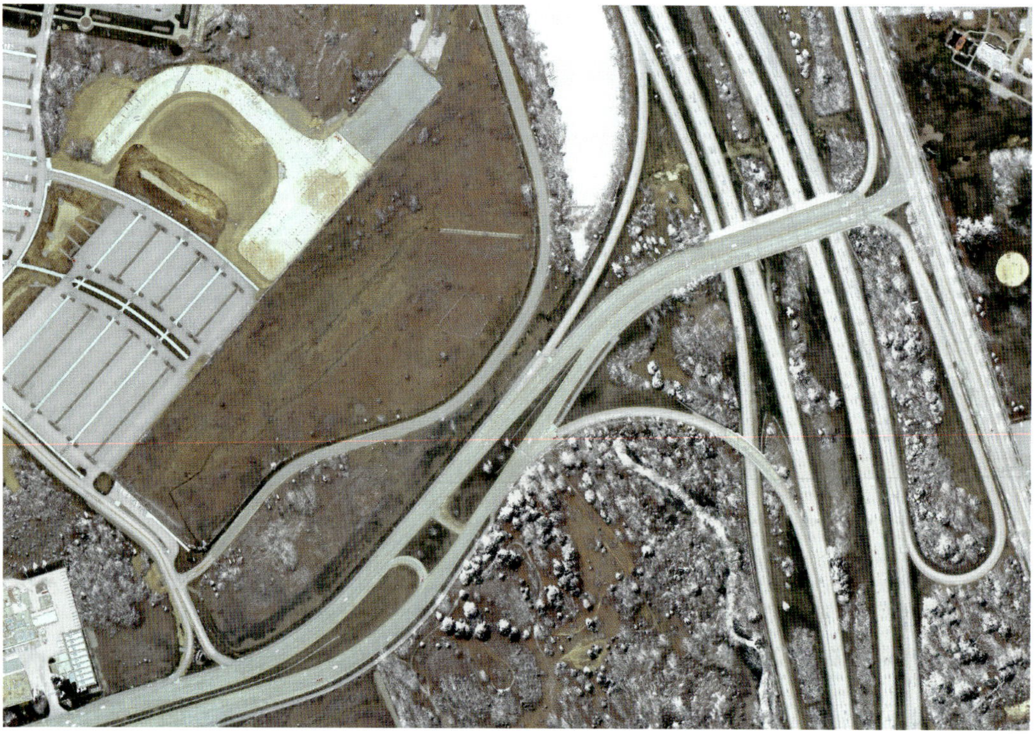

The same view in 2013 shows how the runway was truncated to create more Nassau Community College parking.

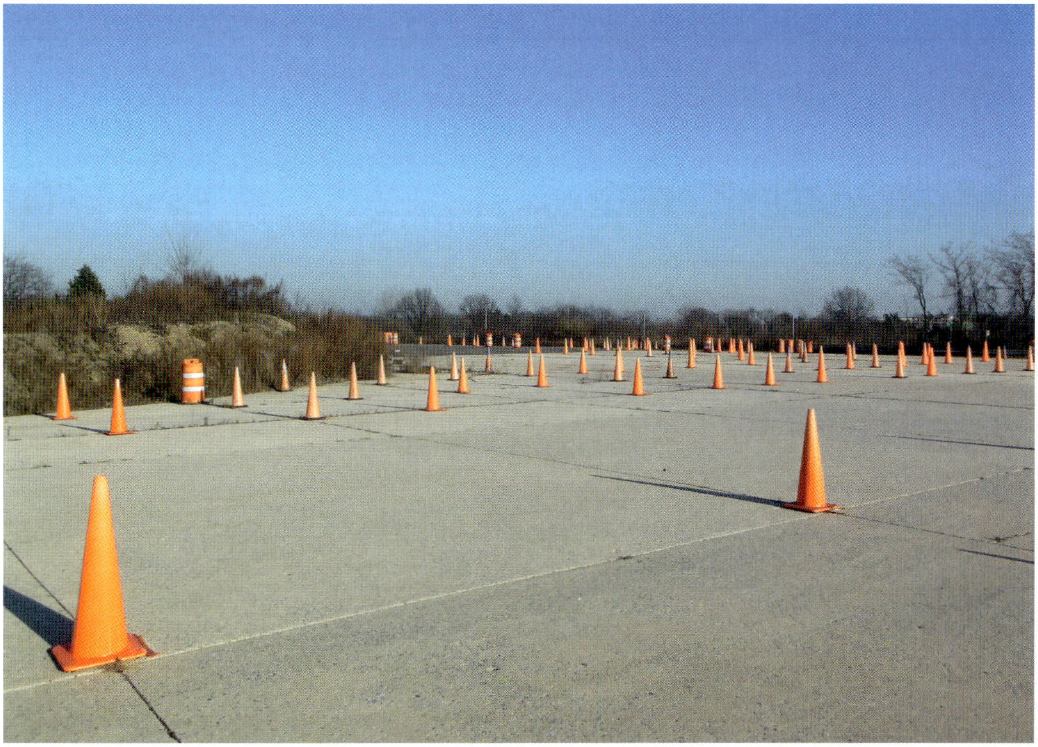

The remnants of the Mitchel Field runway were where the famous toll booth execution scene from *The Godfather* (1972) was filmed. This U-shaped section was a late addition to the Mitchel Field runway system, constructed after 1952.

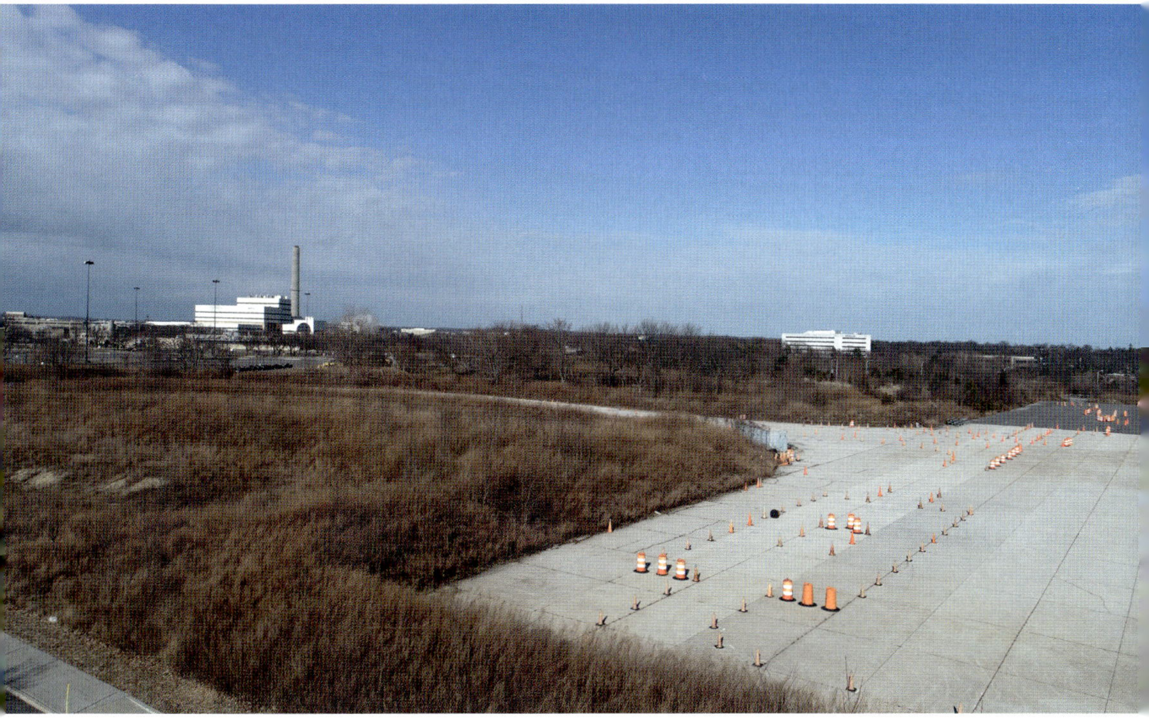

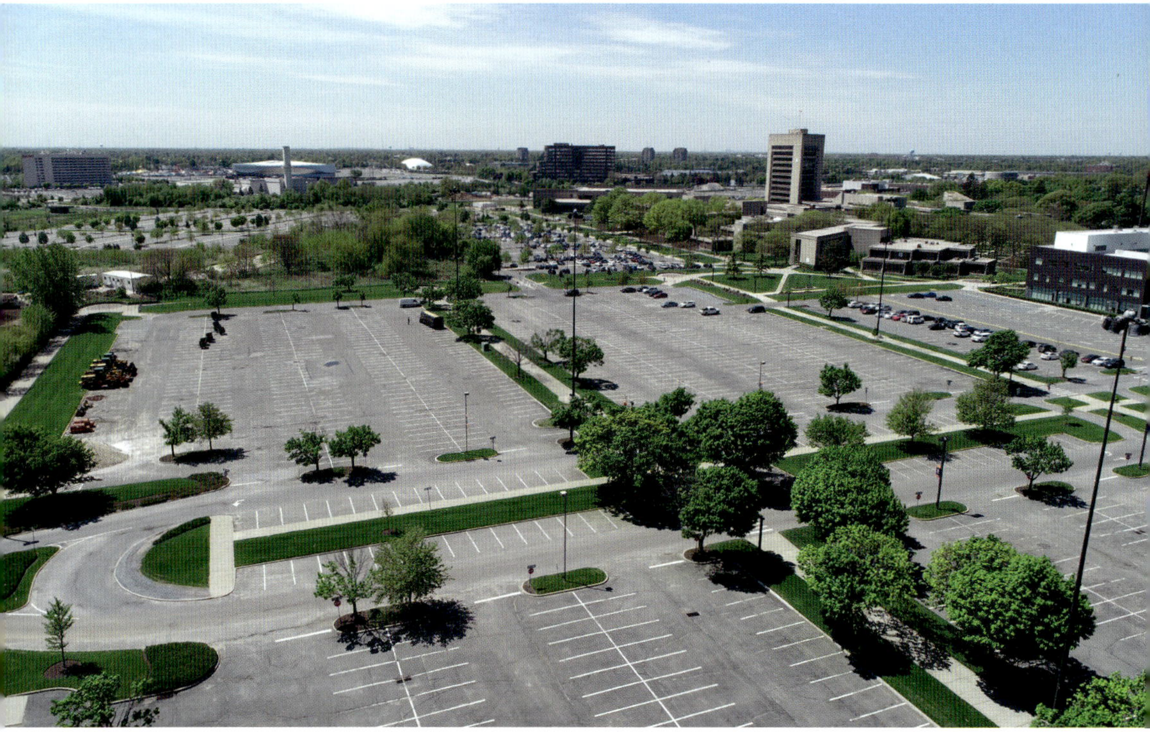

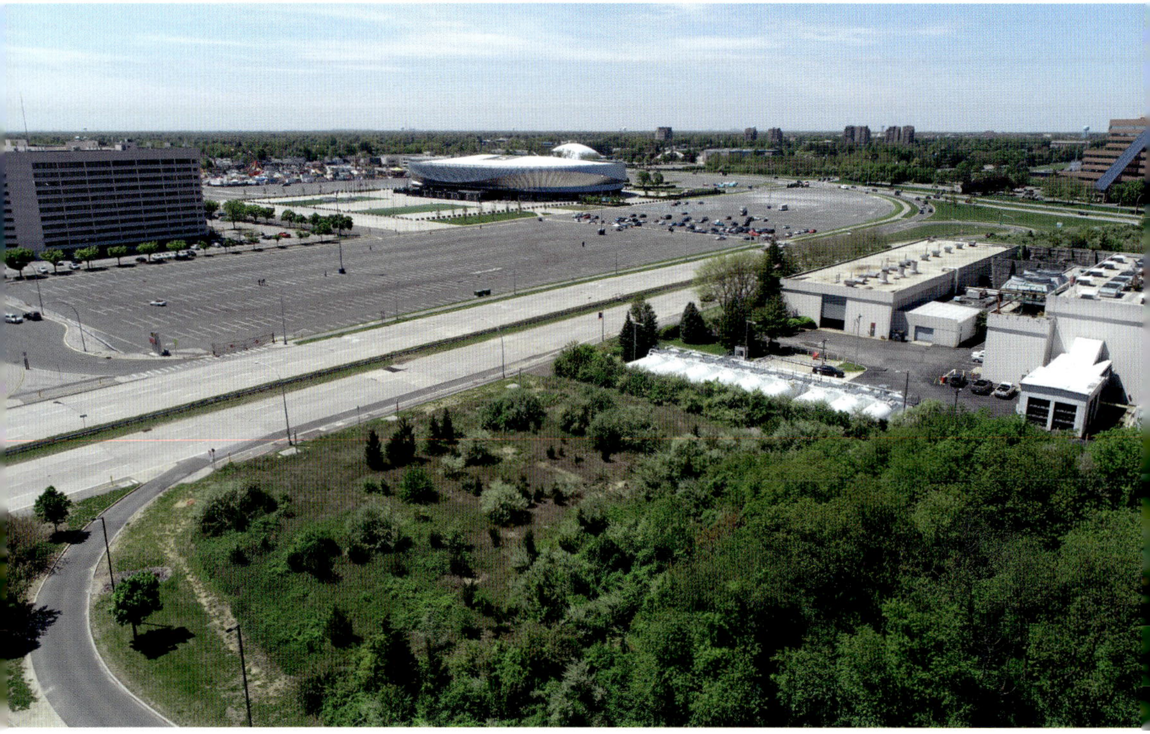

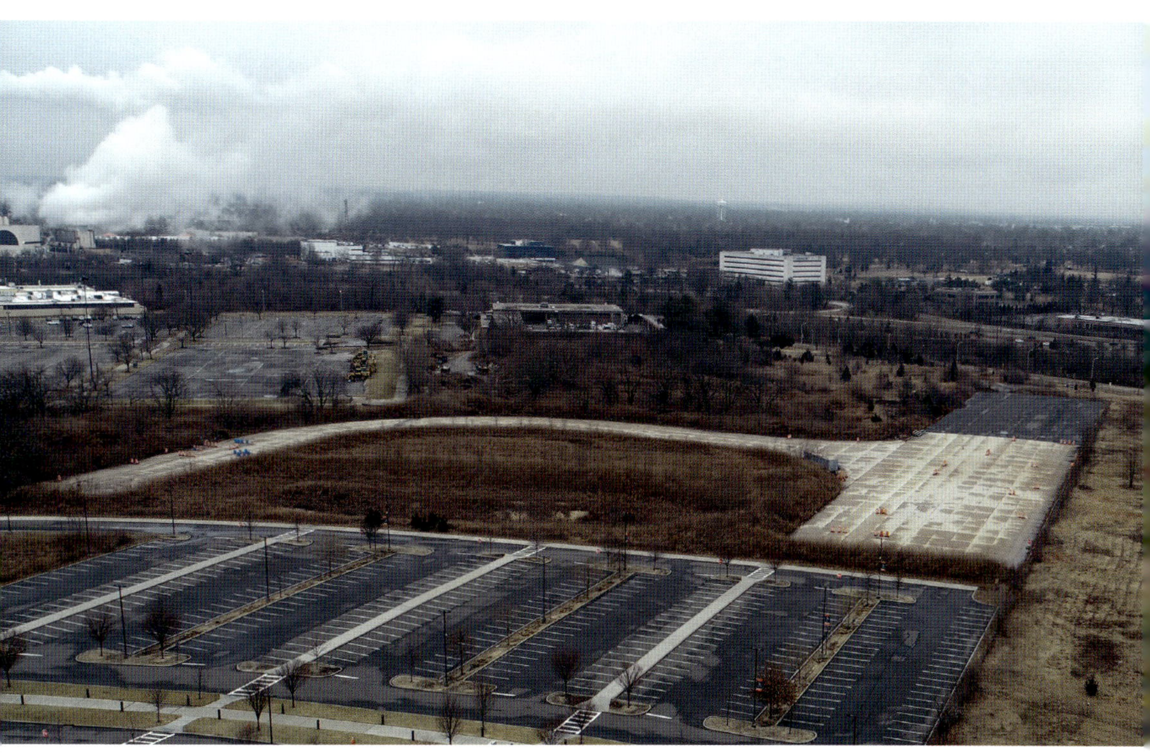

From this view it's easy to see how the NCC parking lot eliminated part of the last remaining Mitchel Field runway.

Above: The Nassau Community College parking fields which occupy much of what was once runway infrastructure at Mitchel Field.

Below: More than two-thirds of Mitchel Field (the southern portion) was occupied by runways and the grassy areas between the runways, and is now in part Nassau Coliseum and the Marriott and their parking lots.

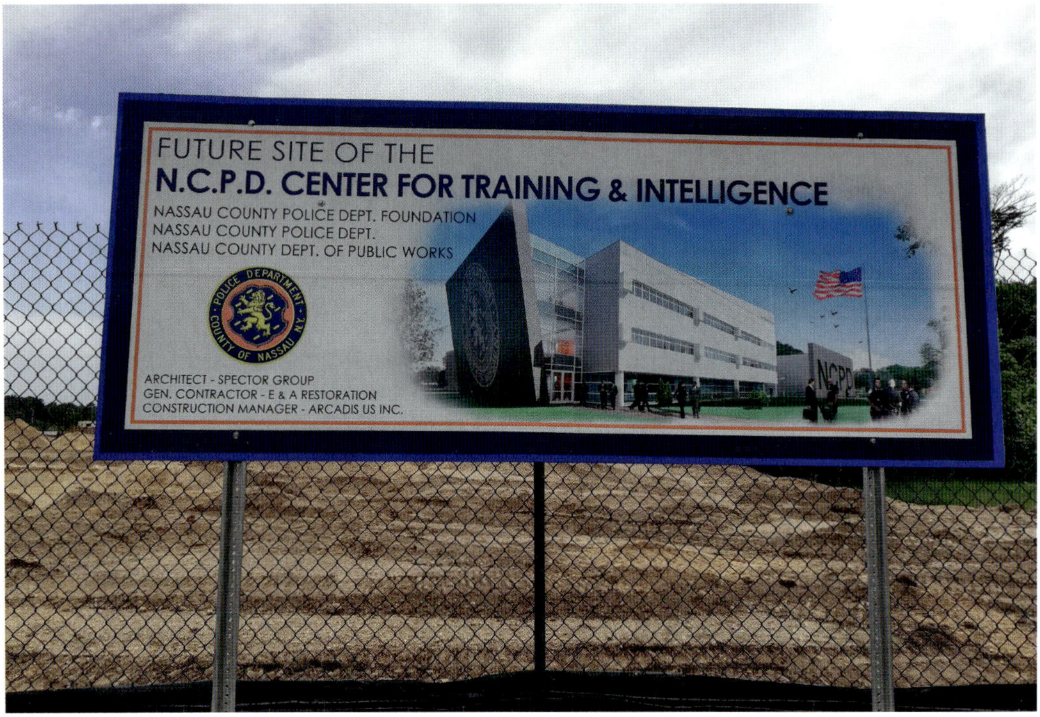

Construction on and near the Mitchel Field runway remnant in 2019 for what was to be the Nassau County Police Department Center for Training and Intelligence.

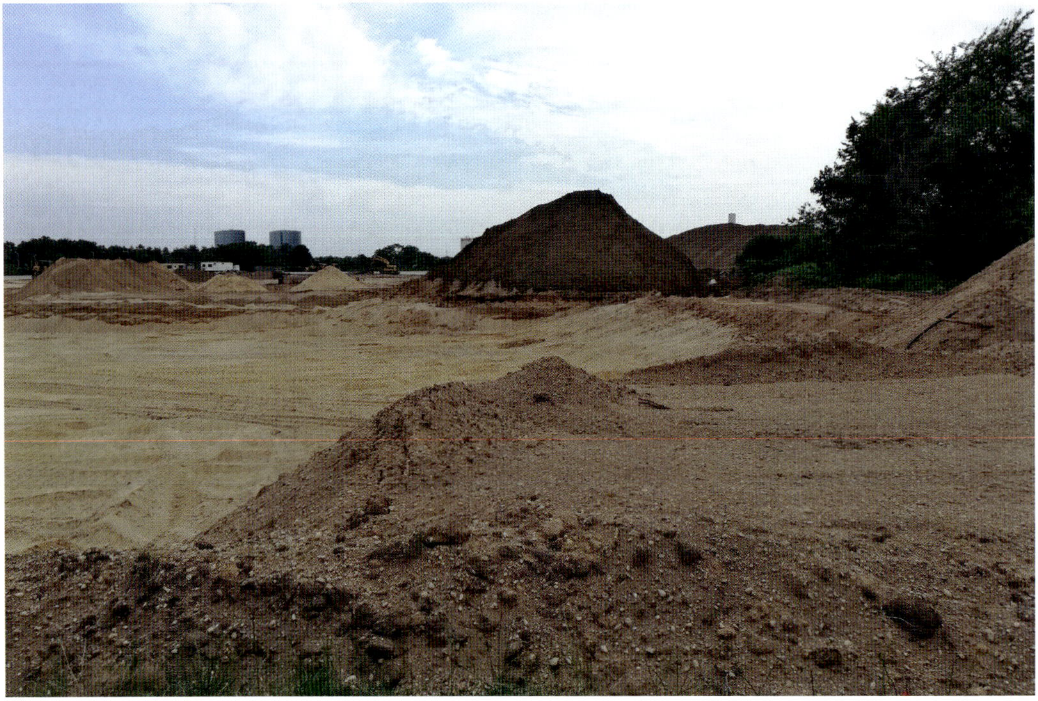

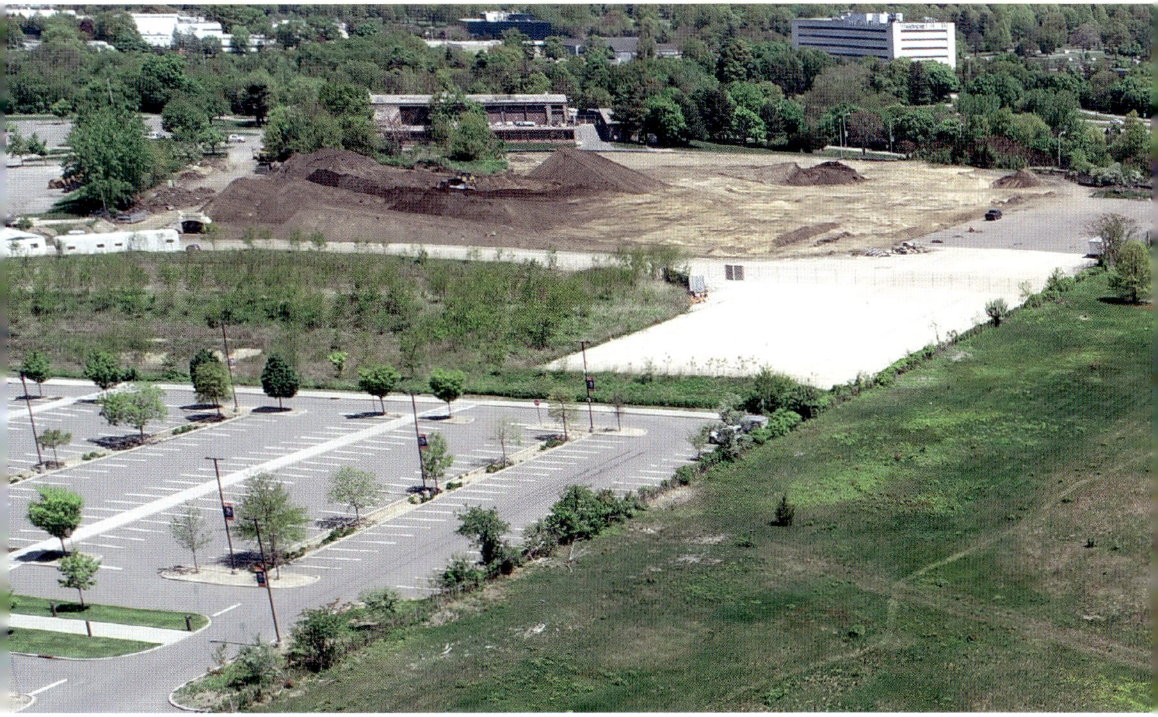

This aerial view shows the construction impinging on what's left of the Mitchel Field runway.

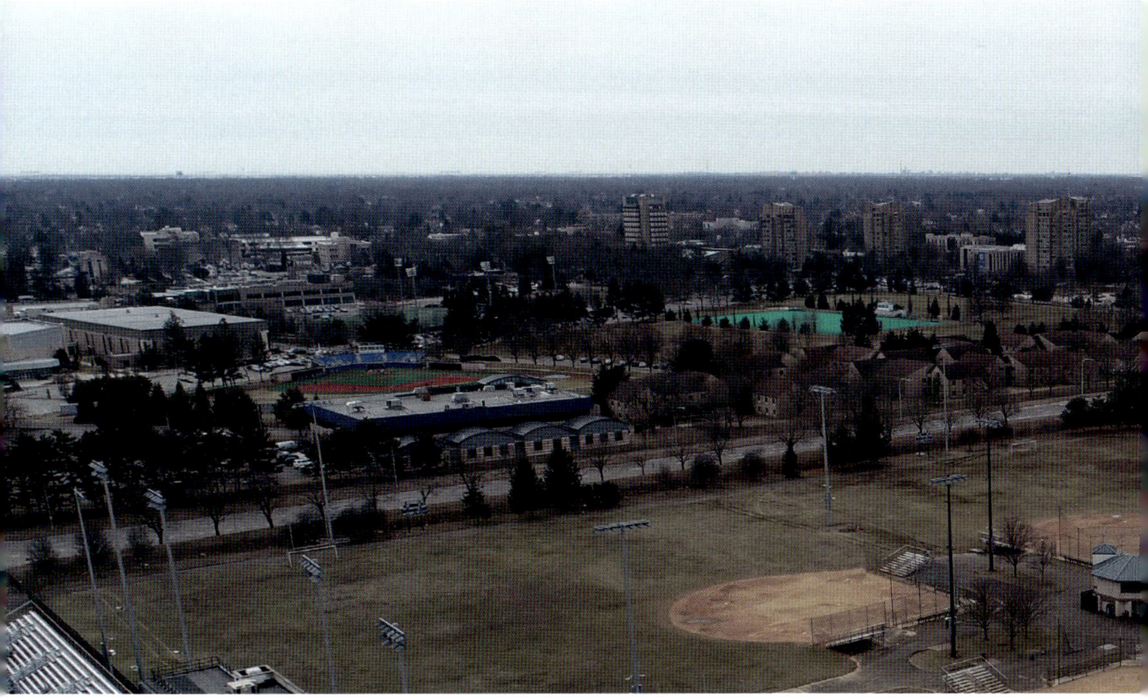

One of Hofstra University's parking lots follows the alignment of the intact runway remnant at the northeast corner of Mitchel Field.

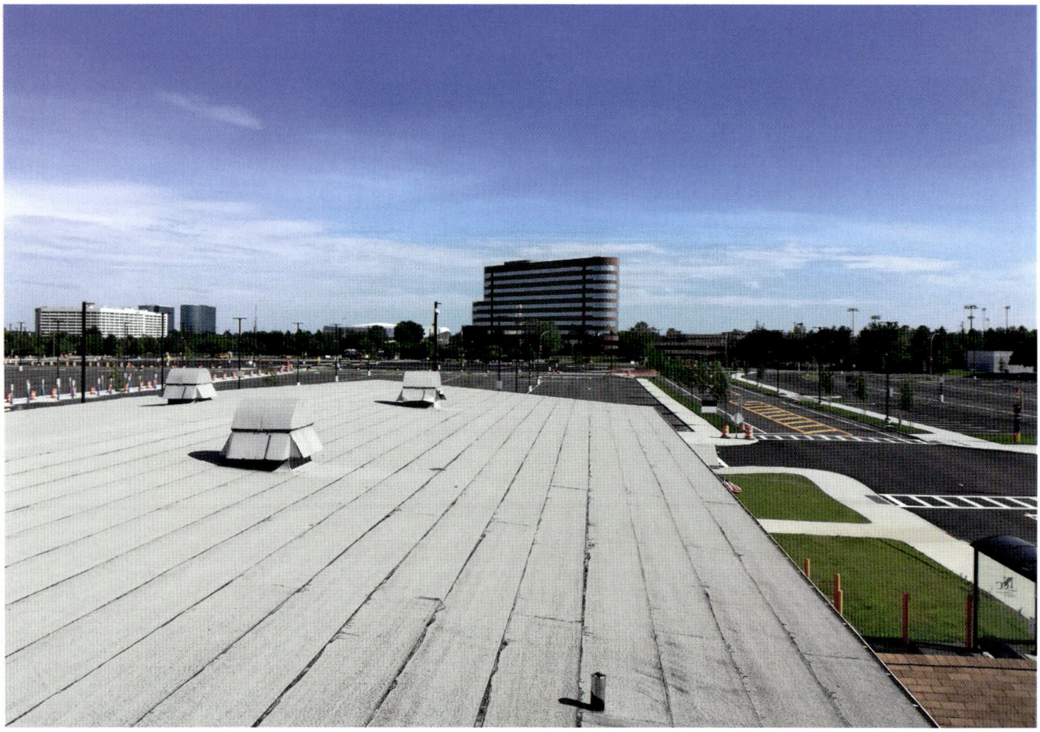

Looking out from the former Operations Building at Mitchel Field (now used by Nassau Community College), toward parking lots that used to be runways.

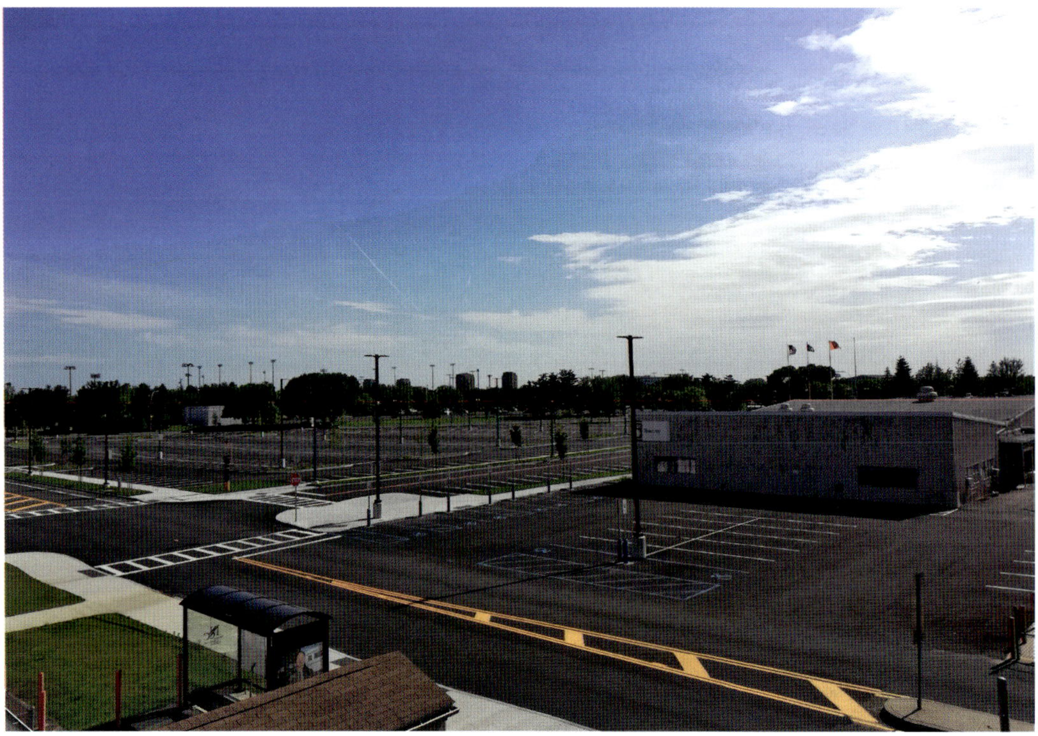

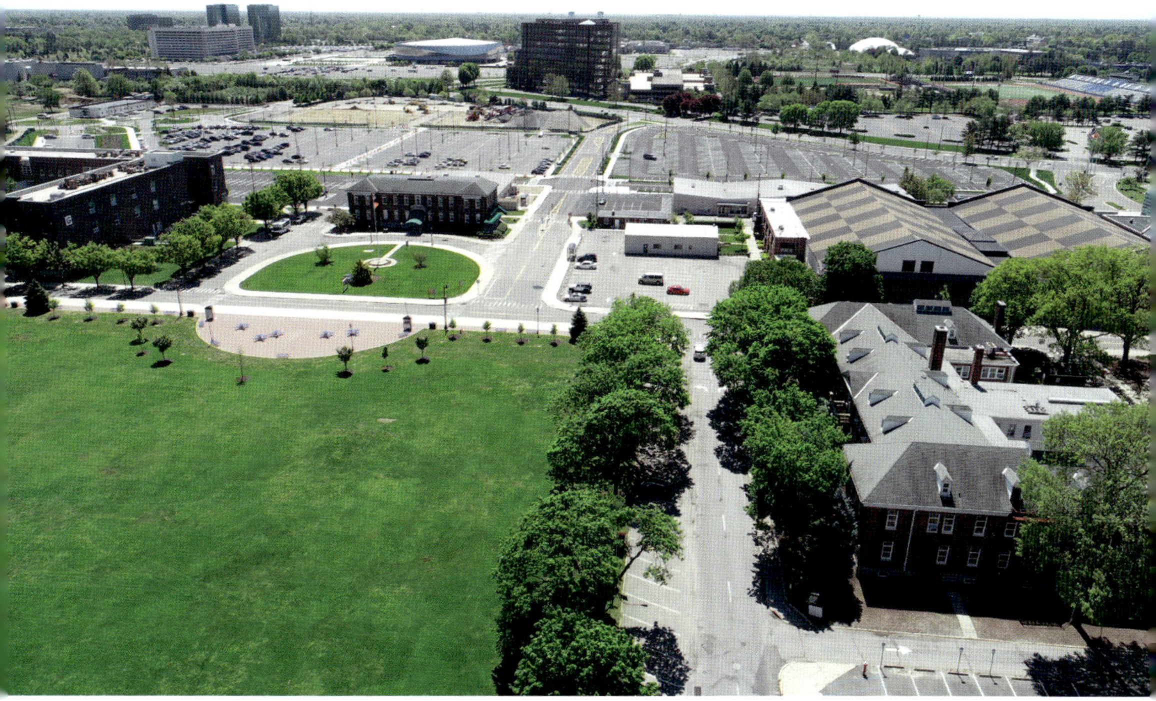

The largest single intact feature of Mitchel Field is the parade ground, a rectangular shaped plot of grass bordered with trees. The former parade ground has been nicely incorporated into the NCC campus and makes for a pleasant place to enjoy the fresh air.

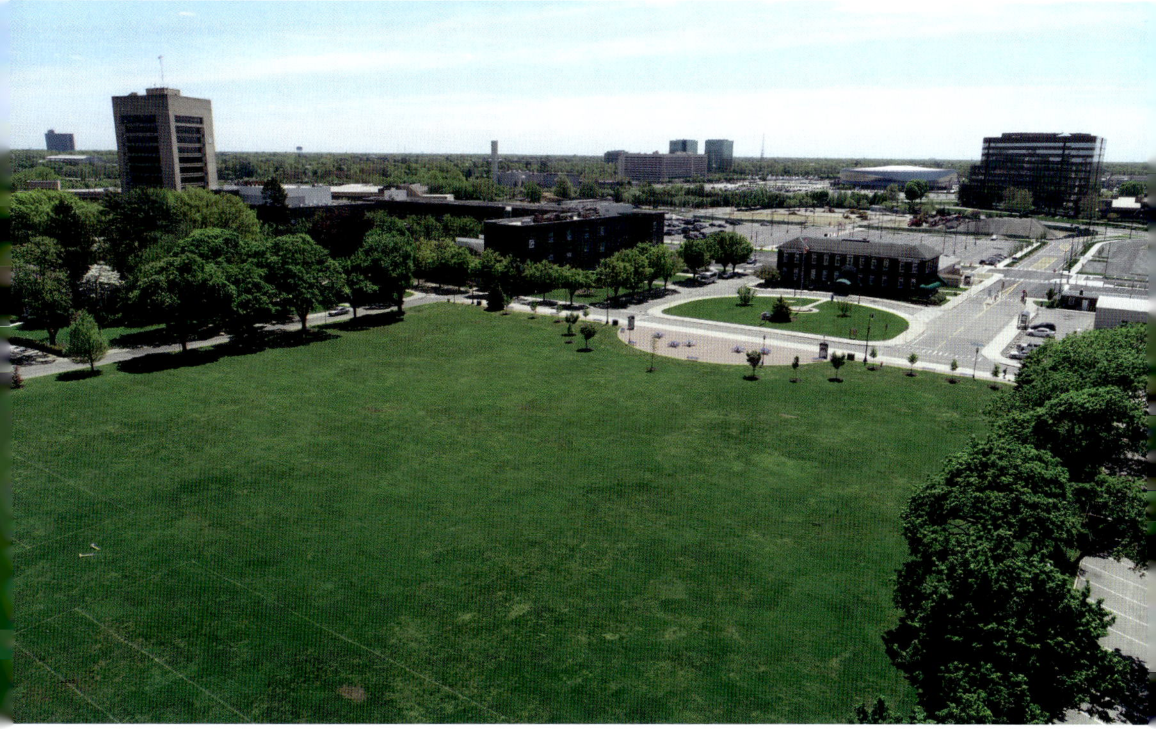

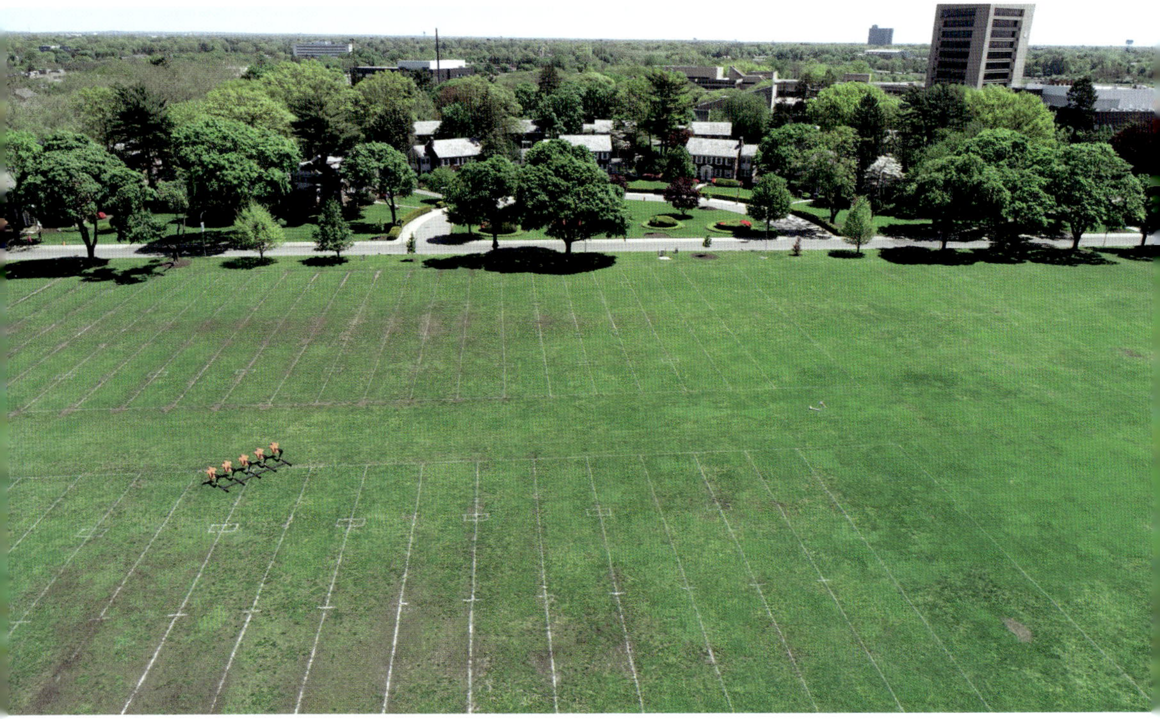

Looking east-southeast from the parade ground toward the newer part of the NCC campus.

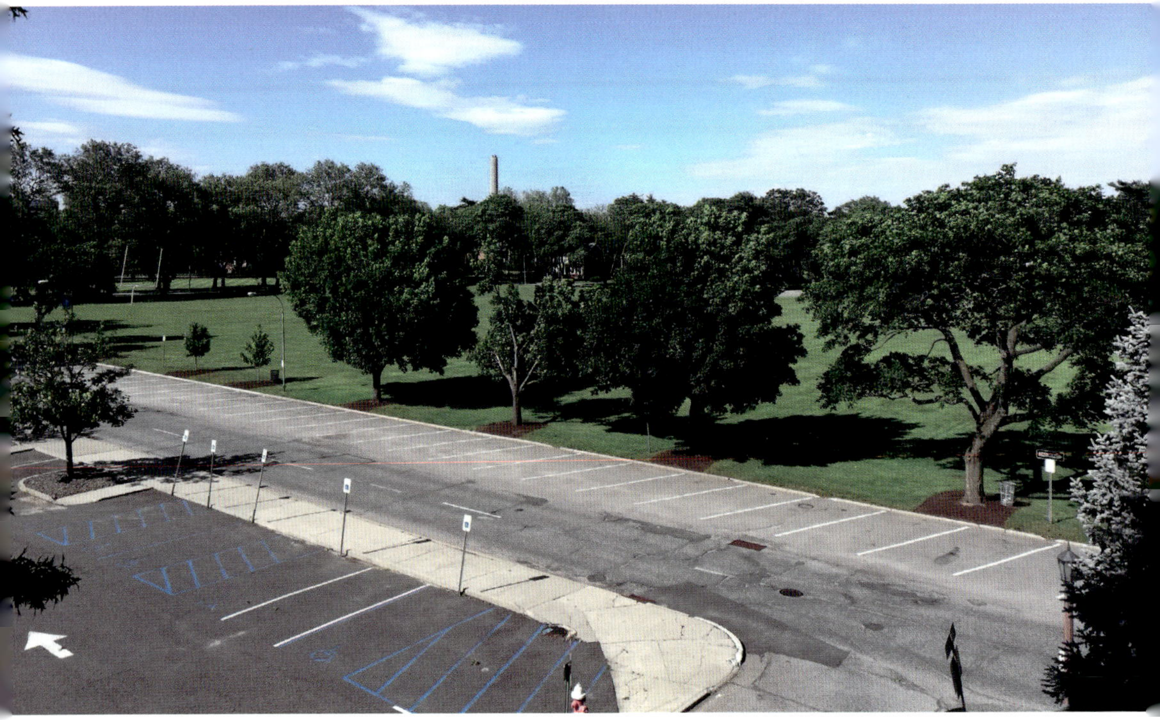

Looking toward the parade ground from one of the former Mitchel Field Buildings. This housing offered pretty views then and now.

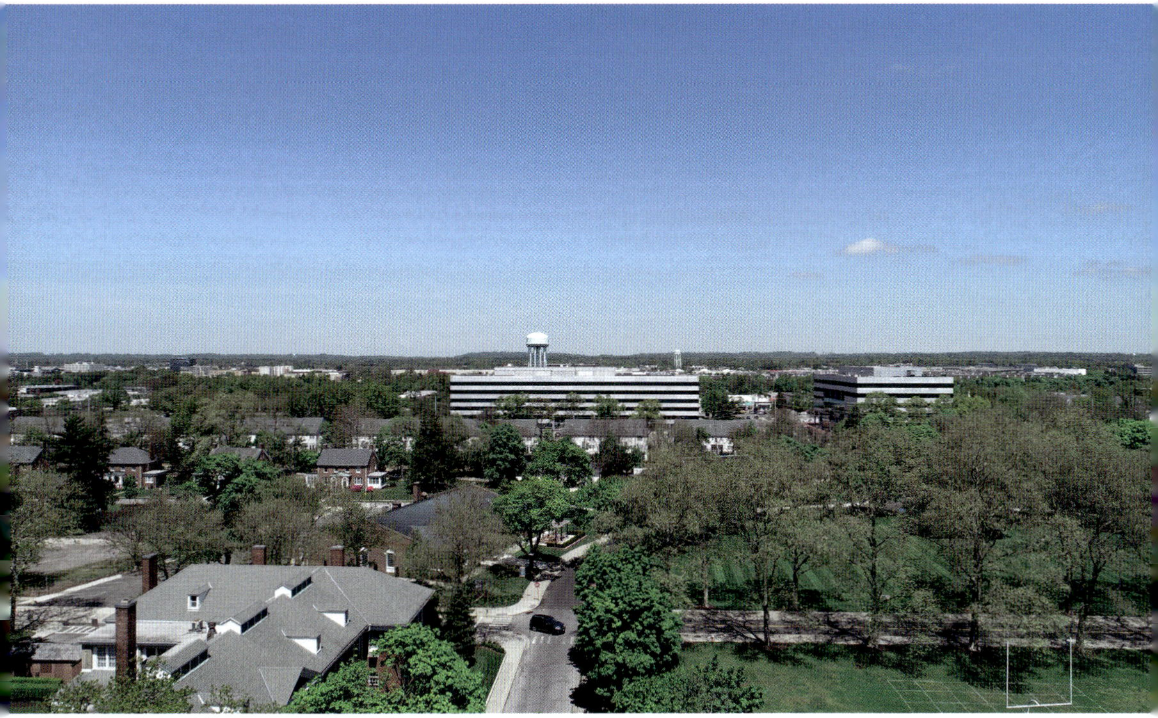

Looking east from the parade ground to where the Meadow Brook club stood until the 1950s.

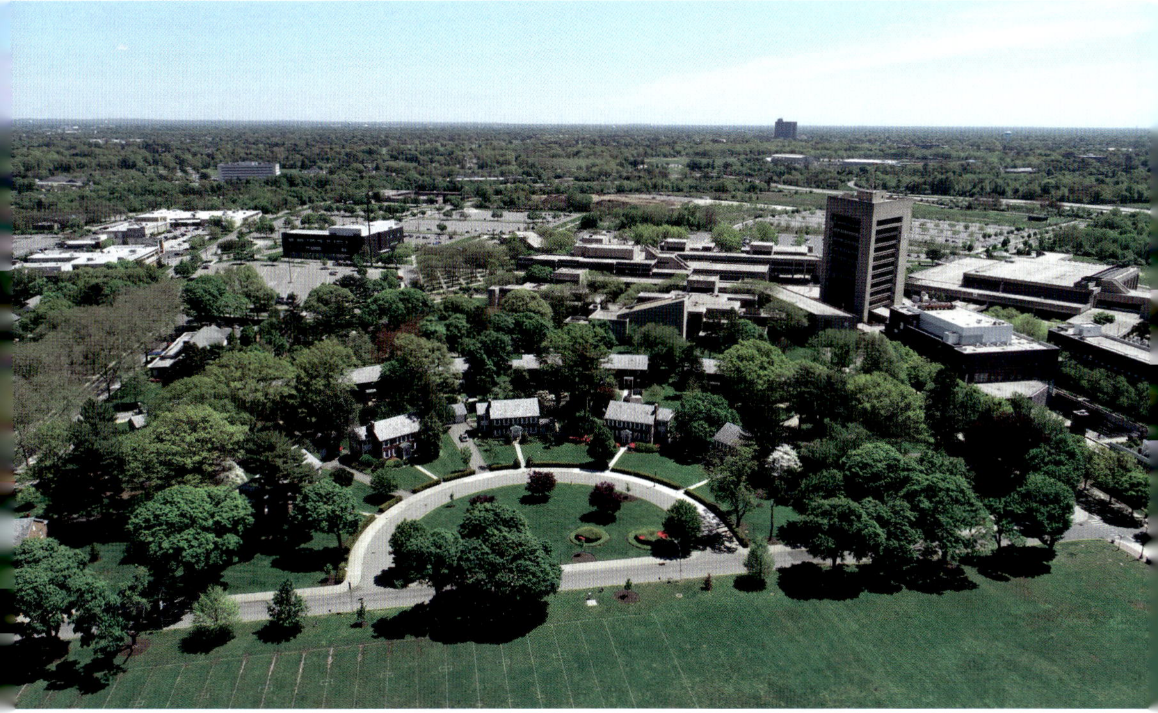

The well-preserved officers' homes along the semi-circle that caps the northern end of the parade ground, with their manicured gardens, are like a time capsule to the days when Mitchel Field was an active air base.

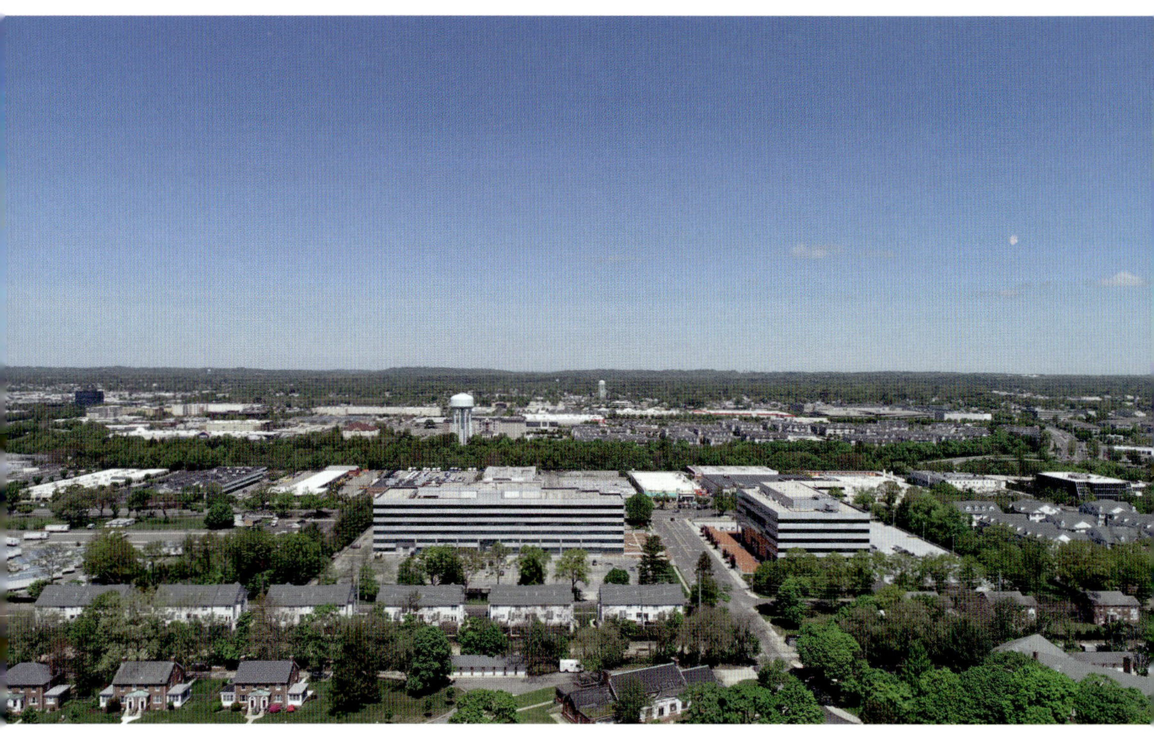

Looking north from the Mitchel Field parade ground at Stewart Avenue. The abandoned Central Branch of the LIRR tracks run south of and parallel to Stewart Avenue. The Long Island Motor Parkway used to parallel Stewart to its north.

At the eastern end of the former Mitchel Field is the modern section of the Nassau Community College campus. The college has been using the former Mitchel Field as its campus since 1962. It is currently fifty buildings on 225 acres.

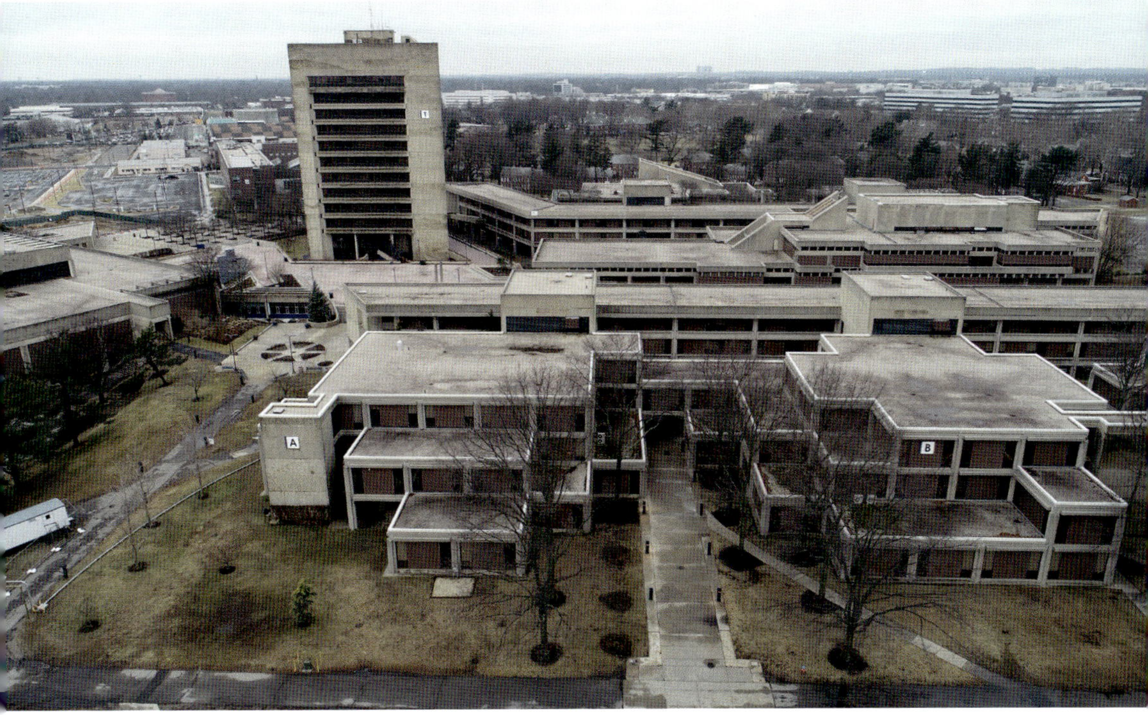

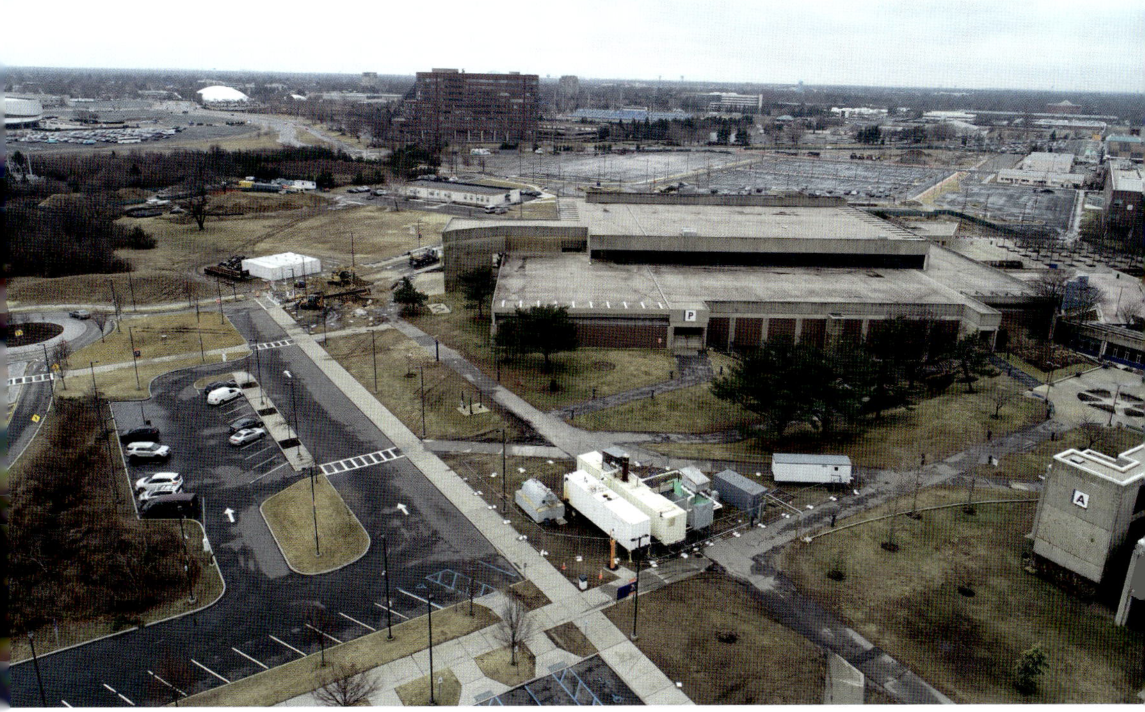

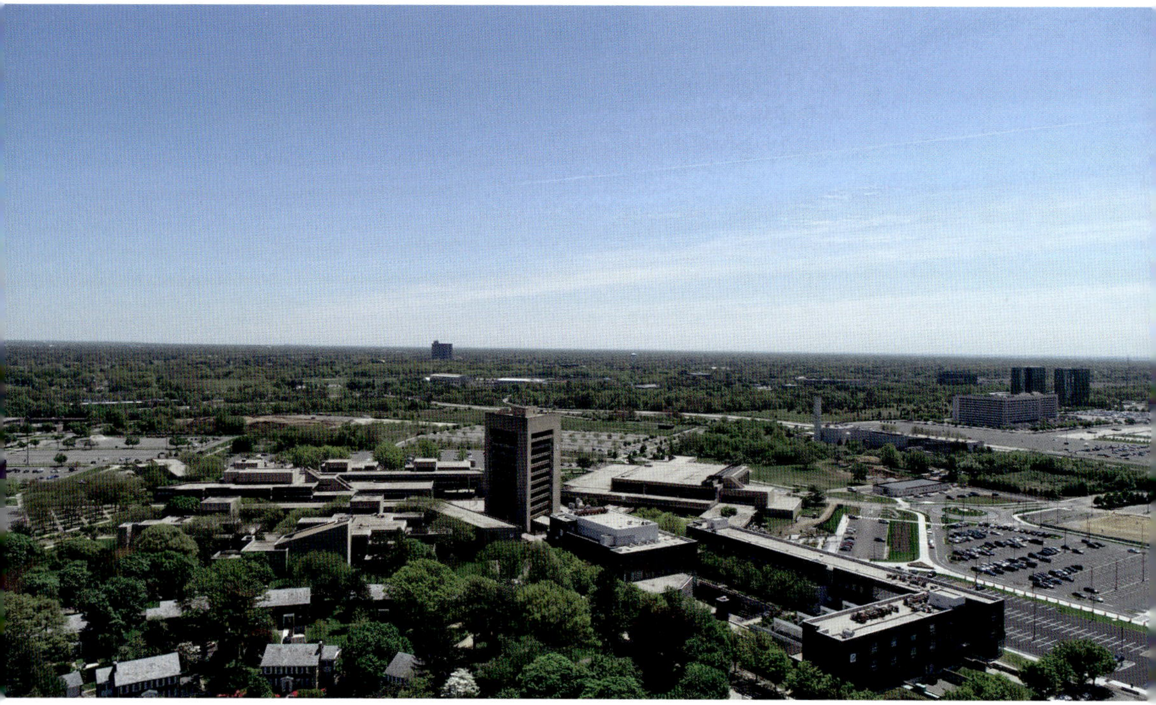

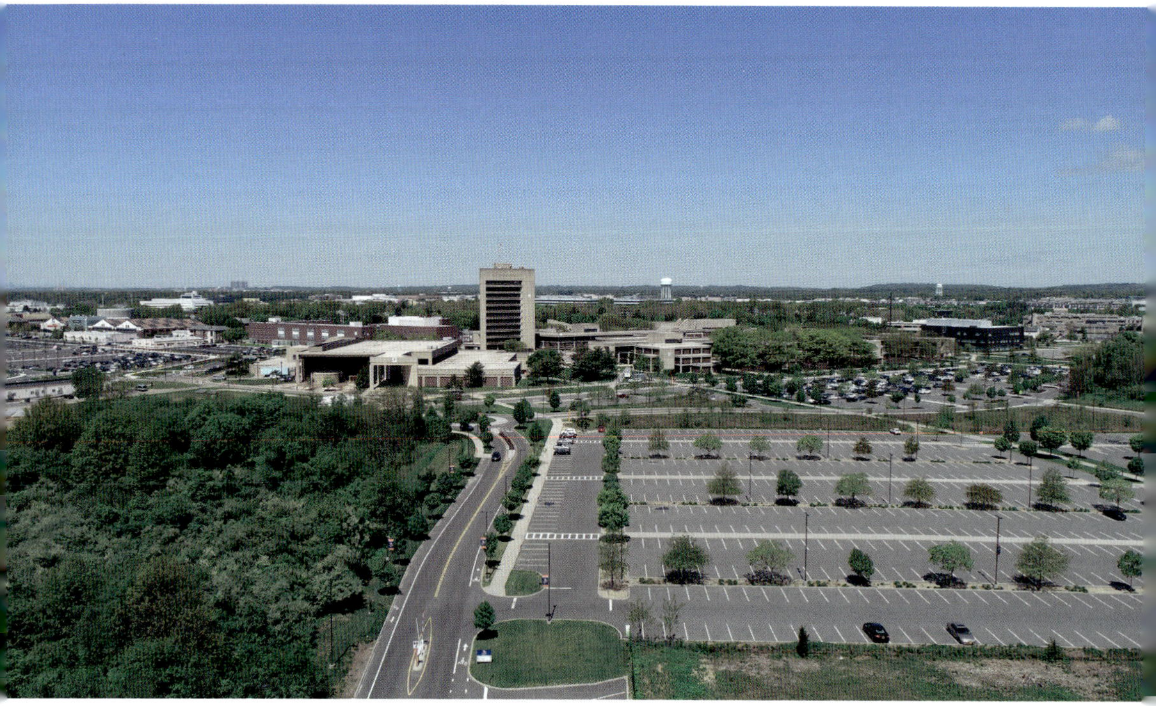

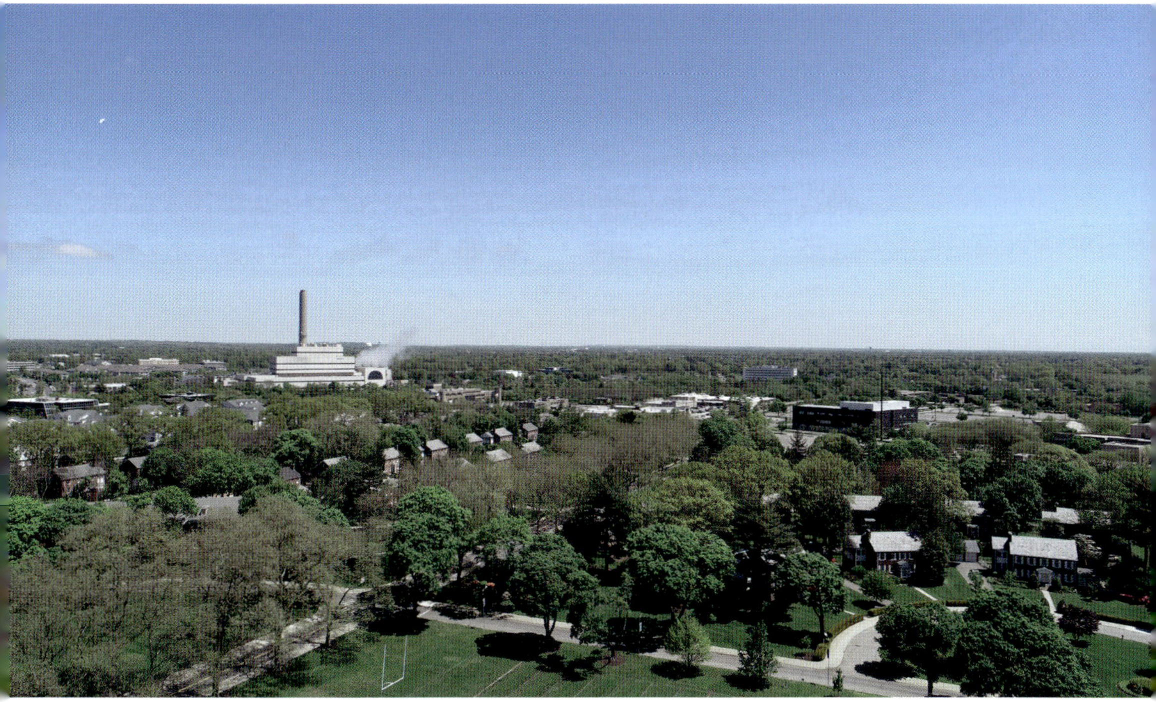

The eastern part of the NCC campus is located adjacent to what was once the property of the Meadow Brook Hunt Club and polo fields. The polo field property began mere feet away from the officers' homes.

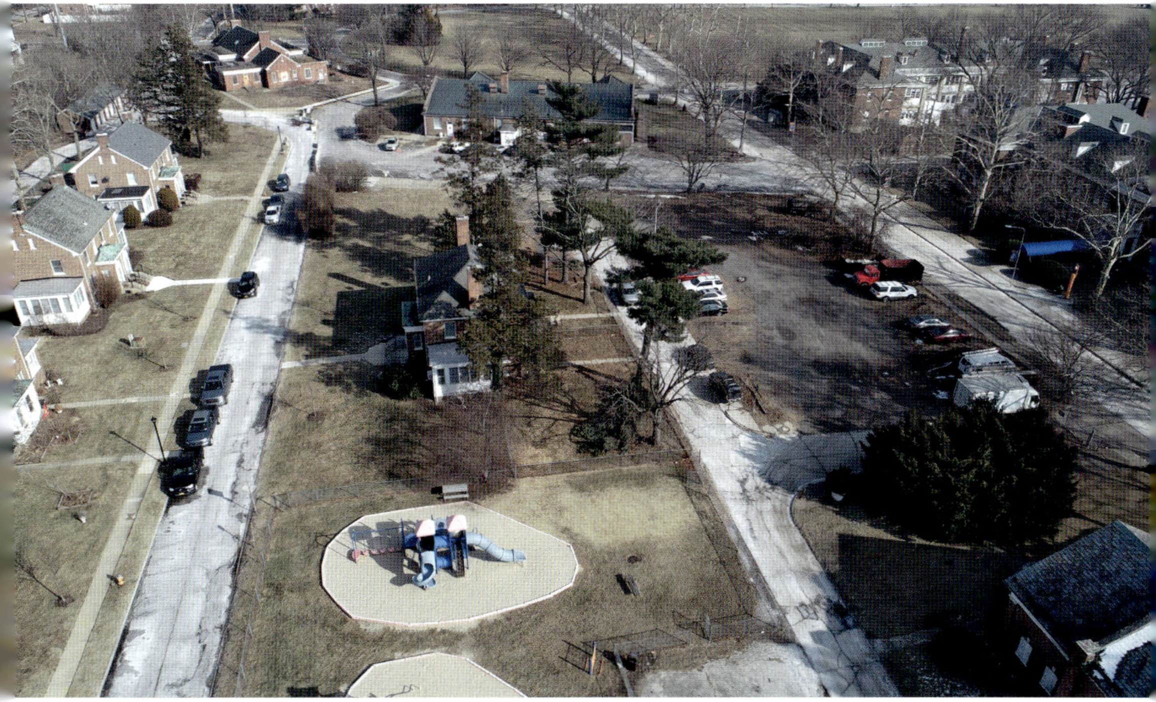

The NCC campus retains much of the original roadway infrastructure of the Mitchel Field base. Many of the streets are one way or dead end.

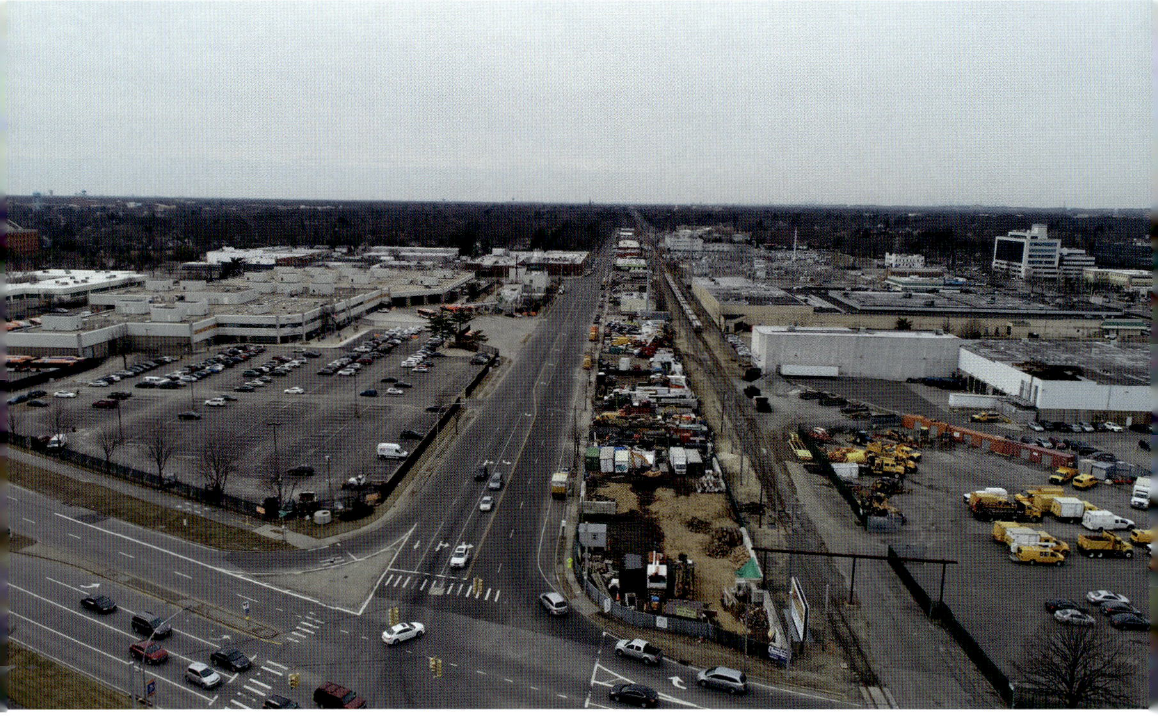

Looking west at the tracks of the defunct Central Branch of the LIRR (parallel to Commercial Avenue), a line that used to supply Mitchel Field and bring passengers to the Meadow Brook Polo Field.

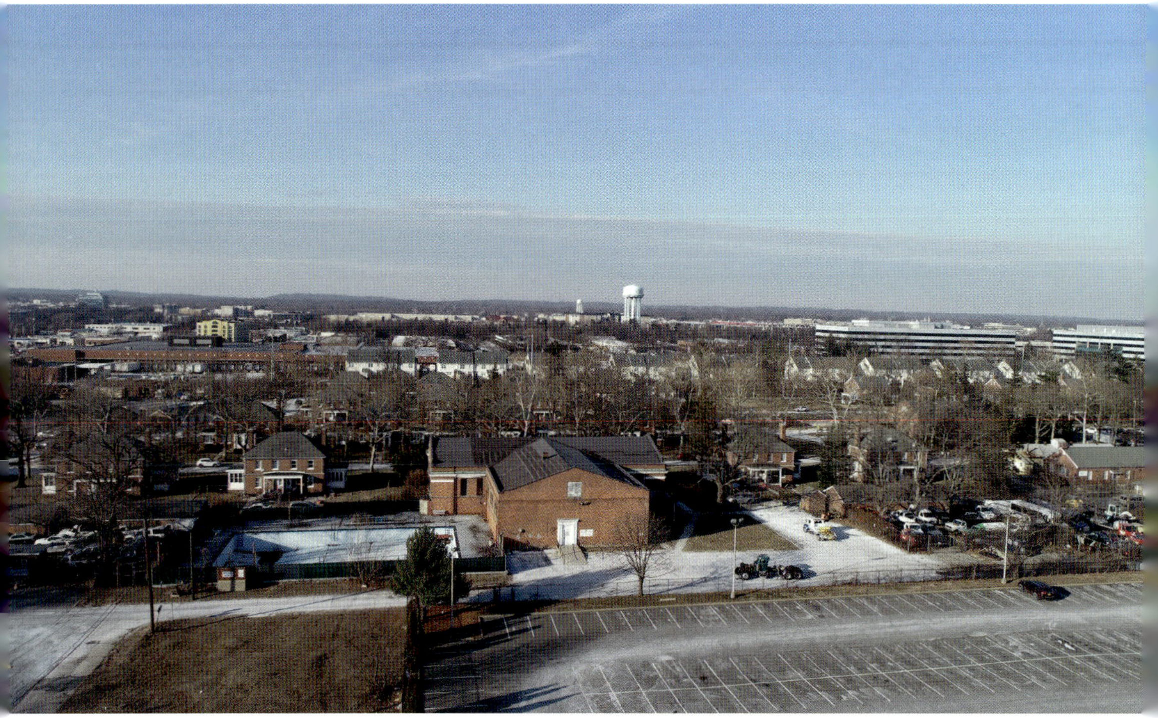

The Mitchel Field Gymnasium building (at center) still stands and retains its original purpose.

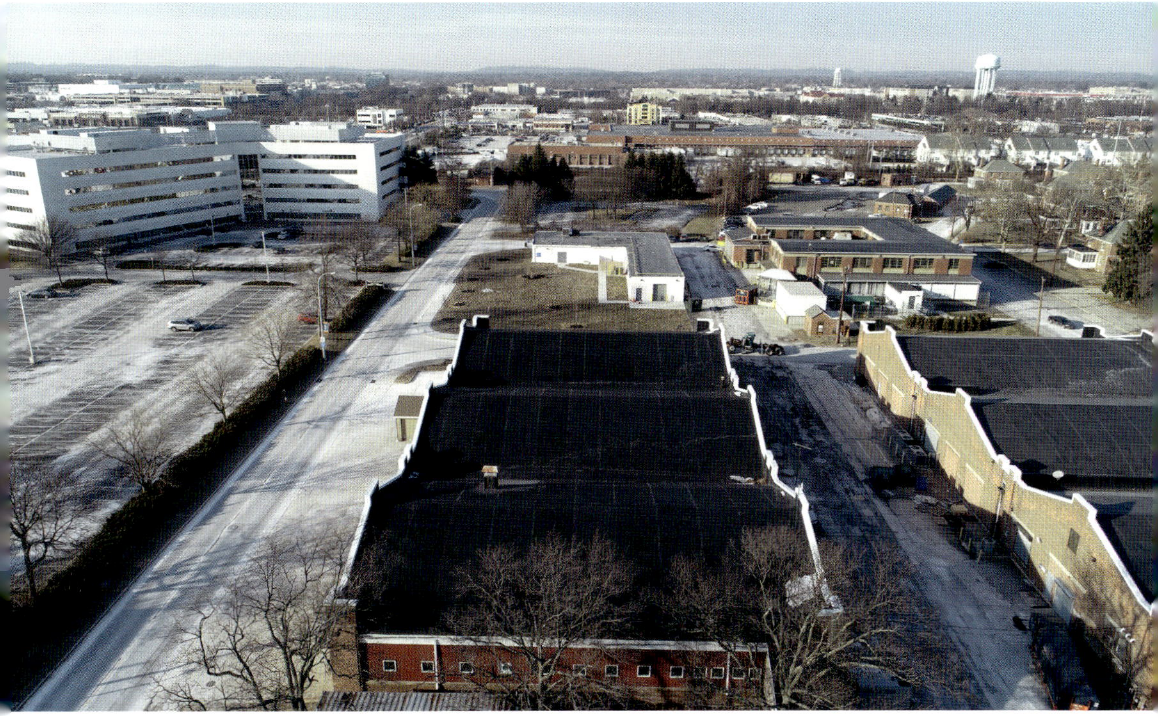

Vintage Mitchel Field warehouses are still in use today. They line an alley that has the remnants of train tracks down the center; back in the day this rail spur off the Central Branch was used to deliver goods to Mitchel Field.

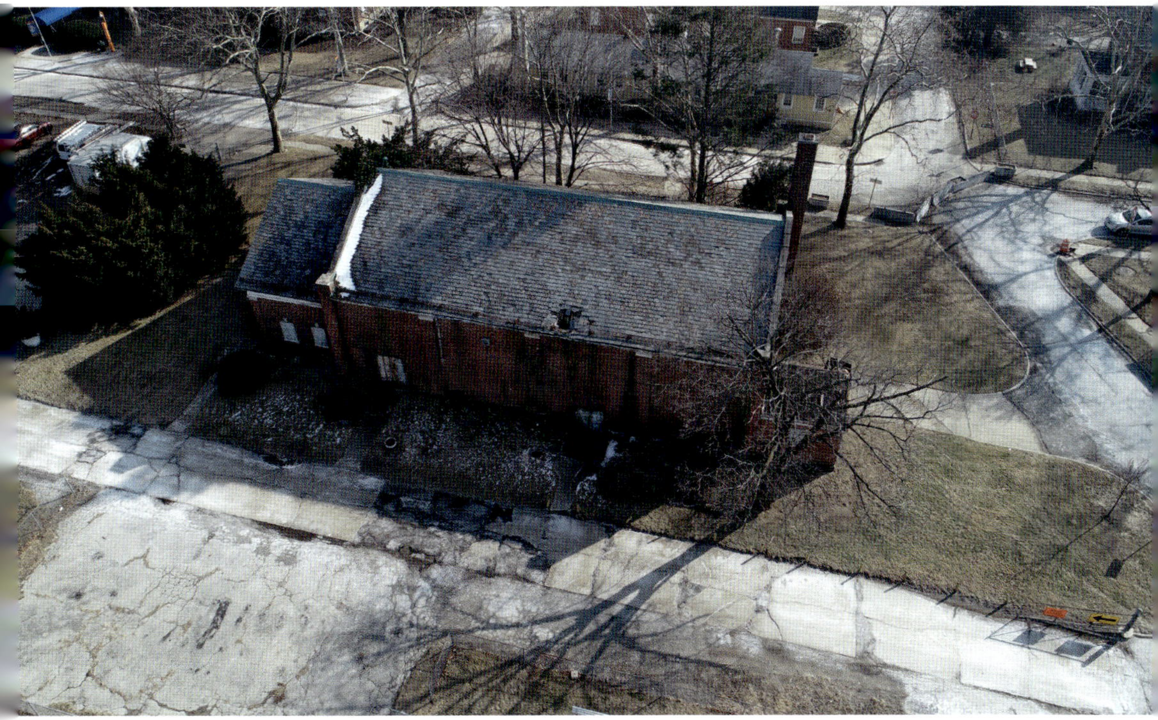

The old Mitchel Field theater dates to the 1930s, and was abandoned *circa* the 1970s or 80s.

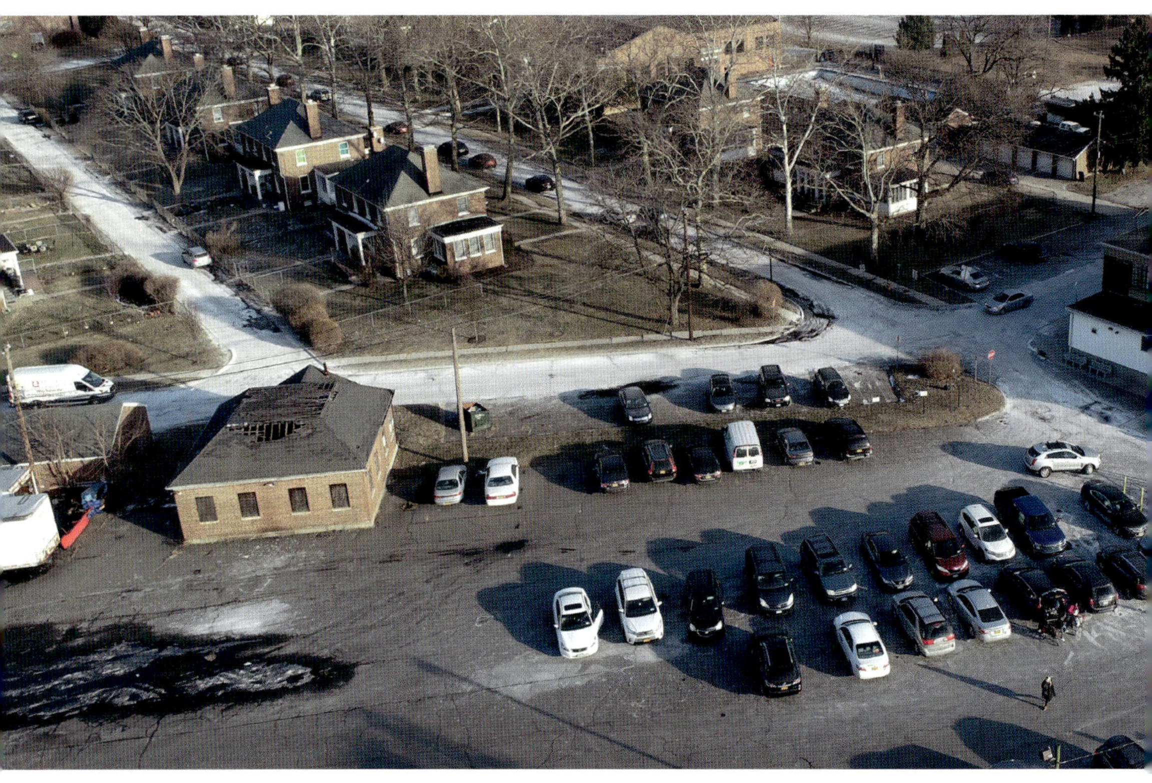

The abandoned former Mitchel Field radio station, later used by the Navy Exchange.

OPPOSITE PAGE:

An abandoned building at the furthest western reaches of Mitchel Field, and below, three other small abandoned buildings just east of that building. These buildings were likely service and repair shops.

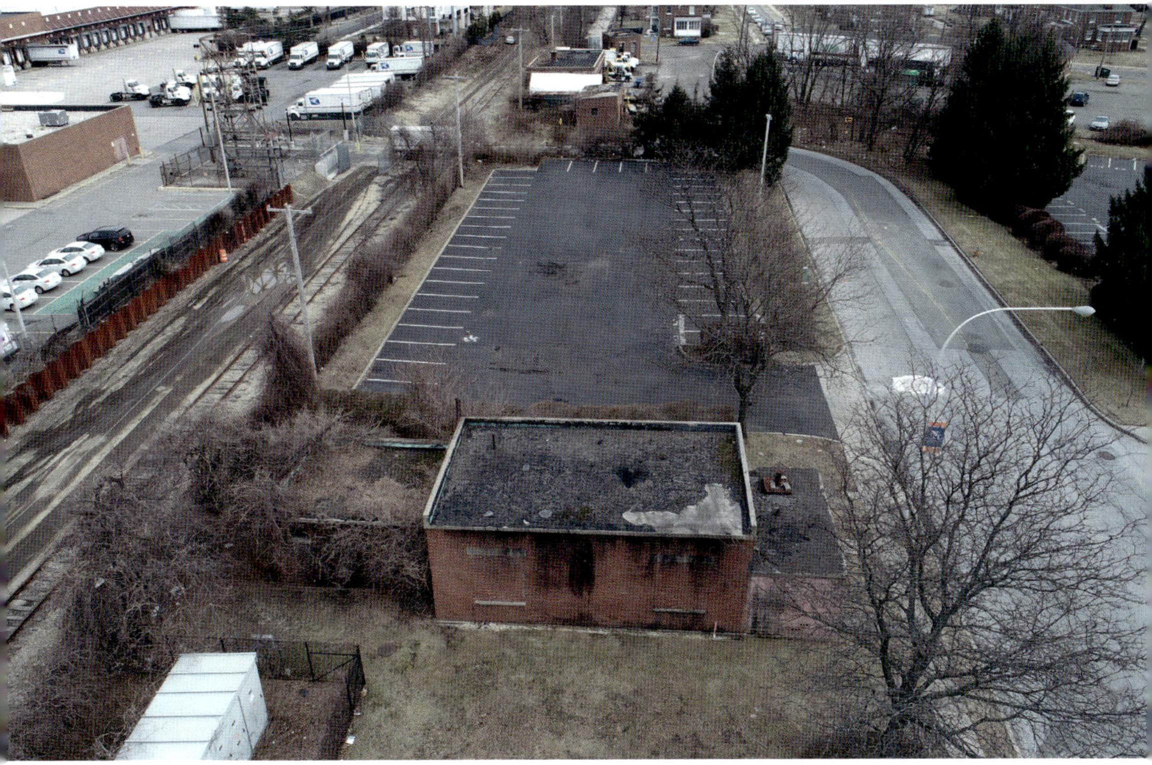

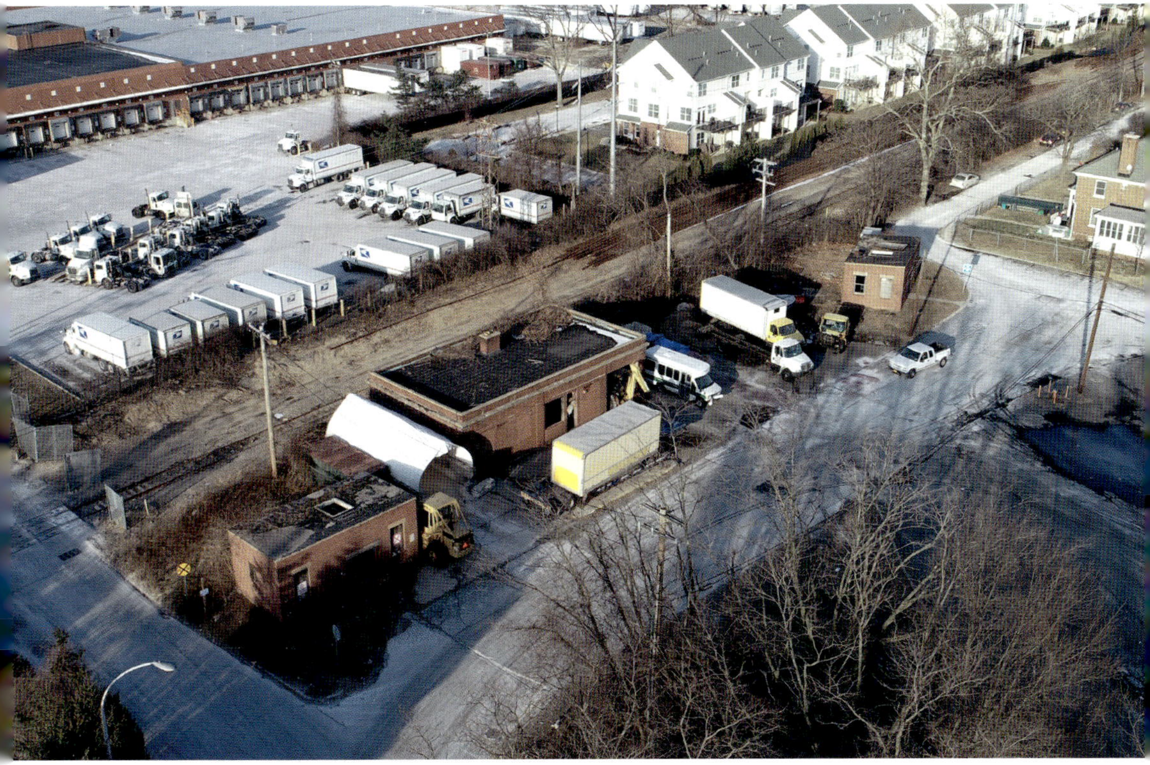

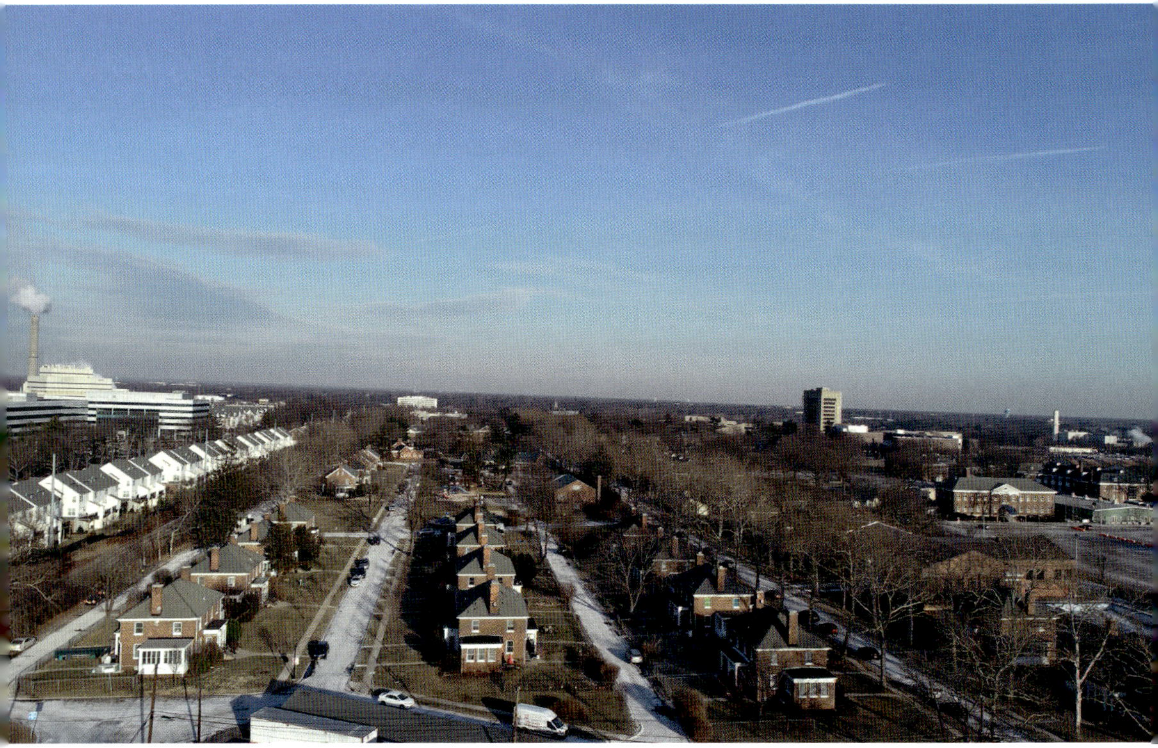

Elegant vintage brick homes that used to house military officers still line Wheeler Avenue, 5th Street, and Miller Avenue. These streets look virtually the same as they did in the 1940s.

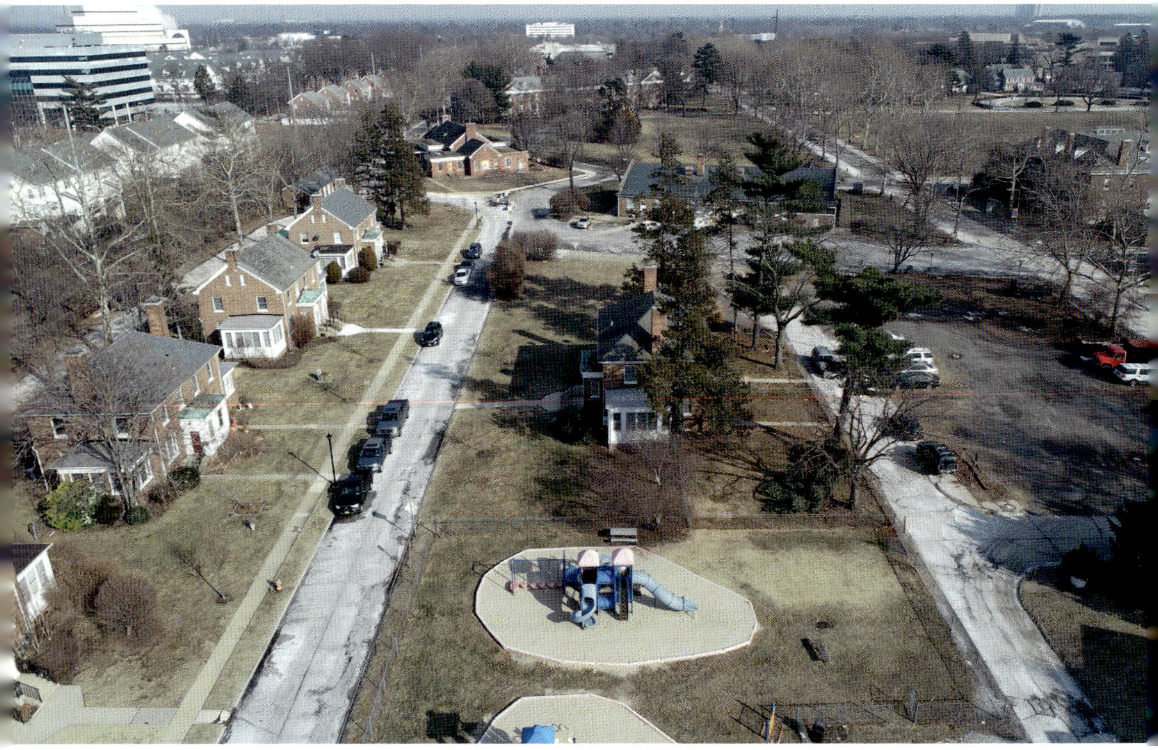

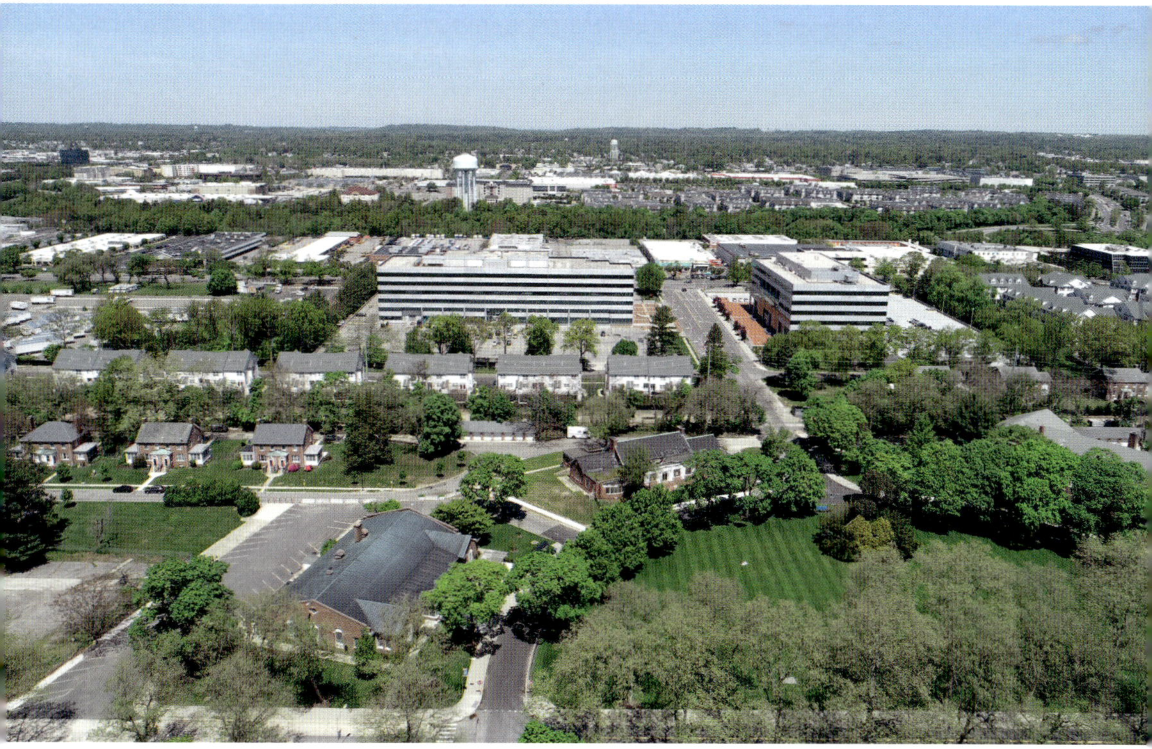

New housing built by Avalon Bay lines Ellington Avenue (north of the railroad tracks) opened in 2012 and replaced some of the old Mitchel Field officers' housing.

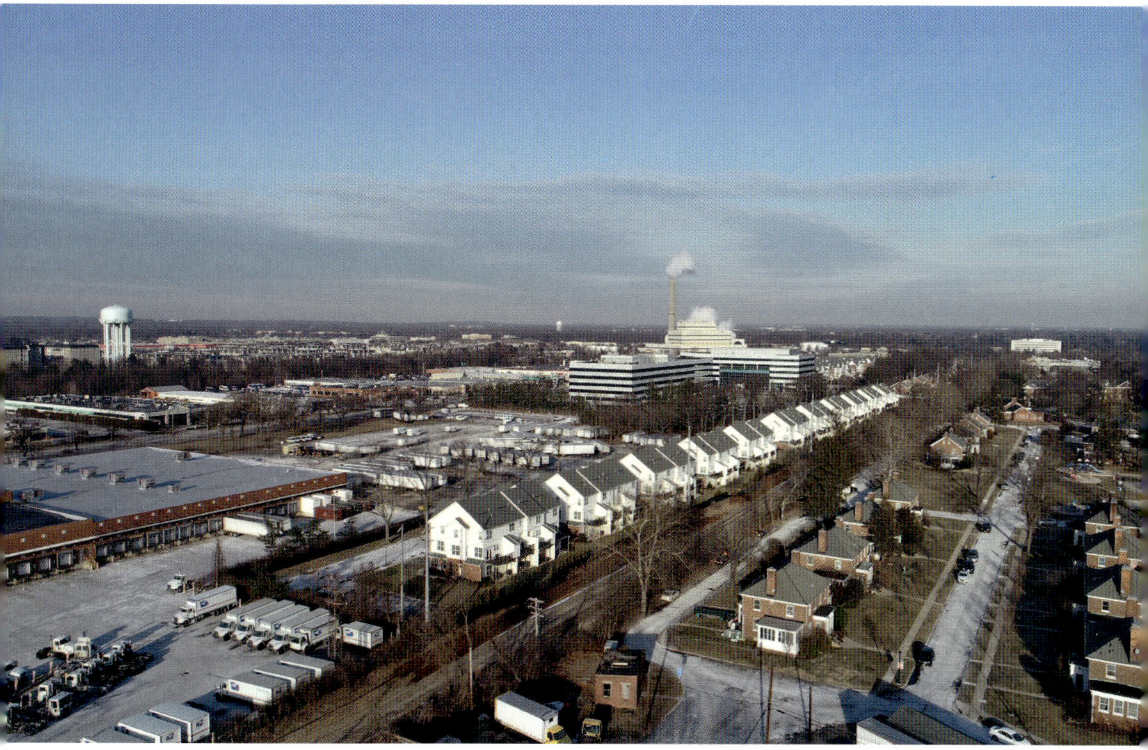

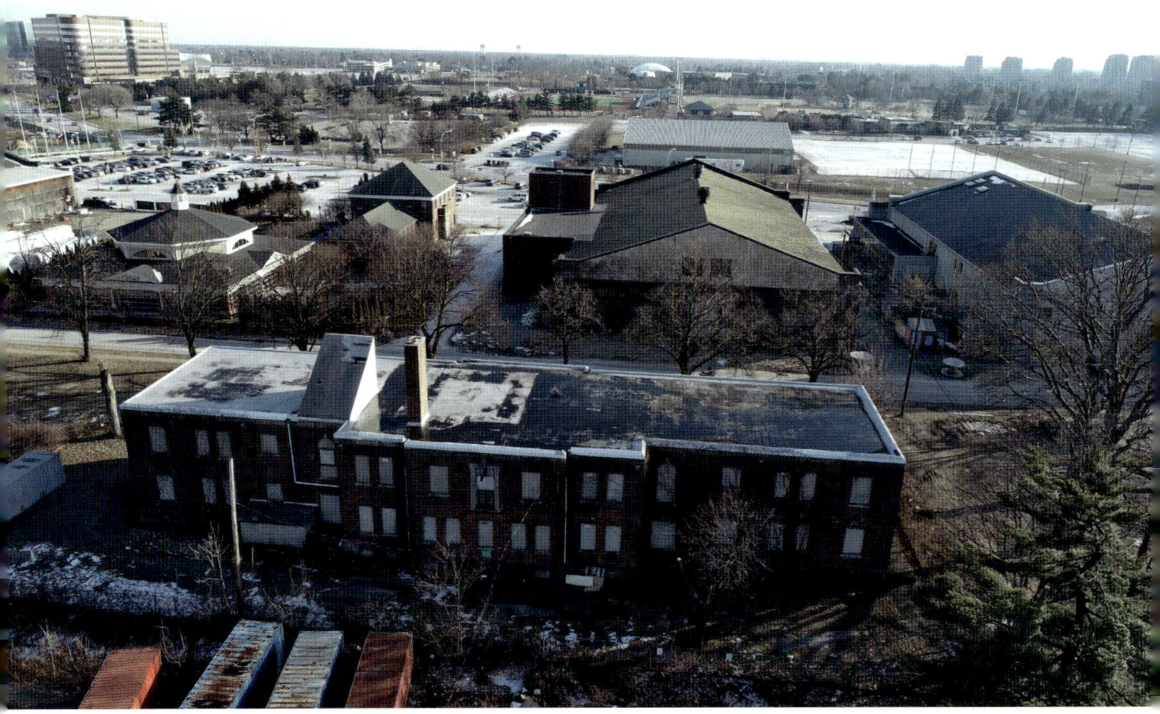

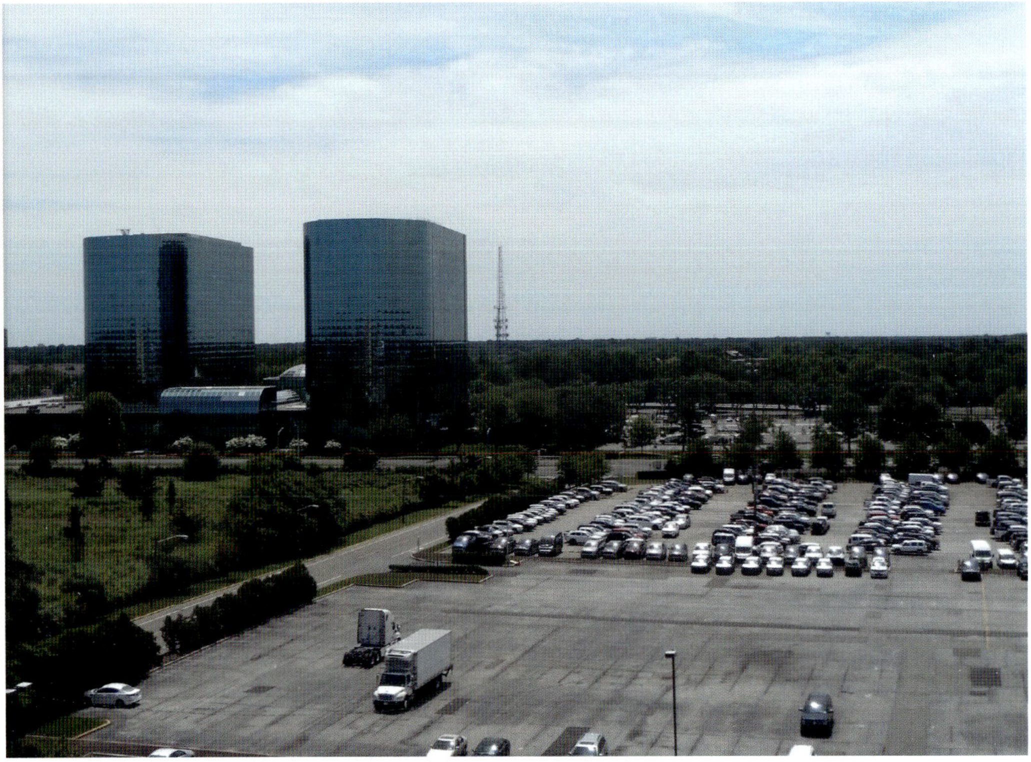

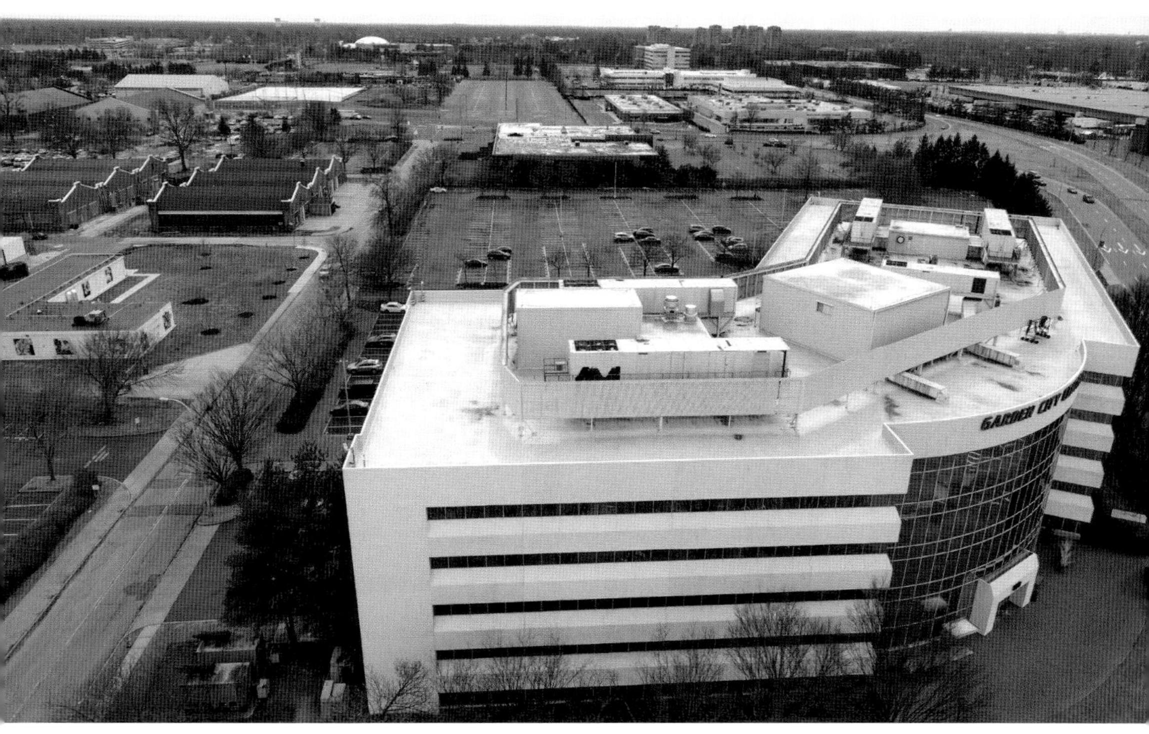

Another office building, at the southeast corner of Commercial Avenue and Quentin Roosevelt Boulevard.

OPPOSITE PAGE:

Above: The former NCO (Non-Commissioned Officers) building sits abandoned just behind the Children's Museum.

Below: RXR Plaza (formerly EAB Plaza) is one of the modern office complexes that is on the southern part of the former Mitchel Field site. Built in 1984, these twin elliptical towers are visible from miles away.

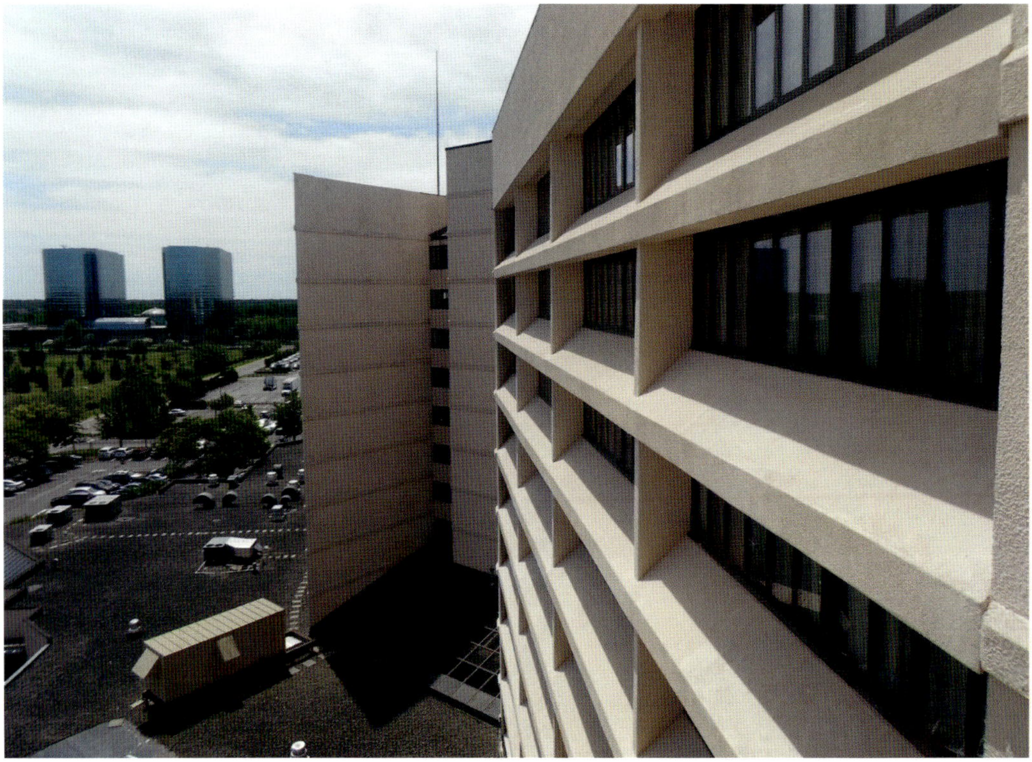

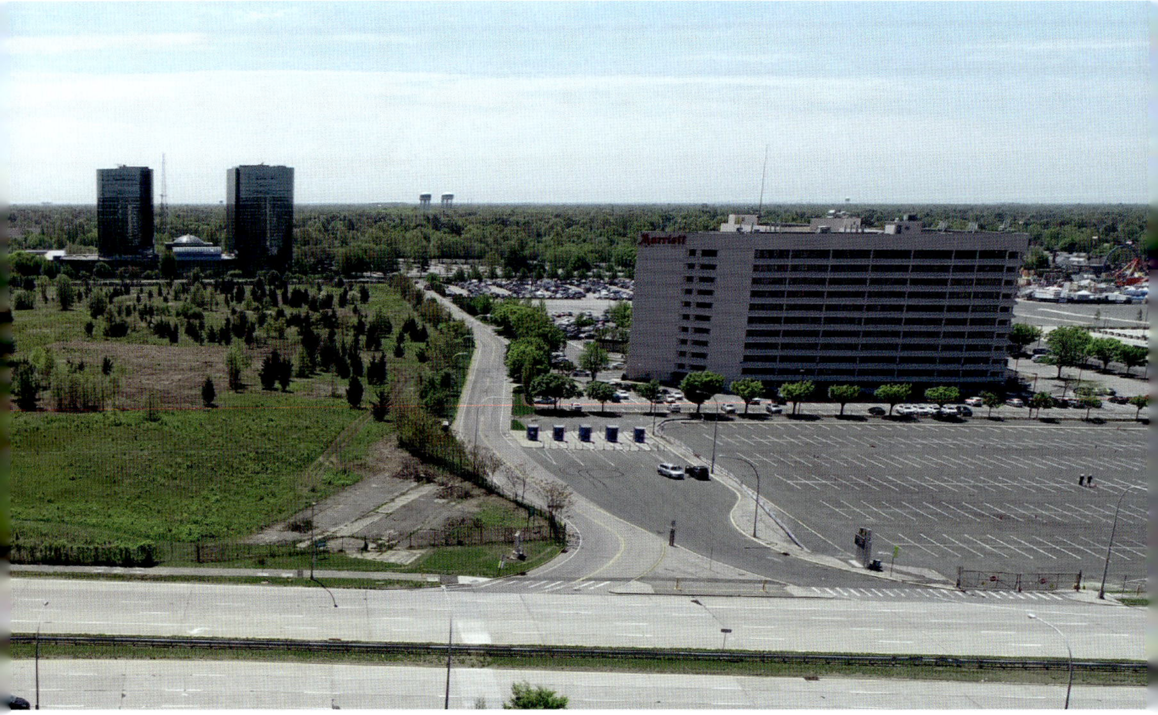

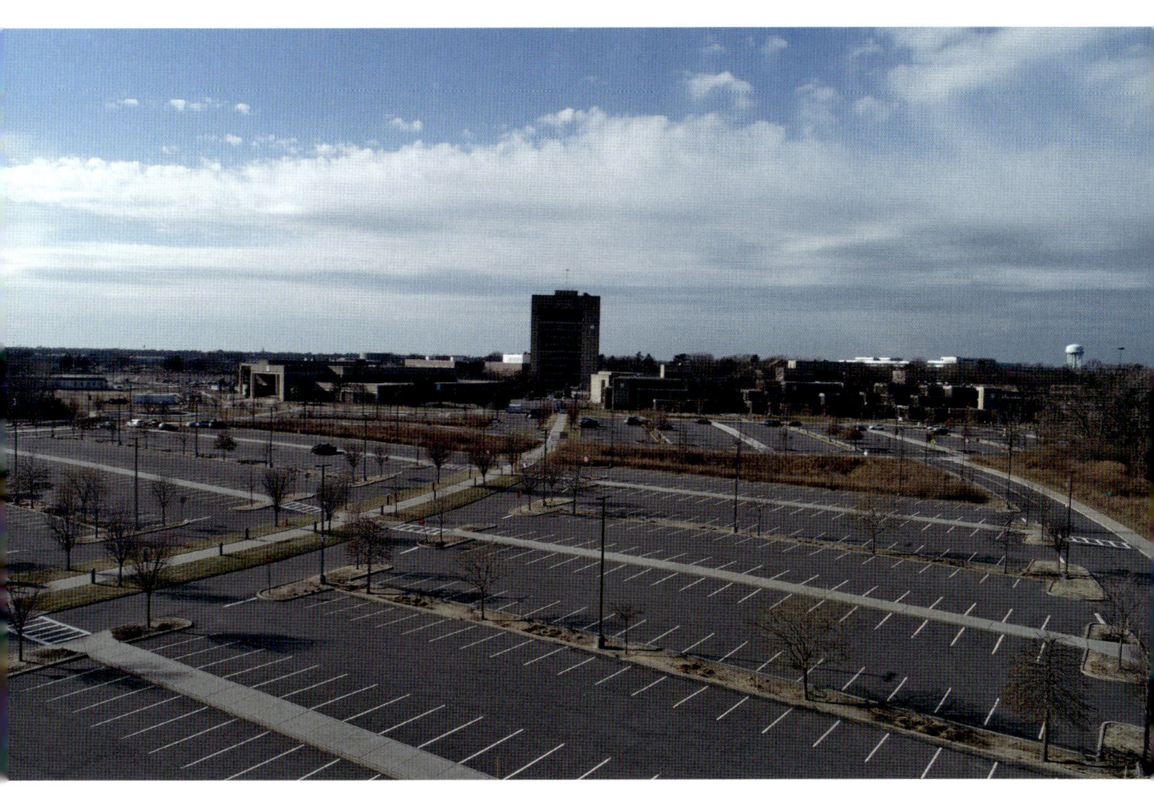

Between Nassau Coliseum, the Marriott, Nassau Community College, Hofstra University, and the Cradle of Aviation and Children's Museums, a good percentage of the former Mitchel Field is now parking lots.

Opposite page:

The Long Island Marriott, built in 1982 next to the Nassau Coliseum on the west side and remnants of the Hempstead Plans on the east side, is eleven floors high.

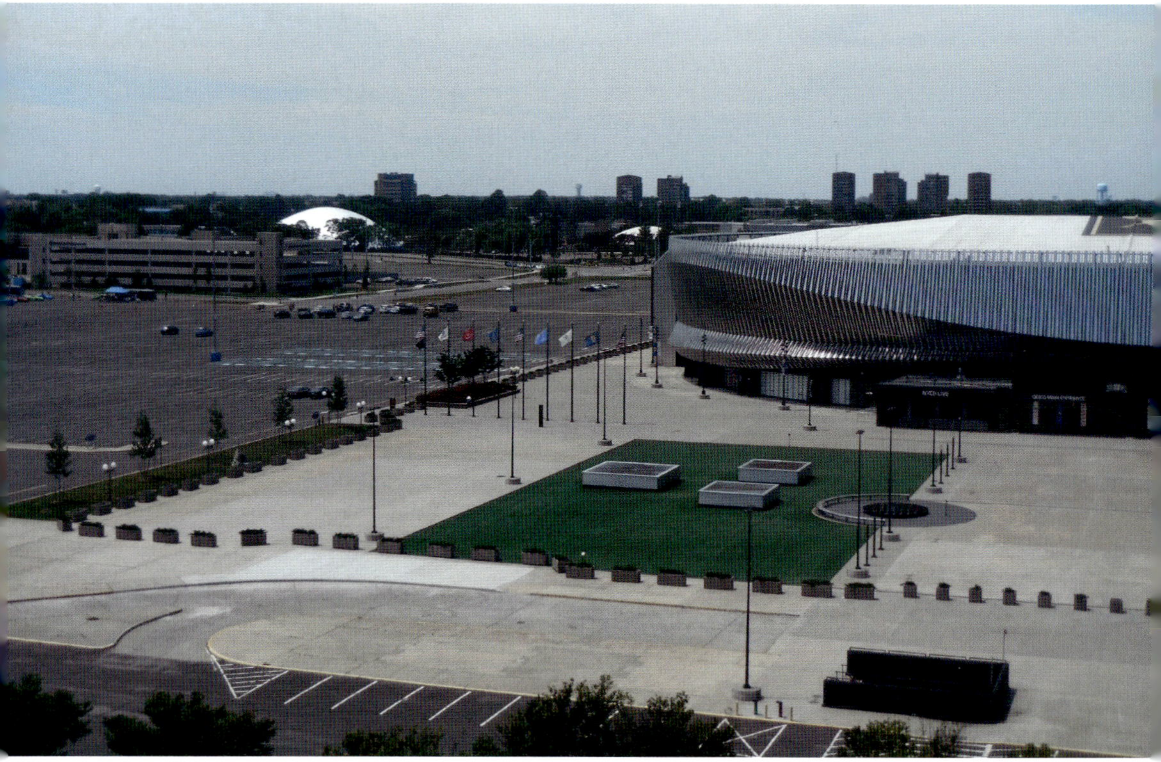

Nassau Veterans Memorial Coliseum was built in 1972, one of the first structures built after Mitchel Field's closure in 1961. It was completely remodeled in 2017.

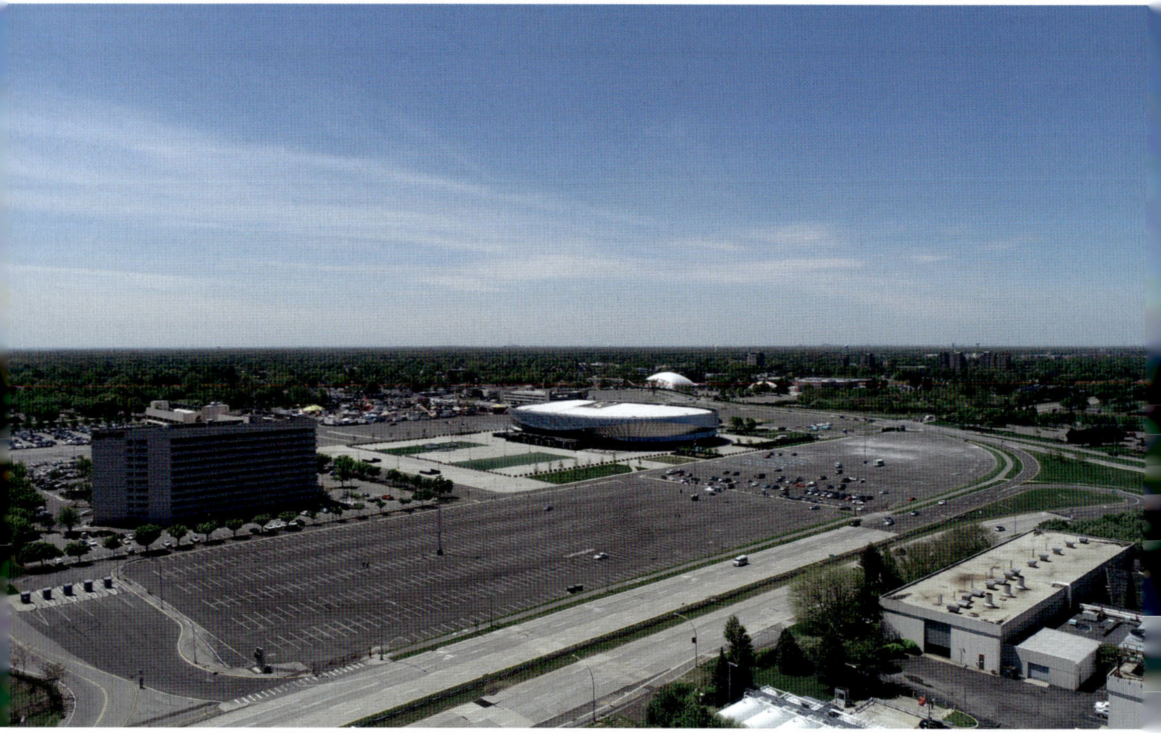

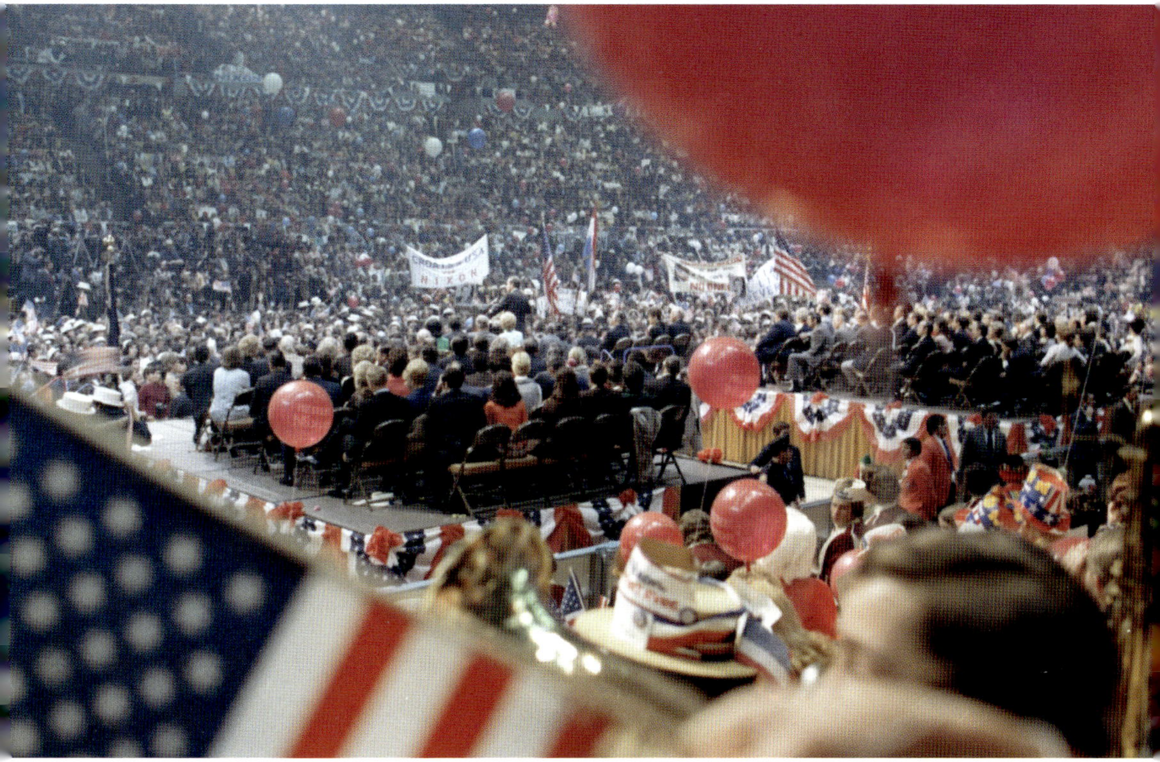

Richard Nixon and Gerald Ford holding rallies at the Nassau Coliseum in 1972 and 1976.

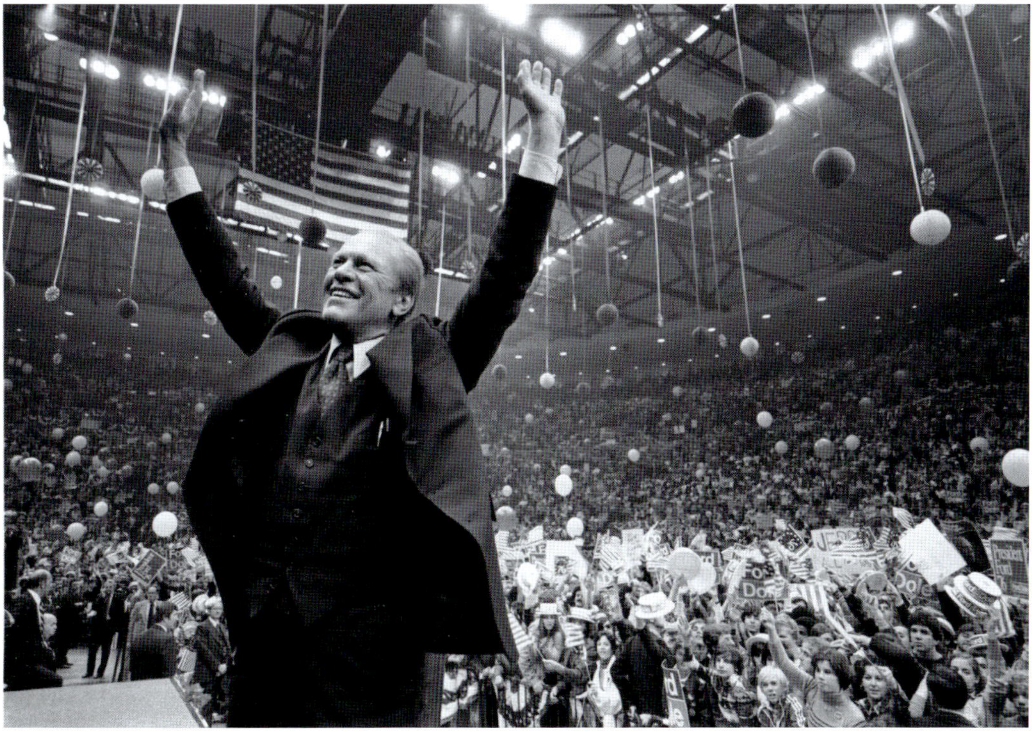

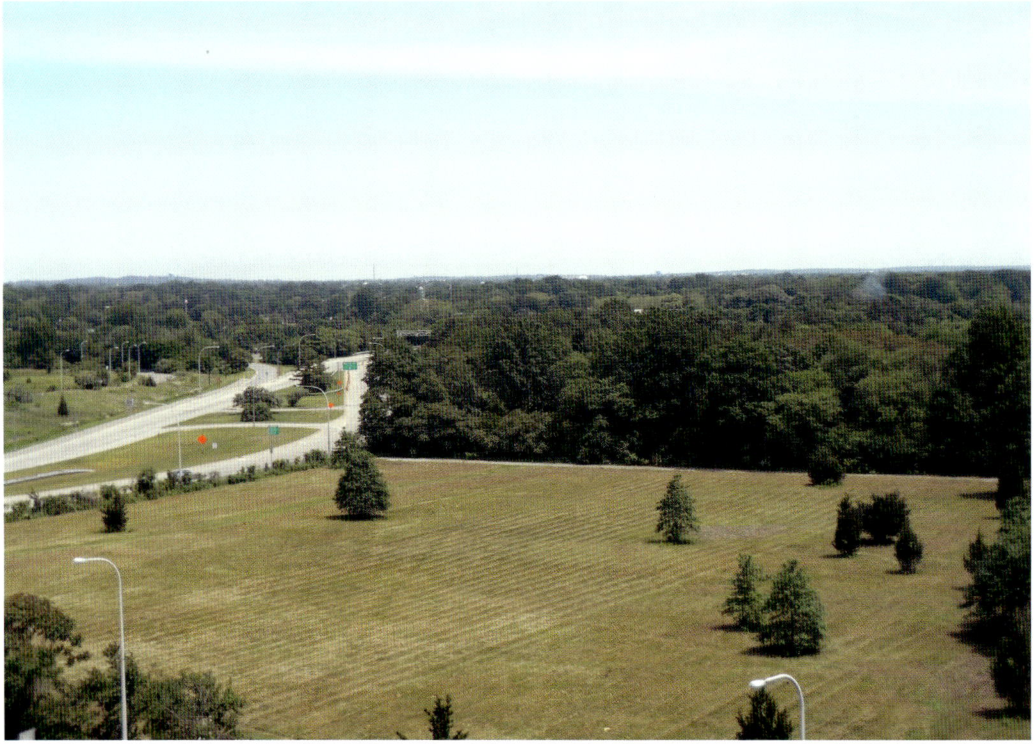

Seen from the Marriott and from across Charles Lindbergh Boulevard, this paved pathway running north-south, that was on the eastern periphery of Mitchel Field and directly adjacent to the Meadow Brook Golf Club, still exists today.

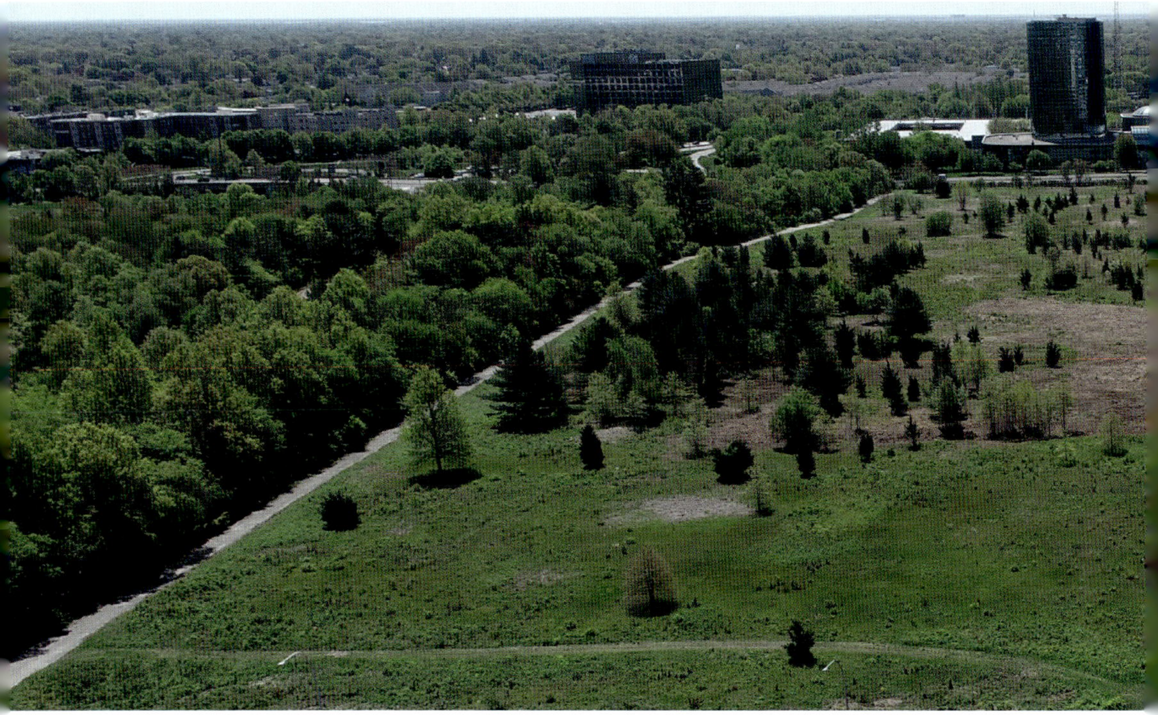

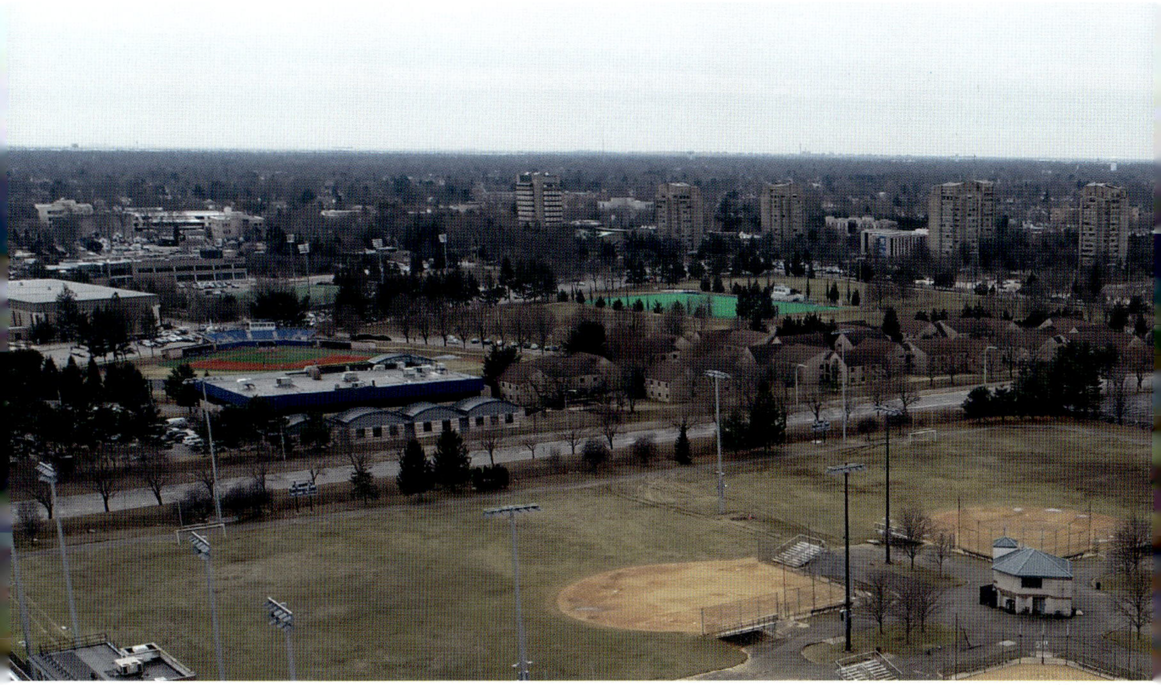

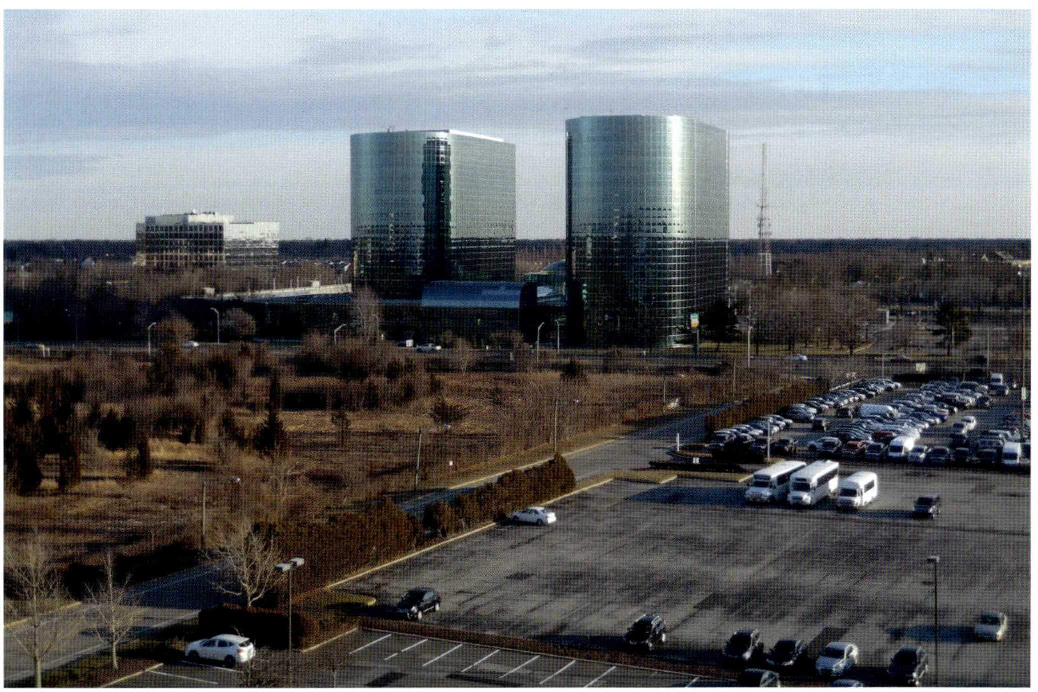

By 1927, there were still several private property owners between the southern edge of Mitchel Field and Hempstead Turnpike. By 1939, Mitchel Field had expanded and acquired all of that land. The northern half of the Hofstra University campus is built on the former Mitchel Field land.

Looking south from the Marriott property. The antenna tower belongs to the Telecare television station, adjacent to the Kellenberg Memorial High School campus. It was once the Santini Annex to Mitchel Field.

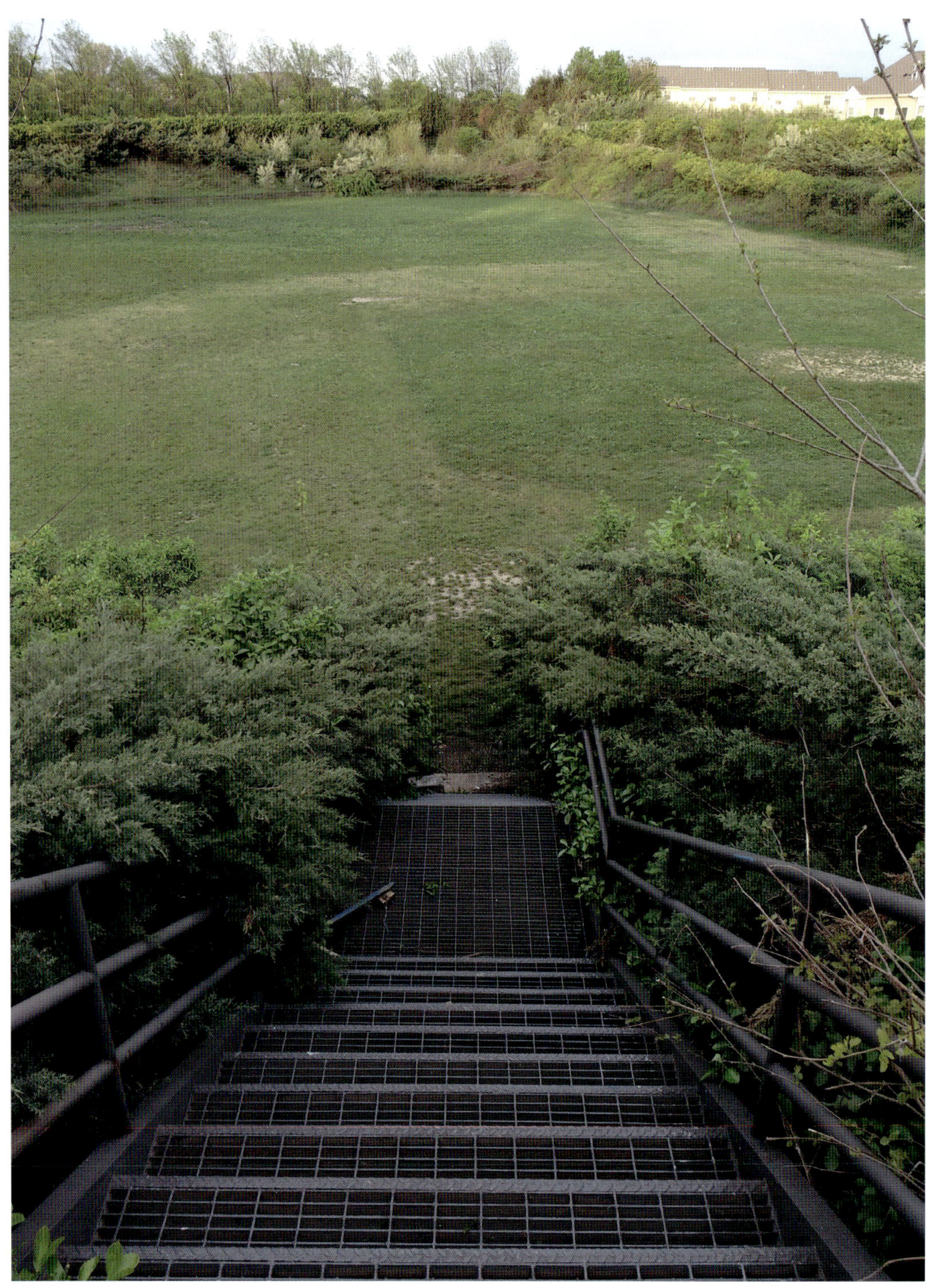

Looking down on what became a baseball field for Kellenberg Memorial High School, once part of the Santini Sub-base that was an annex of Mitchel Field. It was broken into two by the construction of the Meadowbrook Parkway, so a small bridge over the highway was built to connect the two halves.

5

Highways and Byways

The roads and highways of the Hempstead Plains vary widely in age. Some of the older roads include the east-west running Hempstead Turnpike and Old Country Road, which were already there in the golden days when the Cradle of Aviation was still rocking, and were important means for people to get to the airfields and the golf courses and polo fields. The north-south running Post Avenue/Merrick Avenue (then known as Whaleneck Road) was similarly important. The limited access Long Island Motor Parkway was the idea of the wealthy automobile enthusiast William K. Vanderbilt II, and it was the country's first modern concrete highway. The Motor Parkway went straight through the heart of the Hempstead Plains, crossing through Garden City, Mineola, and Westbury, and it offered access to the Mitchel Field and the Meadow Brook Club, among other places, before it closed in 1938. The Meadowbrook Parkway was a major highway that was begun in the 1930s to the south, but finally came north in 1956, cutting through the heart of the Hempstead Plains. After Mitchel Field closed in 1961, new roads (such as Charles Lindbergh Boulevard and Earl Ovington Boulevard) were created over the years where once there were runways. The most recent roadway creation on the Hempstead Plains took place after Roosevelt Raceway closed in 1988 and the property was sold and divided.

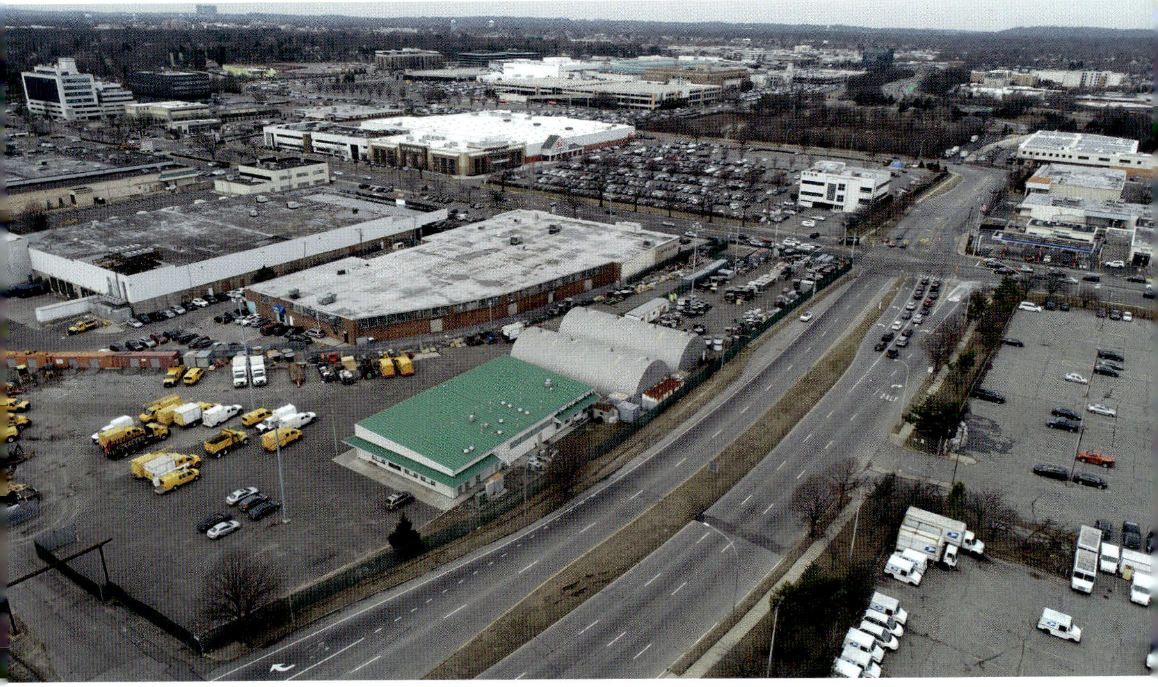

What was once the western end of Mitchel Field is now highly commercial and industrial, matching the name of the street that crosses through it—Commercial Avenue.

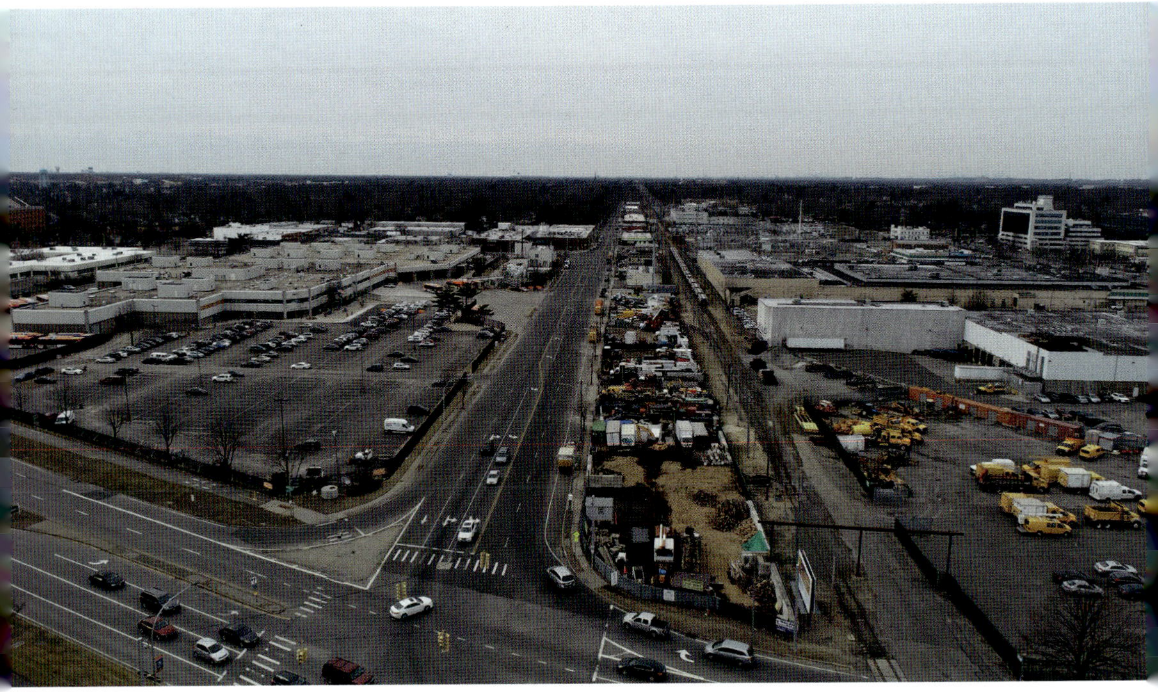

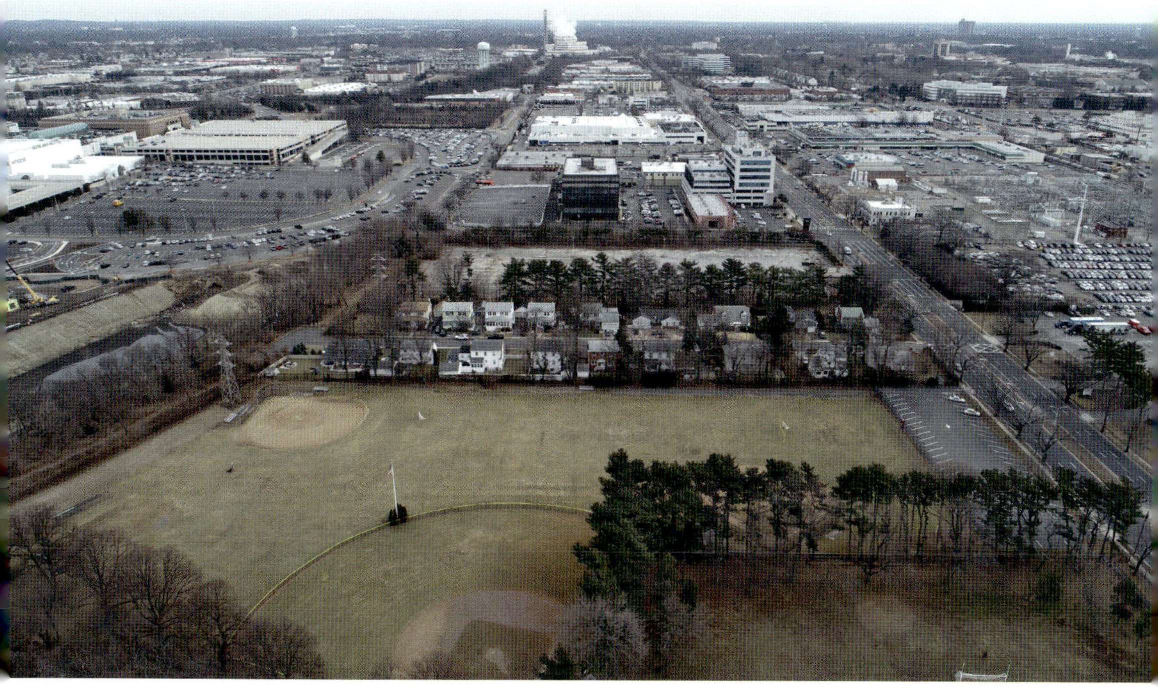

The Long Island Motor Parkway cut through this area north of the intersection of Clinton Road and Stewart Avenue and then ran east-west parallel to Stewart Avenue all the way through what is now Eisenhower Park.

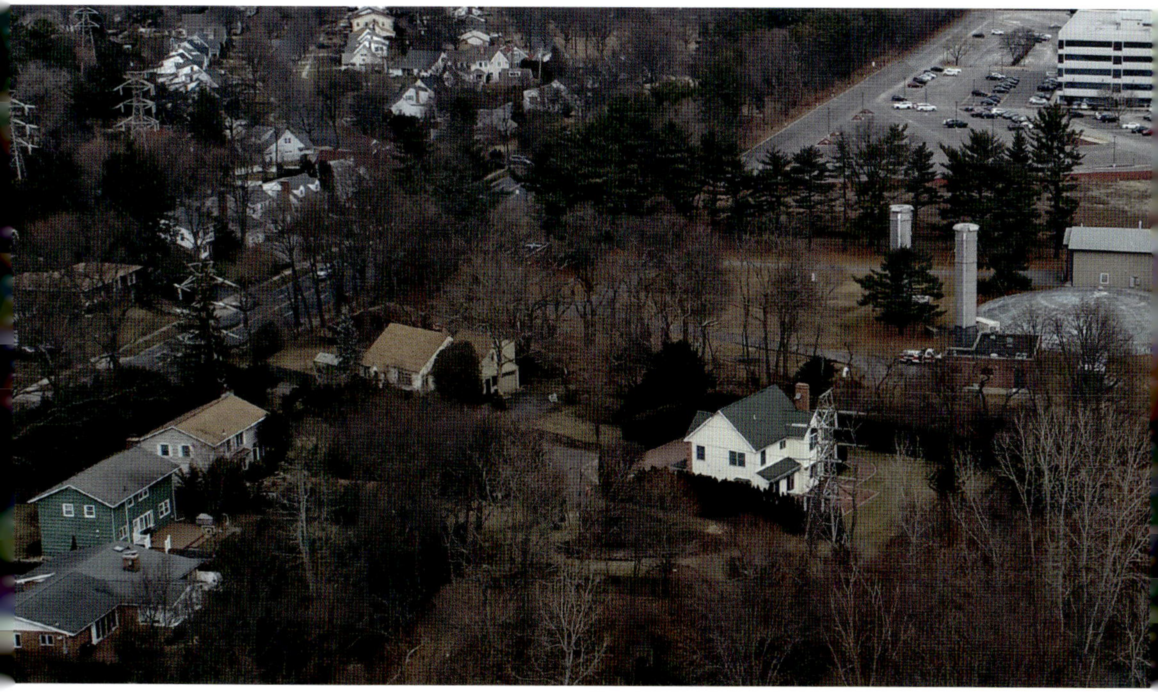

The Long Island Motor Parkway's right of way was where the power lines are, north of Stewart Avenue in this view looking east. The Motor Parkway curved down from the north and then ran parallel to Stewart all the way through what is now Eisenhower Park.

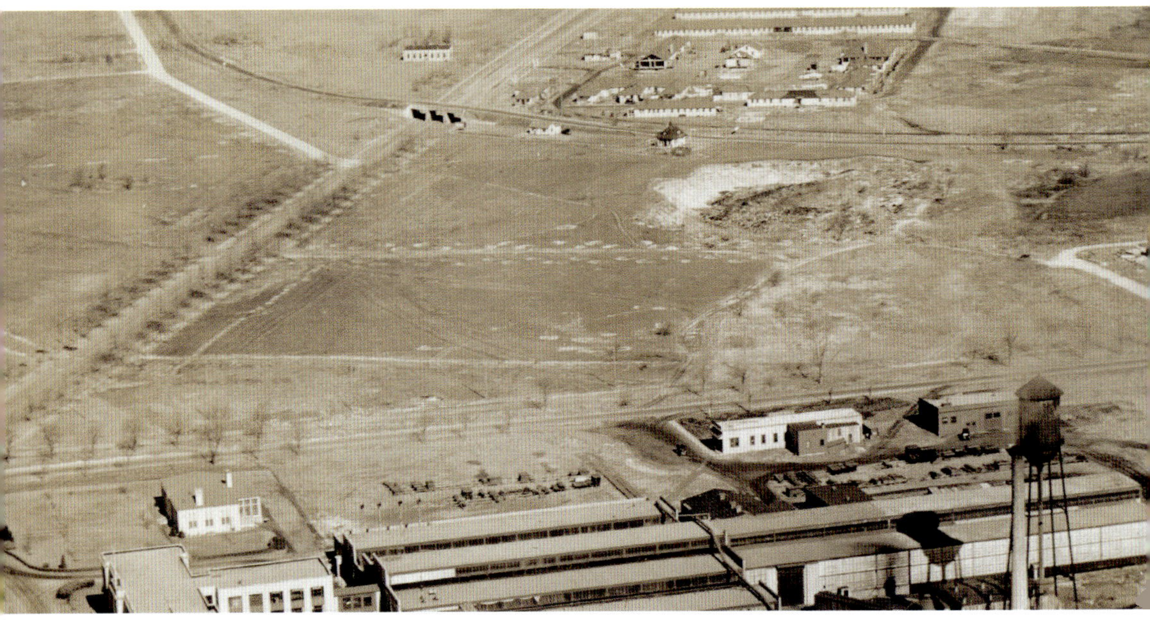

A 1925 aerial showing the Long Island Motor Parkway Bridge over Clinton Road in Garden City. The Curtiss aircraft factory is at the bottom of the image.

OPPOSITE PAGE:

The Meadowbrook Parkway sliced through the heart of the Hempstead Plains and what was once the Meadow Brook Club, offering highway access to Jones Beach from points north.

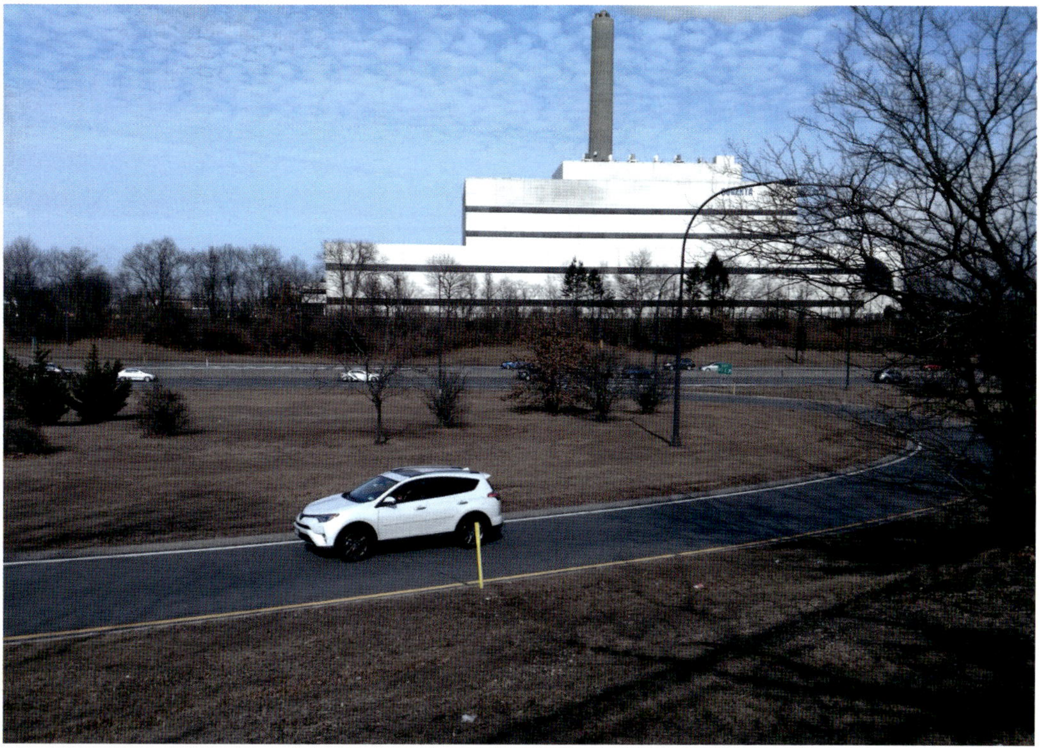

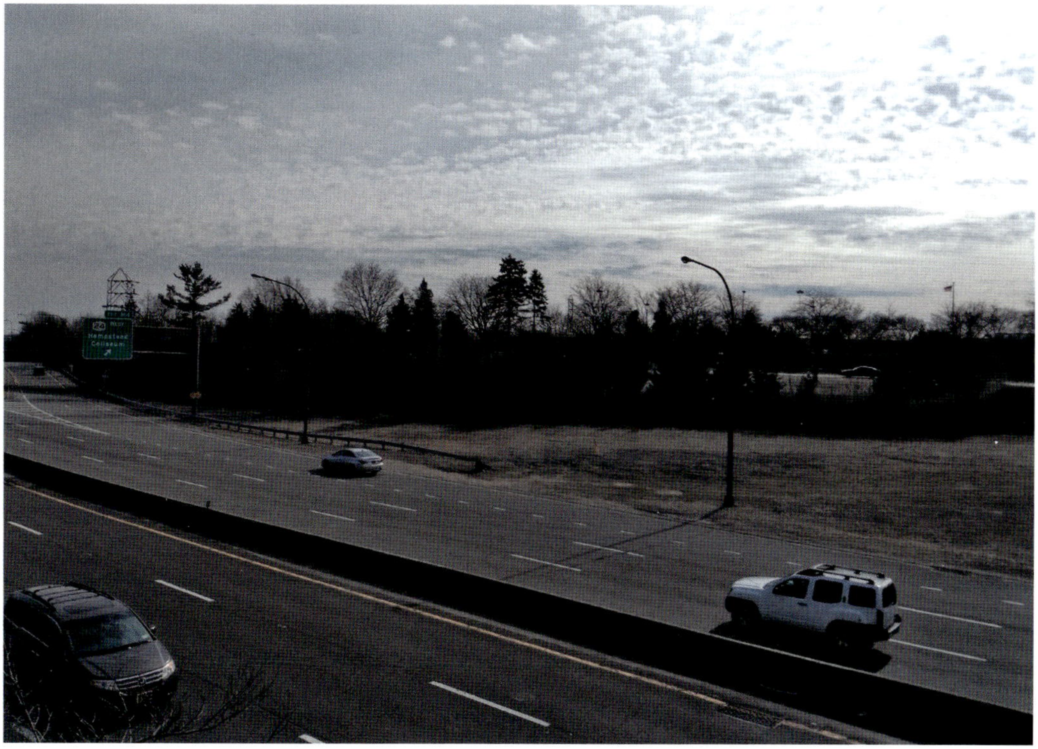

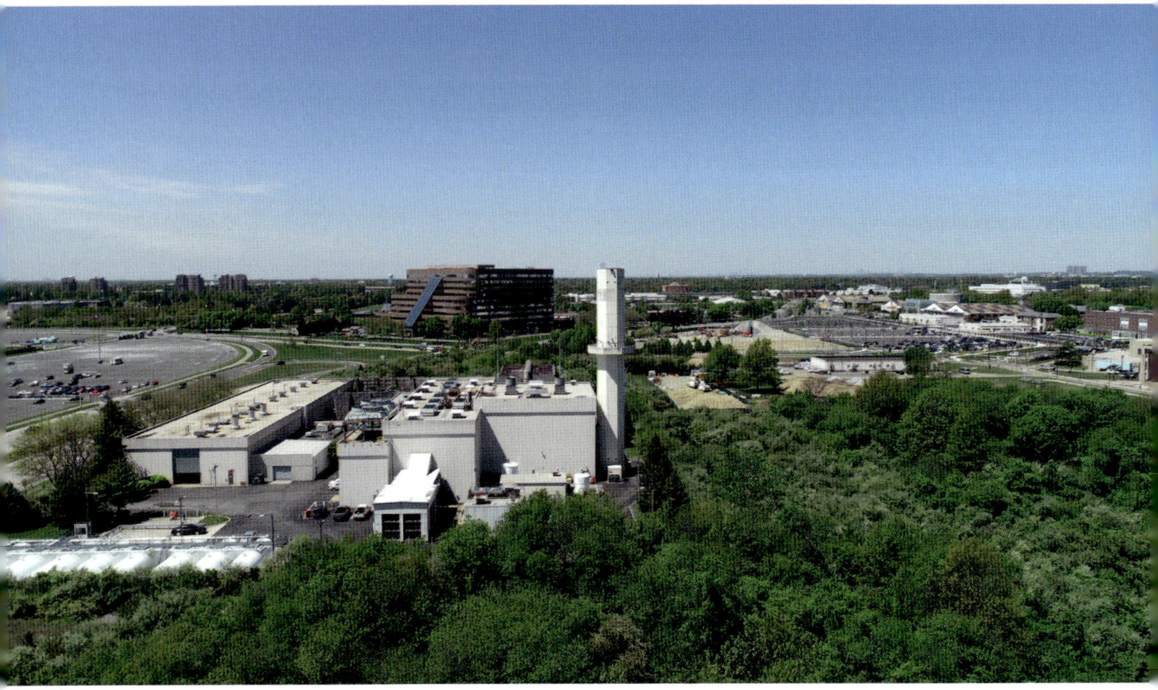

The roadway network within what used to be Mitchel Field includes three pilot-named roads: Charles Lindbergh, Earle Ovington Boulevard, and Glenn Curtiss Boulevard. In this image, Earl Ovington meets Charles Lindbergh. The modern brown building is 333 Earl Ovington Boulevard.

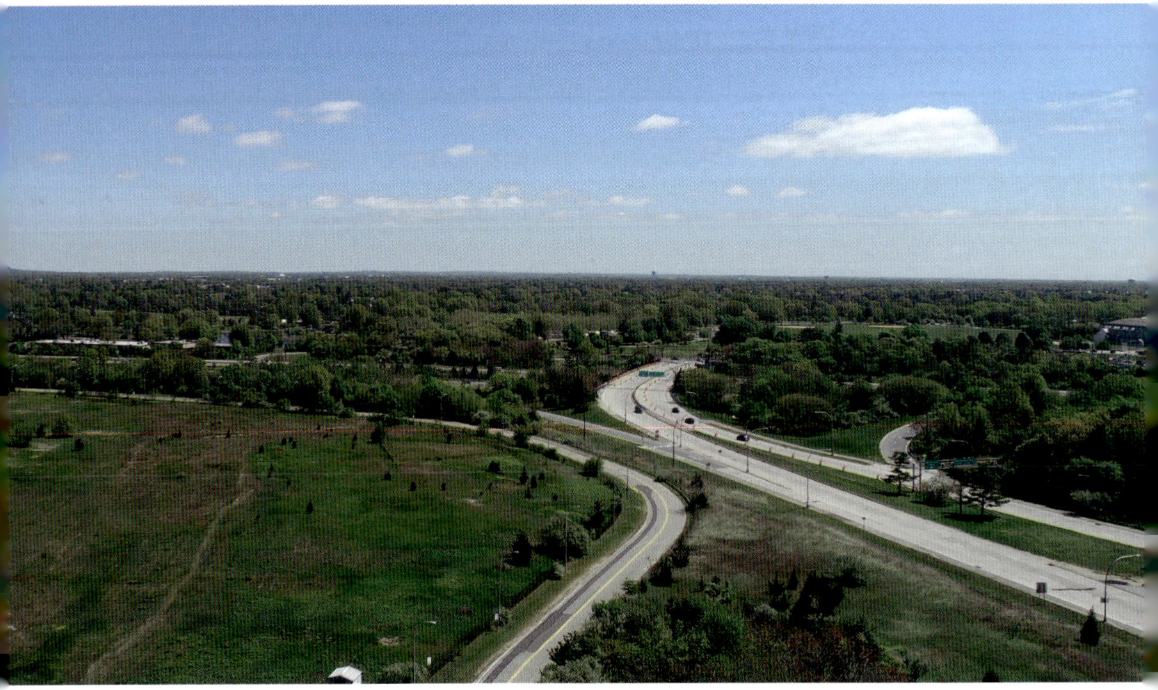

Charles Lindbergh Boulevard offers access to the Meadowbrook Parkway. It skirts very close to the Nassau Community College Campus, as can be seen in this image looking east.

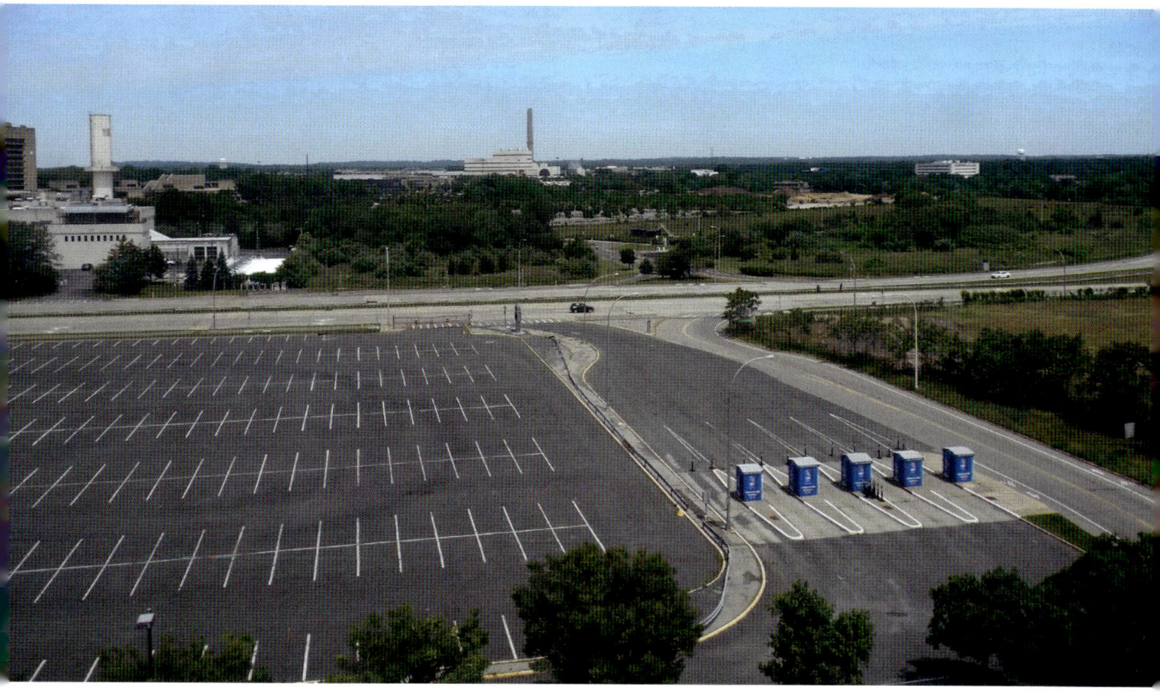

Charles Lindbergh Boulevard is named after an aviation pioneer who flew locally. It offers access to the Nassau Coliseum and the Marriott.

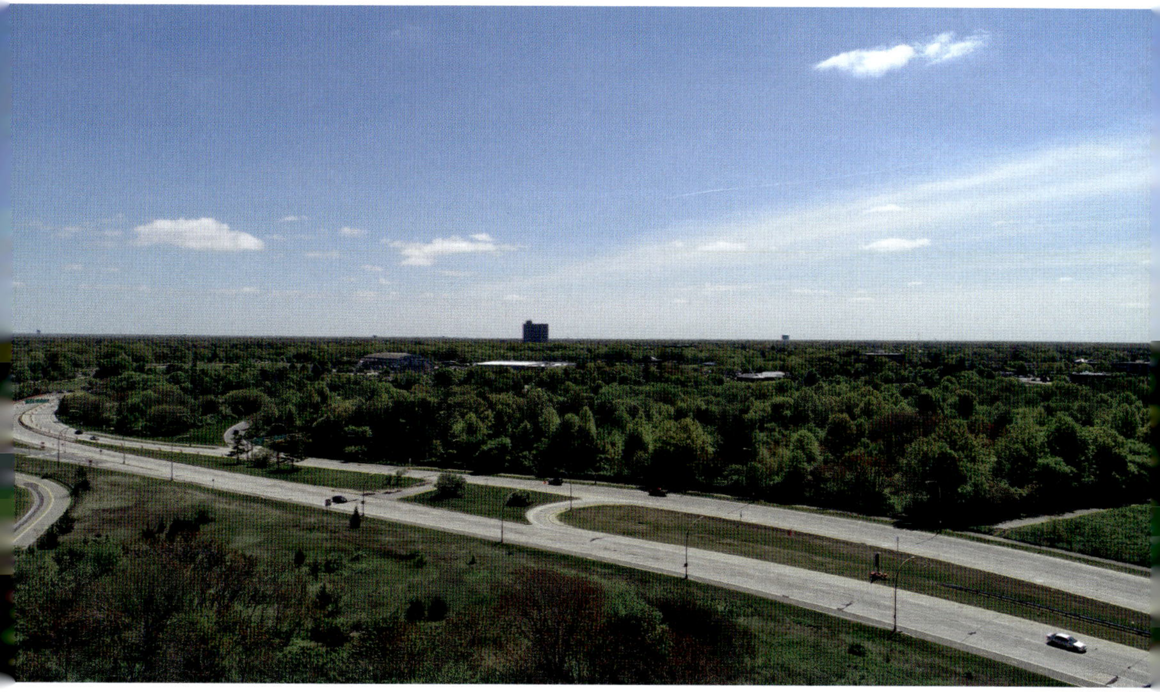

Another view of Charles Lindbergh Boulevard (looking southeast), a road created after Mitchel Field closed.

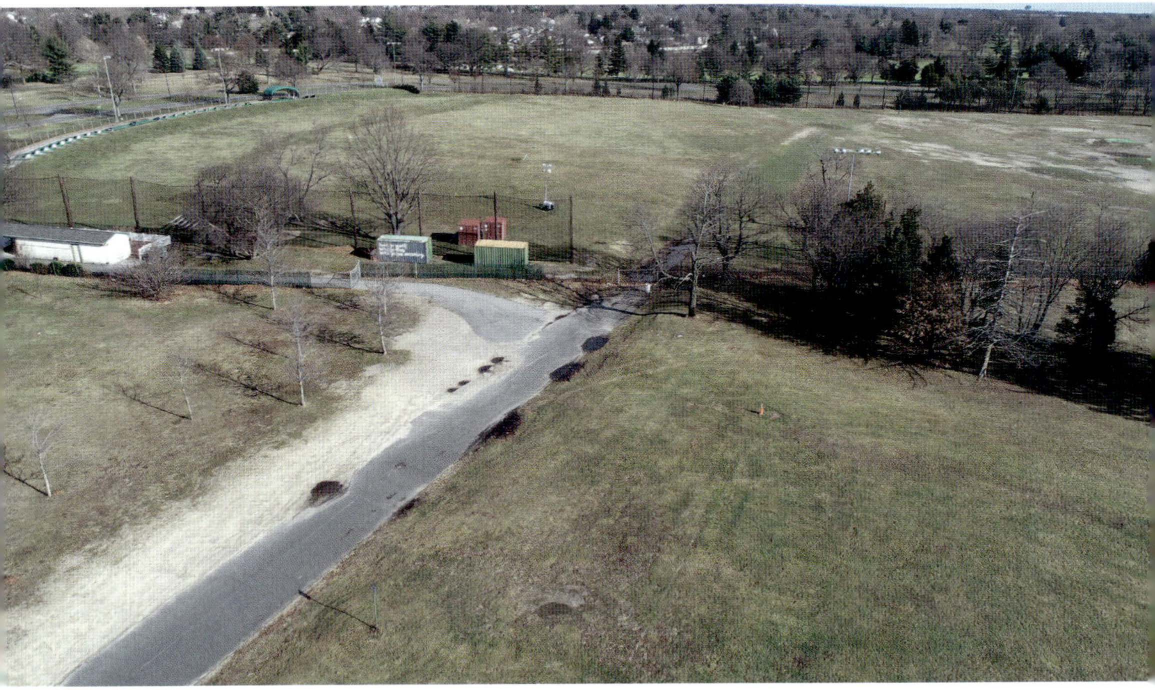

The remains of Stewart Avenue, which used to cut through what is now Eisenhower Park.

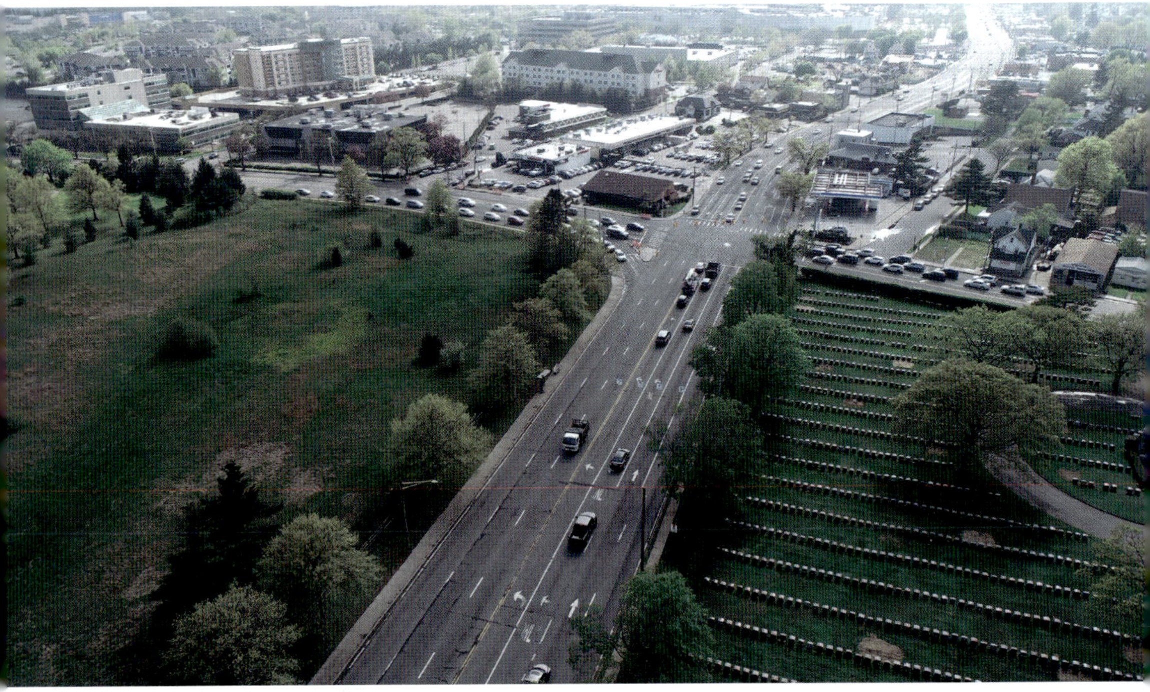

Post Avenue and Old Country Road, for more than 100 years one of the most important intersections of the Hempstead Plains—a true crossroads. To the southwest, the eastern boundary of Roosevelt Field and the Cradle of Aviation. To the southeast, the Salisbury Golf Course (eventually Eisenhower Park). To the northeast the property of the Catholic church. To the northwest, residential neighborhoods that once looked out onto the flying field.